Women of the Roman Aristocracy as Christian Monastics

Studies in Religion, No. 1

Margaret R. Miles, Series Editor

Professor of Historical Theology
The Divinity School
Harvard University

Other Titles in This Series

No. 2   *Acts of God and the People,*
         1620-1730   Peter Lockwood Rumsey

No. 3   *Science and Religious Thought:*
         A Darwinism Case Study   Walter J. Wilkins

Women of the Roman Aristocracy as Christian Monastics

by
Anne Ewing Hickey

59012

U·M·I Research Press

Ann Arbor, Michigan

Produced and distributed by
UMI Research Press
an imprint of
University Microfilms, Inc.
Ann Arbor, Michigan 48106

Library of Congress Cataloging in Publication Data

Hickey, Anne Ewing, 1946-
Women of the Roman aristocracy as Christian monastics.

(Studies in religion ; no. 1)
Revision of thesis (Ph.D.)—Vanderbilt University,
1983.
Bibliography: p.
Includes index.
1. Monasticism and religious orders for women—Rome—
History. 2. Rome—Nobility. 3. Women—Rome—Social
conditions. 4. Asceticism—History—Early church, ca.
30-600. 5. Church history—Primitive and early church,
ca. 30-600. I. Title. II. Series: Studies in
religion (Ann Arbor, Mich.) ; no. 1.
BX4220.R6H53 1987   305.4'8611037   86-19242
ISBN 0-8357-1757-7 (alk. paper)

116369

To my husband, James, whose love and friendship have long sustained me.

Contents

1   The Interpretive Dilemma of the Appeal of Asceticism to Women   *1*

2   Current Studies of the Ascetic Women of Rome   *13*

3   Roman Ascetic Women of Late Antiquity   *21*

4   The Roman *Matrona* of the Late Empire   *49*

5   Parsons' Theory of Action and the Analysis of Asceticism   *67*

6   Images of Women Current in Late Roman Antiquity   *87*

7   Conclusions   *107*

Abbreviations   *113*

Notes   *115*

Bibliography   *145*

Index   *149*

1

The Interpretive Dilemma of the Appeal of Asceticism to Women

The recent interest of contemporary women scholars such as Rosemary Ruether, Elisabeth Schüssler Fiorenza, Elizabeth Clark, and Ross Shepard Kraemer in the attraction of women in the early church period to asceticism comes as no surprise. Ascetic conceptuality and experience seem to have long captured the imagination and hearts of women. From the Therapeutae of Philo to the women of the early monastic movement to women mystics of the medieval period to the Shakers' Mother Ann Lee, there is a thread of development which suggests that asceticism has a special hold on the feminine imagination. While the modern mind chuckles at Margery Kempe's extraction of a vow of chastity from her husband in exchange for agreeing to pay his debts, one cannot so easily laugh off the conversion of countless women to virginity in an earlier age at the beginning of the Christian monastic movement. Nor can one dismiss the disinterested claim of F. Van Der Meer in his detailed study of Augustine that "among the ascetics of the Latin West they [the women] were in the overwhelming majority."[1] This apparent appeal of ascetic spirituality to women over a broad sweep of history poses an interpretive dilemma in view of the misogyny of the ascetic *Weltanschauung* which views the body in general and procreation in particular as impediments to spiritual wholeness. Is the female embrace of ascetic spirituality simply an internalization of patriarchal dichotomies which dissociate woman from the source of her authenticity? Or does the recurrent attraction of women to virginity over a broad sweep of history in such historically diverse phenomena as gnosticism, early Syrian Christianity, and early monasticism force us to consider a more positive perspective on the meaning for women of ascetic denial of the maternal, bodily self? These questions pose the interpretive problematic which provides the inspiration for this study.

While the appeal of asceticism to women throughout the first few centuries of Christian experience sets the contextual stage in which misogynist, ascetic rhetoric seems not to deter female renunciants, this investigation will address the problematic by reference to the Roman women of the early Christian monastic movement generally associated with the names of Jerome and Rufinus of Aquileia. Although a broad sweeping theory which would equally explain the ascetic choice of Thecla of the Apocryphal Acts and Melania the Elder of the early monastic movement would be a worthy goal, it is necessary to focus on one particular ascetic phenomenon in order to give full attention to the historical and sociological data which might inform a thesis. The ascetic protégées of Jerome and Rufinus present themselves as fruitful subjects of inquiry not only because of the intriguing nature of their lives, but because there is sufficient accessible data to glean a reasonably clear account of the social, political, and religious context in which they lived.

My interest in the women of late Rome, who first embodied the Christian monastic ideal inspired by Antony, is not unique. The feminist movement of the early 1970s has channeled more women into academe and sparked their interest in women's experiences in the past which might have points of contiguity with contemporary social and religious struggles. Anne Yarbrough must receive credit for the initial contemporary rediscovery in America of the female monastics of Rome of late antiquity and for reconsidering them in the light of feminist dialogue. Her essay entitled "Christianization in the Fourth Century: The Example of Roman Women" published in *Church History* in 1976 prompted further consideration. In 1979 Elizabeth Clark (formerly of Mary Washington College and now at Duke University) published an innovative study of the women in question called *Jerome, Chrysostom, and Friends*. Also in 1979 Rosemary Ruether included an essay on the protégées of Jerome and Rufinus in a survey of women in the history of the Christian church entitled *Women of Spirit*. In 1981 Elizabeth Clark furthered the analysis of ascetic renunciation in light of the feminist dialogue in an essay entitled "Ascetic Renunciation and Feminine Advancement: A Paradox of Late Ancient Christianity," *Anglican Theological Review* (July 1981). Thus, the subjects of this inquiry are not obscure figures lost for centuries under layers of musty history. Rather, they have a rather wide range of devotees who share an interest in unraveling the secrets of their lives which might inform contemporary women in spiritual quest for wholeness. This study, therefore, is not staking out new ground historically. Rather, the focus is on staking out new ground theoretically, particularly with regard to the interpretative problematic posed by the appeal of asceticism to women despite the misogyny of its categories. It is my view that current studies, while all significant in their own way, do not exhaust the interpretive possibilities presented by these enigmatic figures of the monastic past whose voices never speak to us directly.

While a more detailed account of the current studies of the protégées of Jerome and Rufinus will follow in the next chapter, a few general statements on this point are needed to explain the area of supplementation addressed by this work. Studies to date vary in their focus and in the degree of theoretical reflection brought to bear on the monastic choice of these upper-class matrons of Rome of the Late Empire. Anne Yarbrough's study is a rejoinder to Peter Brown's claim that the Roman aristocracy was Christianized on its own terms, resulting in a syncretistic religious milieu.[2] Yarbrough argues that the rigorous spirituality of the protégées of Jerome and Rufinus was an exception to this move toward a pagan/Christian synthesis.[3] Her questions have to do with uncovering the social background of the subjects of the inquiry within the Roman senatorial aristocracy, describing the typical ascetic woman, and discerning the possible social functions of asceticism for women. At the theoretical level Yarbrough makes reference in a general way to functionalist theory to claim that asceticism had two social functions—to provide women with an alternative to marriage and to spare parents too many costly initiations of children into aristocratic society.[4]

Rosemary Ruether's approach in her essay entitled "Mothers of the Church" in *Women of Spirit* is primarily historical with little theoretical reflection on the question of how to interpret the monastic choice of such figures as Paula, Marcella, and Eustochium. Insofar as Ruether moves beyond an historical survey she makes reference in a general way to a liberation model as interpretive guide.

To date Elizabeth Clark is in the vanguard of those scholars investigating the ascetic women of Rome in the early stages of the Christian monastic movement and has been the most sophisticated in use of social theory. Clark's work includes a book entitled *Jerome, Chrysostom, and Friends*, an essay in the *Anglican Theological Review* called "Ascetic Renunciation and Feminine Advancement: a Paradox of Late Ancient Christianity," and a translation of the *Vita S. Melaniae*. Yet, to date Clark's question has not been the one which fueled my interest in the subjects of this inquiry: what in the historical situation would prompt women to embrace a seemingly misogynist world view? In *Jerome, Chrysostom, and Friends* Clark focuses on the question of how Jerome and Chrysostom exempted their protégées from the general class of inferior females in order to establish bonds of friendship. Here the incompatibility of monastic misogyny and friendship between the sexes focuses the study on the interiority of Jerome and Rufinus rather than on the women. The question in "Ascetic Renunciation and Feminine Advancement: a Paradox of Late Ancient Christianity" more closely approaches mine. Yet, here the paradox for Clark is that whereas the prevailing view of cultured Rome was that monasticism degraded aristocrats, in the case of women monasticism was enhancing or social advancement.[5]

Clark has been the most innovative at the theoretical level by consciously aligning herself with the "social description" school of the American Academy of Religion and the Society of Biblical Literature which uses the insights of the social sciences, psychology, and social anthropology in order to bring a fresh perspective to historical studies of early Christianity. Beginning in 1973 as a study group under the auspices of the AAR and SBL, the group is now formally organized to bring the resources of many scholars to bear on the question of the social world of early Christianity.[6] In this vein Clark has most aptly applied the insights of Victor Turner's studies of liminars undergoing status transition in *The Ritual Process* to the questions posed in *Jerome, Chrysostom, and Friends.* In "Ascetic Renunciation and Feminine Advancement" Clark has made use of no supplementary theoretical source but has pressed further the sociological perspective on the women in question by arguing that asceticism constitutes social advancement for women. Thus, to date scholars have not fully used social theory to account for the ascetic conversion of scores of aristocratic women despite the seemingly misogynist monastic world view. Therefore, the interpretive dilemma posed by women of the early monastic movement has not been fully explored by current studies nor has the theoretical aid provided by social theory been exhausted.

My study, following the lead of scholars such as Peter Brown, Elizabeth Clark, W. H. C. Frend, and others who use sociological theory to enhance historical investigation, will attempt to uncover something within the historical context which prompted the monastic choice of such figures as Marcella, Melania, and Paula by means of references to theories of social dynamics. It goes without saying that this historical/sociological approach to asceticism suspends for the moment the spiritual/theological perspective. While certainly the theological motivation, i.e., the quest for closeness to God, was the dominant consciously articulated motive, it is my view that the historical and social context influenced the monastic choice and further that current theories of social dynamics might illuminate that context.

I have found that the basic principles of the action frame of reference (that is, social theory which analyzes the dynamics between the individual, his web of relationships, and the culture), particularly as explicated by Talcott Parsons in *The Social System,* provide a highly suggestive basis for analyzing the social context of aristocratic women of Rome of late antiquity. Marcella, Melania, and Paula, the first generation of Roman nuns, were caught in a clash of cultures and in clashes within cultures as the senatorial class extricated itself from its tenacious pagan roots. I will argue that late antiquity can be characterized by a highly unintegrated pattern of cultural norms for women. This claim emerges as a result of the historical investigation of the social, economic, and political context of the matron in the Late Roman Empire, but it will be further demonstrated by the construction of a typology of images of women current in late antiquity. Plautus, Terence, Jerome, Juvenal, Ovid, Augustus, and others depicted the ideal woman in terms which demonstrate the ambiguity of cultural expectations for the Roman matron.

Methodological justification for the typology need not be included in this introductory section but will be deferred to the main body of the study. At this point it is sufficient to point out that the typology functions to further the basis for the application of the insights of action theory into the effect of malintegrated norms on a person's relation to society. Should a woman be beautiful? Juvenal will satirize her vanity. Jerome will call her decadent. And Ovid will have her in bed with a lover. Vergil wasn't kind to Dido for betraying the memory of her departed spouse. Yet, Augustus required remarriage as part of his social reform to repopulate a declining citizenry. I will argue that such conflictual views of the Roman matron which were current in the culture point toward an unintegrated pattern of social expectations and, further, that on the basis of insights of the action frame of reference such malintegration can lead to social deviance.

In summary, the thesis of this study is that the unintegrated normative expectations for woman, exacerbated by the closeness and the clash of pagan and Christian in senatorial families of late Rome, prompted the ascetic choice. Thus, despite the misogynist world view of monasticism, the ascetic life would have moved women beyond the ambiguities of Roman expectations.

The apparent attraction of women to ascetic spirituality over a broad sweep of early Christian history in distinct historical movements underscores the significance of the interpretive problematic. The conversion of aristocratic women of Rome to monastic withdrawal is the culmination of ascetic trends long present in Christianity. In the late fourth century these minor ascetic tendencies came into full bloom, capturing the imagination of most of the great ecclesiastical leaders of the day—Ambrose, Jerome, Augustine, Chrysostom, Rufinus, and many others. Certainly, women converts to monasticism drew upon precedents long present in Christianity for their adoption of ascetic spirituality. Jerome's dubbing of Melania the Elder as the new Thecla suggests a conscious grounding in the ascetic precedents of the past. Therefore, a review of the evidence, from the centuries preceding the monastic movement, which points toward the special appeal of asceticism to women, sets the contextual stage for our more in-depth investigation of Roman aristocratic women renunciants of the late fourth century.

A special function of asceticism for women is suggested by the prevalence of stories about women in the Apocryphal Acts of the Apostles which have their roots in the ascetically oriented Christianity of Syria and Asia Minor of the second and third centuries. The prominence of female figures in the Apocryphal Acts caught Harnack's attention in *The Mission and Expansion of Christianity in the First Three Centuries* and is now being noticed by current scholars.[7] Ross Shepard Kraemer, with John G. Gager, Jr. as advisor, wrote a Ph.D. dissertation at Princeton University on the function of asceticism for women, using the Apocryphal Acts as one of the foci of analysis.[8] Steven L. Davies has also noted the feminine presence in the Apocryphal Acts in his new book *The Revolt of the Widows: The Social World of the Apocryphal Acts.* Whether the women converted in the Apocryphal Acts are historical or (more likely) products of literary imagination, their prominence in this literature of ascetic conversion in the East supports the claim that asceticism had a special appeal to women. While Thecla's dramatic commitment to virginity is well known (receiving attention in Elisabeth Schüssler Fiorenza's overview of women in earliest Christianity in *Women of Spirit*[9]), there are in the Apocryphal Acts other conversion stories of such figures as Maximilla, Trophina, Drusiana, and Xanthippe for whom Thecla is a paradigm.

An historically distinct phenomenon in which asceticism and female presence also go hand in hand is early Christian gnosticism. Recent scholars, such as Carol Christ and Elaine Pagels, have taken seriously the charges of Irenaeus and Tertullian that women converts were prevalent among gnostic circles.[10] This observation isn't new. Harnack, in *The Mission and Expansion of Christianity in the First Three Centuries,* noted the appeal of gnosticism to women.[11] While evidence of the inclusion of the feminine in gnostic conceptuality of the divine abounds in the treatises discovered at Nag Hammadi, these secret gospels are primarily theological in nature, including mythic female figures but little about actual women adherents to gnosticism. Thus, one must depend upon the heresiologists to supply data about the actual role of women gnostics in their respective factions.[12]

Historical evidence supplied by the heresiologists about actual women gnostics is scant. Further, its reliability has to be considered in the light of the usual license taken by the ancients in disparaging an opponent and by noting the tendency for any female power to loom larger than its reality to offended men. Thanks to Tertullian, we have some reliable evidence of an improved social and cultic role for women in Christian heresy. The following, often quoted statement alludes to advancement for women despite Tertullian's intended disparagement: "The very women of these heretics, how wanton they are! For they are bold enough to teach, to dispute, to enact exorcisms, to undertake cures—it may be even to baptize."[13] Tertullian also gives us the name of one actual gnostic woman—Philumene.[14] Irenaeus gives us the name of one gnostic woman, Marcellina, who if misguided at least received attention for her effectiveness as a proselyte: "From among these [the Carpocratians] also arose Marcellina, who came to Rome under Anicetus, and, holding those doctrines, she led multitudes astray."[15] Irenaeus also alludes to the appeal of gnosticism to women in his reference to Marcus who seemed to have unique success in converting women to heresy.[16]

Despite the paucity of historical evidence about particular gnostic women, Elaine Pagels thinks the data sufficient to claim a correlation between the feminine God-language (evidence of which is considerable in the gnostic literature) and an improved social role for women in gnostic circles. On the basis of Pagels' claims about gnostic social progress, some scholars argue that the authority accorded to Mary in the gnostic literature itself (in the ending of *The Gospel of Mary*) is reflective of the social reality in gnostic communities. In this essay of esoteric teaching, Mary's authority is such that she becomes the mouthpiece of the Lord. When she speaks at others' initiative about what the Lord related to her, Peter challenges her testimony on the grounds that female speech has no authority.[17] Yet, the other disciples defend Mary's authority to teach them what the Lord has taught her. Fiorenza considers *The Gospel of Mary* (along with sections of the *Pistis Sophia*) political allegory in which Mary represents the gnostic view which legitimates female authority and Peter represents patriarchal exclusion of women from authoritative roles.[18] Clearly the struggle with gnosticism was a watershed in terms of the role of women in positions of authority in the church.[19] Even Harnack implies this.[20] However, discerning what social reality lay behind the allegorical expression of conflict in a document such as *The Gospel of Mary* is difficult. Nonetheless, what evidence there is, supplied by disparaging defenders of orthodoxy or gnostic writers engaging in political propaganda, points in the direction of movement toward an improved social and cultic position for women in gnosticism.

While Pagels explains this improved social position as having its source in the use of feminine language and images of God,[21] the apparent cultic inclusion of women in the circles of Marcion, Carpocrates, Valentinus, and others could be casually related to their asceticism. Pagels' thesis has some stumbling blocks to which she alludes. The Marcionites and the Carpocratians, about whom we have specific evidence of the role of women, maintained a largely masculine view of God.[22] An element more uniformly common to gnostic groups than inclusion of the feminine in theological imagery was their asceticism. With the exception of the libertine Carpocratians, gnostic groups embraced an ascetic spirituality which despised the flesh, the body, and this-worldly concerns. While there are many unanswered questions regarding the actual role of women in gnostic groups and the theological and social source of these roles, it is sufficient for this study to observe the evidence, emerging out of current gnostic studies, which points toward the appeal of gnostic asceticism to women.

The literature of the early monastic movement provides us with ample evidence of the appeal of virginity and the ascetic ideal to women in the early stages of Christian monasticism. The aristocratic women of Rome schooled in monasticism by Jerome and Rufinus of Aquileia, who will be the historical focus of this study, are not alone in the late fourth century in their zeal for asceticism. In addition to the ascetic groups organized in Rome by such figures as Marcella and Asella there were organizations of virgins associated with many of the great names in the Latin church of the day.[23] Augustine's sister, whose name is never supplied, headed a convent at Hippo where, fortunately for historians, a discipline problem prompted Letter 211 which informs us of the little that is known of this convent. Ambrose wrote of an order of virgins at Milan,[24] and women comprised a segregated section of the monastic community fostered by Paulinus of Nola.[25] *The Lausiac History* of Palladius which chronicles the early monastic movement in Egypt abounds with stories of the dedication of women to the monastic life.[26] According to Palladius there was a woman's monastery across the Nile from Pachomius' original foundation at Tabennesi.[27] Palladius also writes of twelve monasteries for women in Antinoe, the size of which might be indicated by the claim that there were sixty women in one of the monasteries.[28] Chrysostom witnesses to the Promethean struggles of women ascetics in the deserts of Egypt whose feats were no less than those of men.[29] Female participation in the monastic movement of Egypt was not limited to the cenobitic form, according to Palladius. Alexandra imitated the anchoritic style of Antony, when she retreated to a cave where she lived for ten years.[30] While the debate begun by Weingarten in the nineteenth century about the historical reliability of *The Lausiac History* continues,[31] one can at least claim that the evidence points to widespread participation of women in the early stages of the monastic movement in Egypt and participation in both the anchoritic and cenobitic styles. Specifying numbers of women and the percentage of women relative to men in the monasteries of Egypt may not be possible, however, and certainly lies beyond the scope of this study.

The apparent appeal of asceticism for Christian women in the ascetically inclined milieu of Syria and Asia Minor of the second and third centuries (reflected in the Apocryphal Acts of the Apostles), for women converts to the gnostically defined Christianity preserved in the Nag Hammadi tracts and for women of the early monastic movement (both in the Latin West and Pachomius' Egypt) lies shrouded in a paradox in view of the misogynist rhetoric of most ascetic literature. While the ending of the *Gospel of Thomas* has almost become a cliché, it bears repeating insofar as it represents the strand of misogyny which runs through much ascetic literature:

> Simon Peter said to them [the disciples]: Let Mary be excluded from among us, for she is a woman, and not worthy of Life. Jesus said: Behold I will take Mary, and make her a male, so that she may become a living spirit, resembling you males. For I tell you truly, that every female who makes herself male will enter the Kingdom of Heaven.[32]

Gnostic literature is replete with such misogyny. In the Greek *Gospel of the Egyptians* the Savior says, "I am come to undo the works of the female" by the female meaning lust, and by the works birth and decay.[33] In the *Dialogue of the Savior* found at Nag Hammadi, Matthew claims that the Savior says, "Pray in the place where there is [no] woman, (and) Destroy [the] works of femaleness."[34] Any theory regarding social improvement for women in gnostic circles requires some attention to the contradiction raised by this recurrent misogynist strand in gnostic literature. Elaine Pagels in her essay in 1976 on gnostic conceptuality of the divine in feminine terms, published in *Signs: Journal of Women in Culture and Society,* neglected to mention this contradiction, but she corrected this oversight in her reworking of the essay in her book *The Gnostic Gospels.*[35] However, Pagels remains much more positive toward the gnostic view of women (if gnosticism can ever be considered monolithic enough to have "a" view of women) than Elisabeth Schüssler Fiorenza. Fiorenza explains the misogynist rhetoric of gnostic literature as an expression of the gnostic use of female as a cosmic symbol of the principle of degeneracy, transience, the body, etc., and even goes so far as to conclude that gnostic dualism participates in patriarchal dichotomies.[36] Despite the fact that the term female does not refer to actual women, the casting of the feminine as a cosmic symbol of evil requires actual women to deny their feminine identity in order to attain spiritual life. While Fiorenza faces honestly the misogynist strand in gnostic writings, the paradoxical situation of apparent female leadership among gnostic circles whose literature is couched in misogynist rhetoric remains unexplained. Fiorenza does not explain the incompatibility of her conclusion that gnosticism "shares in the patriarchal paradigm" with her subsequent documentation of the gnostic argument for female leadership.

Orthodox writers of the monastic movement are no less misogynist than gnostic writers of the second century. The watchword of the monastic movement, "Beware of priests and women," suggests the threat posed by social structure to the monastic ideal of disengagement. Palladius' commendation of a man who "by God's grace ... has had no traffic with a woman, not even in a dream, except in resistance" illustrates the prevailing monastic attitude toward women.[37] Despite the generally antagonistic view of monks toward women, an occasional exceptional woman like Melania the Elder appears to win favor by her ascetic feats. While Palladius does not mention this as a source of monastic esteem, I am sure her generosity with her enormous wealth doubtless appeased a few misogynist monastic feelings.[38] According to Jerome, Paula was enchanted with the Egyptian monks during her tour of monastic Egypt and initially wished to remain there with them. I wonder, but will never know, whether they welcomed Paula as willingly as Jerome claims, for Paula quickly revised her plans.[39]

Not since Juvenal had the foibles of the Roman matron received such a scathing review as that of Jerome's. According to Jerome classical culture is of one mind with regard to the inadequacies of women:

Whole tragedies of Euripedes are censures on women. Hence Hermione says, "The counsels of evil women have beguiled me"... Herodotus tells us that a woman puts off her modesty with her clothes. And our own comic poet thinks the man fortunate who has never been married.[40]

Thus, in the person of Jerome the paradox of female attraction to an ascetic world view which is invariably cast in misogynist language finds a clear and full expression from the male, patriarchal perspective. On the one hand, Jerome found the self-indulgent foibles of the typical Roman matron who painted her face and embellished her body with fine raiment almost intolerable. And sentimental fondness for hearth and home had no place in the writing of one who described a grandson as "some little fellow to crawl upon his [the grandfather's] breast and slobber his neck."[41]

Yet, on the other hand, Jerome's praise for the ascetic Christian female had no bounds. The depth of his love for such figures as Paula, Eustochium, and Blaesilla prompted him to preserve their memories in glowing terms and prompted others to gossip about his intentions.[42] Clark addresses the ambiguity of Jerome's attitude toward women in terms of reconciling the classical view of friendship which required equality between the parties with Jerome's apparent genuine friendship with women who by definition are socially inferior. Thus, Jerome found himself in the paradoxical situation of experiencing genuine attachment to those whose sex represented a threat to the ascetic disdain for procreation and the body.

From the perspective of Paula, Eustochium, Melania, and other women of the early monastic movement, the problematic becomes one of reconciling their eager choice of the monastic way with the misogyny of the ascetic world view reflected in *The Lausiac History* and Jerome's acerbic satire of the Roman matron. Why would women embrace an ascetic *Weltanschauung* which degraded their bodily natures and required them to deny the maternal part of their identities? Letter XXXIX clearly expresses Paula's cruel dilemma when her maternal grief at the death of Blaesilla is impatiently ridiculed by Jerome. And, further, how could a degree of social improvement, which the leadership of women in gnostic Christian circles and in the monastic movement suggests, develop in a misogynist context?[43] These questions address the paradox of the apparent appeal of asceticism to women over a broad sweep of history as outlined in the preceding paragraphs.

The following study will investigate the women associated with Jerome and Rufinus in the early stages of the Christian monastic movement with this interpretive problematic in mind. The approach will be two-faceted in that it will press further the historical and prosopographical investigation of the women in question and then will refer to social theory to gain an interpretive perspective. Chapter 2 will be a more in-depth account of studies to date on the Roman aristocratic women of the early monastic movement and what they have to say about the problematic addressed by this study. Chapter 3 will focus on what historical data we have about the women in question, with particular attention to their place within the senatorial aristocracy of late Rome. Chapter 4 provides insights into the historical, political, and social context in which the women found themselves by investigating the life of the Roman *matrona*. Clues of the many contradictions in the life of the Roman *matrona,* emerging out of chapter 4, point to the conceptualization of the social context of women such as Paula, Melania, and Marcella in terms of the malintegration of cultural norms. This will be demonstrated more dramatically in chapter 6 by the construction of a typology of images of women as they appear in the ecclesiastical and classical literature which informed late Roman consciousness. However before attempting to reconstruct the cultural milieu of late Roman society, I will examine the basic paradigm of Talcott Parsons' action frame of reference and the categories it provides for disassembling the dynamics in which the aristocratic women of Rome had their social existence. The paradigm of social dynamics found in action theory aided by the reconstruction of the cultural milieu in the typology of images of women will be the basis for my thesis that the monastic choice can be explained in terms of the malintegration of cultural norms for aristocratic Roman women who lived on the borderline between pagan and Christian in late antiquity.

2

Current Studies of the Ascetic
Women of Rome

For purposes of clarity it is necessary to define the Roman ascetic women who are the focal point of this work. The group of Roman Christian women, usually associated historically with the names of Jerome and Rufinus of Aquileia, forms a fairly cohesive group for the purpose of study. Often related by blood or marriage, the women had their roots in the same social network of the elite aristocracy of the city of Rome at the end of the fourth and early part of the fifth centuries. This group of ascetic women had one foot in Egyptian style monasticism in the persons of Melania the Elder, Paula, Eustochium, and Paula the Younger[1] and the other foot in a less rigorous style of monasticism resembling the philosophical *otium* in the persons of Marcella, Asella, Lea, Principia, and others.[2] The women whose names come to us primarily from the pen of Jerome (although Palladius and Paulinus of Nola preserve the memory of Melania the Elder, and Gerontius that of Melania the Younger), insofar as they have their roots in the same social milieu in Rome, respond to the first stirrings of the monastic movement, and interact with each other during the living out of their ascetic lives, form an identifiable group for consideration. While similar monastic practices were occurring concurrently in Milan with Ambrose as mentor, in Hippo with Augustine as mentor, in Pachomius' Egypt, in Caesarea under the direction of Basil's sister Macrina,[3] and in the East according to the model of Olympias, the ascetic women discussed in this study are distinguished from these.[4] The distinguishing characteristic of the friends of Jerome and Rufinus is their interwoven lineage among the senatorial families of the city of Rome. Paula's daughter, Paulina, was briefly married, before her premature death, to Pammachius, possibly a cousin of Marcella's.[5] The only surviving son of Melania the Elder, Valerius Publicola, whose secular ambitions rebuffed the ascetic call, married a descendant of the family of Marcella's uncle.[6] Even Paula and Melania the Elder who fit into the rival monastic camps of Jerome and Rufinus may have been linked by marriage in that their sons, Julius Toxotius and Publicola, married women whose fathers may have been brothers.[7] Thus, the three leading female figures of the first generation of Roman nuns, Marcella, Paula, and Melania, saw their families linked together by marriage among the second generation; therefore, their genealogy as well as their monastic experiences tie them together as a group for study.

Until the current work by contemporary women scholars (Clark, Ruether, Yarbrough, and Moine), studies of the ascetic women in question were largely historical and historical-critical in nature. In 1947 Francis X. Murphy noted that the historical studies of his immediate past centered on the figure of Melania the Younger because of the availability of texts of the *Vita S. Melaniae,* an ancient biography of the younger Melania credited to Gerontius.[8] At the turn of the century Cardinal Rampolla had assembled a major study of Melania the Younger which included Latin and Greek texts of the *Vita S. Melaniae,*[9] and this study spawned an interest in Melania the Younger as evidenced by studies in French, German, and English.[10]

Current studies, which owe their origin to the recent interest in women's studies resulting from the feminist movement of the early 1970s, are also primarily historical and historical-critical in nature. Yet, some movement has been made on furthering the theoretical reflection on the question of how to interpret the monastic choice of these ancient figures whom we glimpse in the writings of Jerome, Paulinus, and Palladius. What follows will be an examination of the current work on the ascetic women of Rome with the interpretive question primarily in mind, since the purpose of this study is to push interpretive reflection further by reference to some fundamental insights of action theory.

Anne Yarbrough's seminal essay entitled "Christianization in the Fourth Century: The Example of Roman Women," was written as a rejoinder to Peter Brown's description of the syncreticism of late ancient Christianity. A largely historical study, Yarbrough draws on the work of social historians such as A. H. M. Jones and M. K. Hopkins in order to uncover the social context in which women such as Melania the Elder and Paula chose ascetic conversion. Exploring the social background of the female associates of Jerome and Rufinus, Yarbrough places them among the elite of the Roman senatorial class, the so-called "inner aristocracy," but detects the possibility of the inclusion of some lesser blood from the provinces and religious mixture in their prestigious families.[11] Considering asceticism socially and economically, Yarbrough discovers the threat to the economic status quo posed by the ascetic conversion of members of the senatorial class whose aristocratic duty was to hand on the vast wealth accumulated over centuries. Yarbrough's approach to interpreting the rise of asceticism among women of the Roman aristocracy in the Late Empire is a kind of implied functionalism. Yarbrough concludes that the success of the ascetic call to virginity among the bluebloods of Rome suggests that it had a particular function for society as a whole:

"These indications, impressionistic as they are, suggest that asceticism was increasing in the West and, therefore, that it had a function to fulfill in the society."[12] This point of view has its roots in functionalist theory which conceives of society as an organic whole whose parts have a useful function for the maintenance of the equilibrium of the whole.[13] While Yarbrough doesn't engage in reflection on her use of functionalist theory (referring to no theoretical studies), she certainly applies a very general tenet of functionalism to her study of the social, economic, and religious status of the Christian ascetic women of the Late Roman Empire. The positive function which asceticism had for maintaining the equilibrium of Roman society, according to Yarbrough, centered on offering an acceptable alternative to marriage for the Roman matron and providing parents with an acceptable escape from the burdensome cost of too many expensive initiations for children into adult aristocratic society.[14] In summary, Yarbrough's interpretation focuses on the pragmatic social function of ascetic renunciation for the aristocracy, nuanced by reference to functionalist theory. However, the possible internal conflict posed by ascetic denigration of the maternal is not at issue for Yarbrough.

Rosemary Ruether's early work on the ascetic movement of the late patristic era with regard to the question of women focuses on the misogyny of patristic anthropology as found in the writings of Augustine and Gregory of Nyssa.[15] The positive view of the virginal woman in late antiquity in no way mitigates the misogyny, according to Ruether. Rather, it simply expresses another dimension of a world view which denigrated the maternal aspect of woman's being. Without denying the misogynist anthropology out of which asceticism emerges, Ruether recently acknowledged the potentially liberating consequences of the ascetic choice in an essay entitled "Mothers of the Church: Ascetic Women of the Late Patristic Age" in *Women of Spirit* (Ruether and McLaughlin, eds.). This essay, largely historical in nature, summarizes the lives of the major figures among the Roman ascetic women— Marcella, Melania the Elder, and Melania the Younger. Relying almost exclusively on historical sources, Ruether engages in little reflection on the hermeneutical question. Her introductory remarks contain a reference to the suitability of a "liberation" model in viewing the ascetic women. Without much reflection on the character of a liberation model, Ruether defines liberation in terms of moving toward self-definition:

> What individuals find "liberating" is relative, but perhaps the most important common denominator of the liberating choice is the sense of taking charge of one's own life; of rejecting a state of being governed and defined by others.[16]

Disregarding for the moment the question of the suitability of the liberation model, clearly liberation as defined by the concept of self-definition is not universally applicable to the ascetic women in question. While the dramatic departure of Melania the Elder from Rome where she deposited her remaining child was a slap in the face to patriarchal values and could be interpreted as a move toward self-definition, other ascetic women appear at times to be molding themselves unwillingly to Jerome's monastic fantasy just as their pagan sisters were molding themselves to Ovid's erotic fantasy.[17] The tragic case of Blaesilla aptly illustrates the point. Blaesilla, whose beauty and charm later haunted her mother's memory, only converted to asceticism after the premature death of her husband of seven months, and a serious illness. Blaesilla's newfound monastic ardor did not agree with her constitution, and she died within three months of her ascetic conversion. The untimely death of Blaesilla scandalized the non-ascetic Roman aristocracy and calls into question the interpretation of her choice as "self-definition."[18] Rather, it appears that, weakened by grief, the young girl succumbed to the ardent pressure of Jerome and her mother to assume a monastic style entirely too rigorous for her.

The case of Blaesilla illustrates the limited legitimacy of a liberation model defined as "movement toward self-definition." It also illustrates the difficulty of developing an integrative theory to interpret the asceticism of a group of women whose experiences and motives diverge despite their cohesiveness as a social group. Therefore, if a liberation model of interpretation is used, further reflection is needed on the meaning of "freedom" or the model will be contradicted by aspects of the historical data, particularly the degree to which Jerome's vision defined their experience.

In summary, Ruether's writing to date on Roman ascetic women of the early monastic movement grasps the interpretive dilemma addressed by this study insofar as her early essay was written from the perspective of ascetic misogyny, while the later essay assumes the positive, liberating dimensions of monasticism.

Elizabeth Clark is in the vanguard of the women scholars currently doing research on Christian ascetic women in late Roman antiquity. Beginning with an essay entitled "John Chrysostom and the Subintroductae" (*Church History* 46 [1977]), in which she explained the practice of spiritual marriage in late ancient Christianity, Clark's work has blossomed to include a wide array of studies on the women in question. Scholarly study of such figures as the Melanias and Olympias, friend of Chrysostom, has been advanced by Clark's translations of ancient documents. *Jerome, Chrysostom, and Friends* (published in 1979) contains translations of *The Life of Olympias*, Sergia's *Narration Concerning St. Olympias*, and two of Chrysostom's treatises on the *subintroductae* whose chaste cohabitation with men offended skeptical Chrysostom. Clark's translation of the Greek version of the *Vita S. Melaniae*, a biography of Melania the Younger written by one of her contemporaries, has recently been completed with encouragement from the National Endowment for the Humanities. Clark also published an essay on Christian ascetic women of the Late Empire which appeared in the July 1981 edition of the *Anglican Theological Review* under the title "Ascetic Renunciation and Feminine Advancement: A Paradox of Late Ancient Christianity."

Clark's approach can be characterized as that of an historian of the classics insofar as she often focuses on the material in terms of issues of classical theory. For example, in *Jerome, Chrysostom, and Friends,* Chrysostom's criticism of the advancement of women described in Plato's *politeia* of Book 5 of the *Republic* is considered paradigmatic of Chrysostom's view of the place of women in social structure. Also, the attitude of Jerome and Chrysostom toward their monastic protégées is examined by Clark in terms of the theory of friendship which emerges in classical literature, i.e., that friendship is based on equality and similarity. In addition, she has shown the greatest methodological reflection by consciously aligning herself with the work of the so-called "social description" school of the AAR/SBL. A methodologically innovative essay, appearing in *Jerome, Chrysostom, and Friends,* draws on current theory in the field of social anthropology. Here she explains the apparent friendship between Jerome and Chrysostom and their respective female protégées, despite their social inequality as males and females, by reference to Victor Turner's theories regarding the liminal state in primitive *rites de passage*.[19] The women monastics are likened to liminars undergoing status changes. The features of the liminal interlude for those moving from one state to another in primitive *rites de passage* are notably similar to the monastic experience. Humility, loss of rank and property, sexual continence, equality, abrogation of duties and ties to one's kin, and the blurring of sexual distinctions are all features of the liminal state which are re-enacted in the perpetual liminality of monasticism.[20] The suspension of ties to one's kin is, of course, one of Jerome's main themes in his proselytizing of aristocratic women of Rome.[21] Clark reminds us of Jerome's impatience at maternal grief in Letter XXXIX and of his romanticizing of maternal abandonment of children in Letter CVIII.[22] According to Clark, the assumption of liminality transforms the women into something other than frivolously feminine matrons concerned with senatorial protocol. The elevation of such figures as Melania and Paula, resulting from this transformation, enables Jerome and Chrysostom to reconcile the classical theories of friendship with their actual fondness for these women.[23] While Clark does not develop this theme, the *communitas* common to those sharing the liminal condition could be at the root of affection between the sexes, for male monastics such as Jerome and Chrysostom embraced ascetic liminality also. Thus, in her use of the theory of liminality found in the work of social anthropologist Victor Turner, Clark opens up an innovative avenue of interpretation which moves beyond the prereflective stage apparent in other writers.

However, Clark uses the theory of liminality primarily to explain the interiority of Jerome and Chrysostom as they seek (perhaps unconsciously) to reconcile their fondness for their female ascetic protégées with the reality of social inequality as males and females. While this is unquestionably a legitimate use of Turner's theories, I would like to explore the application of the model of liminality in terms of insights into the interiority of the women themselves. Thus, the question would be not what Turner's work can tell us about female acceptability as liminars in the eyes of Jerome and Chrysostom but what Turner's work on primitive *rites de passage* might suggest to us about female choice of monasticism. Did the *communitas* of the liminal state which was mirrored in monasticism hold a special appeal to women whose social background was characterized by the senatorial obsession with rank and protocol? Was the *communitas* of the liminal state, which Turner defines as a moment of pure relationship, the goal of the ascetic women with whom we are dealing or was their goal the post-liminal reaggregation present in Turner's analysis and as yet undefined in terms of a monastic parallel? And could the liminal-like condition of monasticism be considered a parody of general female marginality which our women largely escaped as part of the elite of the senatorial class of the Roman Empire? These are the kinds of questions which the application of Turner's work on primitive *rites de passage* raises when directed toward the interiority of the ascetic women themselves rather than toward their male mentors. While this line of questioning cannot be carried through in this study, the questions have been raised not only to illustrate the provocative potential in applying Turner's analysis of liminality to the ascetic women themselves but also to reiterate the view that interpretive possibilities have not been exhausted.

In "Ascetic Renunciation and Feminine Advancement: a Paradox of Late Ancient Christianity," Elizabeth Clark appears to suspend the effort to find interpretive models in the social sciences. Here Clark develops the thesis that, contrary to the prevailing classical view of monasticism as degrading of aristocrats, asceticism for women was actually a form of social advancement. Clark considers female monasticism a form of advancement for two reasons. First, contrary to the subordinate status of women relative to men in the secular world of the Roman aristocracy, in the ascetic world the monastic experiences of men and women were "strikingly similar" (to paraphrase Clark).[24] The similarity between male and female monasticism in the Latin West centers on two features of Western monasticism—its form as "house monasticism" and the absence of physical labor.[25] Second, monasticism sanctioned activities which would have been taboo for the socially conscious

Roman matron.[26] The most obvious privilege accorded the monastic woman was the right to travel extensively under her own direction.[27] The ambitious journeys of Melania the Elder, Paula, and Egeria which strike us today as highly risky were undertaken with zest. In addition, according to Clark, monasticism opened up the intellectual arena to intelligent women. Clark's point is well-taken when one contrasts the praise of Jerome for his scholarly protégées with the disdain Juvenal heaps upon the erudite woman in apparent agreement with conservative pagan circles who held up for emulation an idealized model of the simple, virtuous woman of the Republic. Granting some excess common to eulogies which are often written in a rush of sentiment, the intellectual accomplishments of Jerome's protégées, highlighted in his eulogies of them, are indisputable and receive Jerome's highest commendation.[28]

Thus, the thrust of Clark's argument is that the sanctioning of independent travel and intellectual accomplishment in monastic circles as indicated in the ancient sources makes a case for viewing asceticism as social advancement for women. Yet, this essay suspends for the moment reference to theoretical models drawn from the social sciences as a means of interpretation; the social theorizing is Clark's own and contains no reference to external models.

In summary, it is my view that current studies, while marked by scholarly depth and insight, have not fully accounted for the monastic choice of these Roman aristocratic women and particularly have somewhat neglected the misogynist strand in asceticism. While Rosemary Ruether fully recognizes the ambiguity posed by monastic misogyny,[29] her interpretation of the ascetic choice of women of the Late Roman Empire by reference to a liberation model does not solve the dilemma. Further, Ruether's liberation model, based loosely on the concept of self-definition, fails to take account of those women whose ascetic choice seems to be foisted upon them by the overwhelming personality of Jerome. Insofar as asceticism reflects monastic devaluation of maternity, a liberation model has limited legitimacy; a freedom which demands denial of the maternal has limited authenticity for women. Anne Yarbrough carries theoretical reflection further than Ruether by reference to functionalist theory as interpretive key. Yarbrough views the ascetic choice of aristocratic Roman matrons pragmatically in terms of the function it had for satisfying two social needs of the aristocracy, i.e., an alternative to unwanted marriages and alleviation of expensive childrearing burdens. Yet, Yarbrough's account does not address the negativity of the monastic repression of the maternal, bodily self. Perhaps, the unstated implication of Yarbrough's interpretation is that the positive social functions mitigated monastic misogyny; however, such an account of monasticism's negative side remains unaddressed. While Elizabeth Clark fully recognizes the ambiguity of the monastic choice in view of ascetic misogyny so clearly articulated by Jerome, her work to date has not specifically worked toward interpretive categories which would find something in the historical situation to account for the embrace of asceticism by Paula, Marcella, and others despite its misogyny. In *Jerome, Chrysostom, and Friends,* monastic liminality may account for female acceptability in the eyes of Jerome, Rufinus of Aquileia, Chrysostom et al., but an account of female choice of monasticism is not self-evident as a result of casting monasticism in the categories of *rites de passage.* The implication of "Ascetic Renunciation and Feminine Advancement" would be that the social benefits associated with monasticism, highlighted here by Clark, mitigated its anti-maternal ground.

My study will address the interpretive dilemma defined in the first chapter of this study not only by considering what drew women toward asceticism but also what stresses in the aristocratic world repulsed them. Before we review the social, political, and economic context of the *matrona* of late Roman society which might provide clues about certain stresses for women in late antiquity, it is important to press further the historical account of the subjects of this study—Paula and family, Melania and family, and Marcella. By maintaining a skeptical eye on Jerome's rhetorical flourishes, I have gained some surprising insights into the social status of his favored protégée, Paula, among the elite circles of the Roman aristocracy which will be explained in the following chapter.

3

Roman Ascetic Women of Late Antiquity

Before applying the insights of the interaction model to the historical and cultural context of Roman monastic women of late antiquity, it would be helpful to provide accounts of what we know about the women in question and on what basis we know it. The following biographical sketches of the major figures of the female monastic movement among Roman aristocrats rely primarily on Jerome, Palladius, and Gerontius, but make critical use of supplementary sources of historical information set forth in such works as *The Prosopography of the Later Roman Empire* by Jones, Martindale and Morris, *The Later Roman Empire* by Jones, and the *Atlas of the Early Christian World.* Insofar as Jones et al. culled an impressively wide range of documents in compiling *The Prosopography of the Later Roman Empire,* this work provides our reconstruction of social position with a necessary critical check on the biased accounts of Jerome, whose monastic ideology defined and, perhaps, skewed his perspective. In that female status within patriarchal cultures depends upon the status of the men to whom one is linked, careful attention will be given to the worldly status of the male relatives of our subjects.

Paula and Her Monastic Family

Paula

Our account will begin with Paula, the woman whose ascetic feats most closely fit Jerome's monastic vision. The fact that Jerome wrote more about Paula than about other ascetic women less intimately associated with him, coupled with the scope provided by her many familial and monastic connections, argue for beginning with her biography.

Genealogical information about Paula is striking not only for Jerome's extravagant claims but for the actual lacunae. In his eulogy to Paula, Letter CVIII, Jerome, reflecting the value placed on noble lineage among the aristocracy, begins the account in the conventional rhetorical manner, first praising the ancestors which produced such a stellar figure.[1] Paula's ancestry receives the following praise, presumably to emphasize the nobility of ascetic rejection of it: "Of the stock of the Gracchi and descended from the Scipios, the heir and representative of that Paulus whose name she bore, the true and legitimate daughter of that Martia Papyria who was mother to Africanus."[2] According to Jerome, Paula's mother Blaesilla bore a pedigree which could be traced to the distinguished families of Republican times. Paula's father was unsurpassed in familial pedigree in that "he was said, indeed, to have in his veins the blood of Agamemnon."[3] Yet, reference to the research of Jones et al. in *The Prosopography of the Later Roman Empire* calls into question the impeccable pedigree claimed by Jerome. First of all, the entry under Rogatus, father of Paula, lists Jerome's Letter CVIII as the only source of information about Rogatus.[4] No corroborative evidence substantiates Jerome's claims about the distinguished pedigree of Paula's father. Rogatus' name appears nowhere on the "Fasti" of consuls, suffect consuls, praetorian prefects or prefects of the city of Rome.[5] Presumably, Rogatus' failure to hold high public office accounts for his designation as a senator of the lowest rank, a *clarissimus*. As Jones points out, by our period rank within the senatorial order was based on the status attached to the offices one held.[6] *Clarissimi* held the lowest of senatorial rank, claiming senatorial status on the basis of birth but with no prestigious office to boost them out of the lower ranks.[7] All this would suggest that Jerome's claim of Agamemnon as Rogatus' ancestor is not just hyperbole but a way of avoiding the absence of actually existing persons of distinction in Rogatus' background. Yet, Paula's mother, Blaesilla, appears to have had actual ties to the distinguished Republican families.[8] The absence of corroborative evidence about Blaesilla raises fewer suspicions about her pedigree, since, of course, as a female her name would not appear on lists of officeholders.

M. T. W. Arnheim is also suspicious of actual links of these fourth century senatorial families to ancient Romans of the Republic but offers a slightly different interpretation, attributing the elevation of the status of Paula and others less to Jerome's hyperbole than to prevailing senatorial mores which accepted the often contrived linkage of prestigious senators with ancient Republican families.[9] The apparently exaggerated claims of fourth century noble families of ancient roots traceable to the Republic were, according to Arnheim, not invented by Jerome but accepted within the aristocracy due to the actual nobility of the families for several generations and the similarity of their *cognomen* to ancient Republican names.[10] Nevertheless, this writer still notes the significant absence of a verifiable person of senatorial distinction in Paula's immediate background.

A comparison of Jerome's account of the pedigree of Demetrias may be instructive for determining the actual status of Paula's parents within the senatorial order. In Letter CXXX, Jerome seems to relish mentioning Demetrias' father Olybrius, making a pun on his *illustris* grade which ranked him among the elite of the senatorial aristocracy.[11] As consul in A.D. 395, Anicius Hermogenianus Olybrius moved beyond *clarissimus* status to that of *illustris*.[12] One wonders why in the account of Paula's lineage Jerome does not refer to a specific person who held *illustris* rank or one of the highest offices such as consul, proconsul, or prefect. One can only conjecture that no actually existing person of senatorial distinction lay in Paula's immediate background, as Olybrius, father of Demetrias, lay ready for use by Jerome's ascetic ideology.

Thus, the prosopographical evidence suggests that whatever status Paula had in her ancestry came primarily through the maternal line and, probably, generations back. Insofar as status in patriarchy depends upon the status of the males to whom one is related, maternal derivation of position would have resulted in somewhat lower status. While Paula married into a family of noble pedigree, her husband must have been overshadowed by his more successful brother, Julius Festus Hymetius. While Paula's husband, Toxotius, remained on the lower rung of the senatorial ladder, his brother Hymetius attained senatorial distinction by holding numerous public offices, including the proconsulate of Africa.[13] The superior status of Hymetius was paralleled by the superior status of his wife Praetextata whose presumed brother, Vettius Agorius Praetextatus, attained the highest senatorial grade, the *illustris* grade.[14] Thus, the evidence would suggest that Paula had ties to the elite of the Roman aristocracy but remained somewhat on its periphery. In playing the game of one-upmanship among the ladies described by Jerome as "puffed up by their husbands' honors,"[15] Paula would not have fared as well as many.

Just how wealthy Paula was is also difficult to ascertain. The fact that two of her children presumably married into the elite of the Roman aristocracy would argue for the view that their father's undistinguished career was compensated for by ample wealth. Certainly Pammachius and Laeta, mates of Paula's children with presumed links to the Ceionii Rufii family, were not expected to take on charity cases. Pammachius' securing of a proconsulate, probably in Africa, elevated him above the *clarissimus* rank of his father-in-law to that of *spectabilis*.[16] However, Jerome's evidence about the extent of Paula's wealth is ambiguous. While he does refer to Paula's "distinguished, and noble, and formerly wealthy house,"[17] one wonders why there are no references to vast estates such as Gerontius claims for Melania the Younger, given Jerome's penchant for extravagant claims which throw ascetic renunciation into sharp relief. Given Jones' characterization of Symmachus and Melania the Younger, whose vast holdings are well-documented, as somewhere in the middle range of senatorial wealth (based on a criterion gained from evidence in Olympiodorus),[18] suspicions emerge about Jerome's inexplicit references to Paula's wealth. However, while comparison to the criterion supplied by Olympiodorus is precluded by the vagueness of Jerome's references to Paula's wealth, even moderate senatorial wealth was staggering by modern standards. Praising her generous charity Jerome writes: "And all this she was enabled to do not by the greatness of her wealth but by her careful management of it."[19] Perhaps this refers to the depleted state of her wealth following from her ascetic repudiation of her property. Jerome does mention that upon her departure from Rome to the Holy Land, Paula turned over all that she had to her children.[20]

Whatever the extent of Paula's pre-conversion wealth, Jerome reiterates the view that it was depleted by monastic liberality. Financing Jerome's monastic dreams and providing for the poor required Paula not only to use up whatever resources she had but also to borrow heavily at interest.[21] Jerome recounts Paula's financial generosity with the monks whom she visited on her monastic pilgrimage as she traveled from Rome to Bethlehem. At Cyprus Paula was said to have "left, so far as her means allowed, substantial relief for the brothers" of the local monasteries.[22] At Jerusalem she was said to have distributed "money to the poor and her fellow-servants so far as her means allowed."[23] On the monks of Egypt Paula bestowed something which Jerome does not identify.[24] Upon completing this monastic pilgrimage which included financial largesse, Paula began plans to build the double monastery at Bethlehem. As if generosity with the monastic communities on her itinerary and financing a building project weren't enough of a strain on her resources, Paula refused to turn away a needy person empty-handed. She countered Jerome's rebuke about her liberality by pointing out that she could always secure funds (presumably through her aristocratic connections), but the poor had no one to whom they could turn.[25] Such cavalier monastic generosity resulted in the accumulation of a huge debt which Paula upon her death left to Eustochium. Jerome characterizes the extent of the debt by noting that Eustochium could not possibly pay it off by herself.[26] Yet, Jerome views a debt mounted by monastic liberality as a fitting ascetic legacy for Eustochium.[27]

Before describing Paula's experiences as an ascetic convert and protégée of Jerome, it would be instructive for our later moves toward interpretive reflection to consider the character of her maternal sentiment insofar as possible on the basis of the evidence. Whatever her maternal feelings, Paula was more prolific than the average aristocratic Roman woman.[28] Jerome attributes this fertility to her attempt to provide her husband with a male offspring.[29] While Jerome would have us believe that Paula entirely subordinated maternal devotion to monastic devotion, certain pieces of evidence contract his ideological portrayal of Paula's maternal sentiment. In Jerome's portrayal of Paula's departure from Rome he writes of her noble subordination of maternal feeling to her higher devotion to God. The scene includes the image of bereaved children standing on the dock, entreating their mother not to abandom them.[30] Yet, the historicity of this scene must be questioned. For one thing, Jerome had already left Rome in August of 385, some weeks before Paula's departure.[31] While someone could have written an account of the scene to Jerome, I wonder about the dramatic detail such as little Toxotius' outstretched arms and Rufina's self-interested pleas. Further doubts about the historicity of the passage are raised by the similarity of its form to a poetic form common to classical writers called the *proemptikon*. P.G. Walsh mentions the tendency of Paulinus of Nola to use this form, which includes entreaty by the persons left behind in an attempt to persuade the departing one to stay.[32] While Jerome's description of Paula's departure scene does not contain all the elements of the *proemptikon*, its similarity raises the question of the extent to which the scene forces historical data into a poetic mold rather than an objective one. It may be that Jerome is using elements of the *proemptikon* to embellish his monastic view of the subordination of maternal sentiment.

Jerome's claim that Paula, upon ascetic conversion, "knew herself no more as a mother, that she might approve herself a handmaid of Christ" may tell us more about the former's monastic ideology than about the latter's maternal feelings.[33] In contradiction to this claim about Paula, Jerome includes an account of her demonstrative maternal grief as an illustration that she was not without fault.[34] Upon the death of her husband and daughters, Jerome writes, "[Paula's] maternal instincts were too much for her confiding mind."[35] Her bereavement was such that she succumbed to a threatening illness on one occasion.[36] Not even in Paula's eulogy does Jerome seem to sympathize with what he considers a maternal excess or indulgence of worldly feeling, for he notes that his description of her maternal grief might be considered "an invective rather than a eulogy."[37]

Jerome's description of Paula's maternal grief at the death of her daughter Blaesilla in Letter XXXIX also calls into question his hopeful characterization of his protégées' subordination of maternal attachment. Paula was apparently overwhelmed at the premature death of her daughter Blaesilla a few months after her ascetic conversion. In what strikes me as a very honest passage Jerome describes the way in which the memory of Blaesilla haunted the bereaved mother: "You call to mind Blaesilla's companionship, her conversation, and her endearing ways; and you cannot endure the thought that you have lost them all."[38] Paula's maternal grief was such that it apparently compromised the monastic claim of disengagement. Jerome mentions the criticism leveled at the monastics of Rome as a result of Paula's excessive grief. Rumors abounded that Paula's maternal grief indicated that she had unwillingly succumbed to Jerome's monastic pressure.[39] According to Jerome, Melania's maternal detachment should be an instructive example to Paula, for whom monastic ideology and personal feeling didn't always coincide.

Paula's ascetic experience contains four striking elements which will be treated in succession—her monastic pilgrimage, her intellectual growth, her organization of a monastery and her excessive, perhaps pathological, self-denial. Jerome's advice to Eustochium in Letter XXII, "Rarely go abroad, and if you wish to seek the aid of the martyrs seek it in your own chamber,"[40] was flouted by Paula whose monastic pilgrimage was strikingly extensive. The following outline of Paula's travel should give the reader an idea of the vast area she covered.[41]

Paula's departure from Rome must have been prompted not only by the lure of monastic images painted by Epiphanius but by Jerome's recent exit under duress. The scandal associated with the death of Blaesilla, probably due to ascetic excess, coupled with the death of Pope Damasus, Jerome's well-placed ally, made Jerome's position in Rome untenable.[42] Leaving Rome several weeks after Jerome's departure in August of A.D. 385,[43] Paula set sail from Portus, which, along with Ostia, was the port of Rome at the mouth of the Tiber.[44]

Paula's first stop was the small island of Pontia, off the coast of the Campania area of Italy, where Paula allegedly visited the cells of the emperor Domitian's wife, Flavia Domitilla, who had been banished for her Christianity.[45] Pontia's location had made it a favorite place of banishment for rejects of Roman society, both political and religious.[46]

Sailing through the straits of Messina, Paula voyaged from Pontia to Methone in Greece. According to Jerome, Methone held no special interest other than a place to be refreshed for further travel.[47] Jerome skips over the sea voyage from Greece to Rhodes, which, even if uneventful, should have borne some comment because of its length. We know only that Rhodes and Lycia were on Paula's itinerary before setting sail for Cyprus. On Cyprus Paula spent ten days, detained, according to Jerome, by the noted monk and ecclesiastical leader Epiphanius.[48] Jerome does not mention Paula's reaction when she was reunited with this monastic devotee who originally inspired her abandonment of Roman frivolity.[49] It must have been rewarding to visit someone as compatible as Epiphanius, Bishop of Constantia/Salamis, whose monastic devotion, anti-Origenism, and links with Jerome forged lasting ties with Paula.[50] This same Epiphanius, according to Letter CVIII, later lovingly rebuked Paula for refusing the medicinal aid of wine.[51] Yet, Jerome only tells us of Paula's largesse with the monks under the tutelage of Epiphanius.

After leaving Cyprus, Paula sailed to Seleucia, a town of Cilicia. Jerome doesn't tell us why she stopped in Seleucia; Cyprus' location suggests no reason she could not have sailed straight to Antioch. Egeria's famous pilgrimage to the holy places may provide a clue and proves to be an instructive parallel for comparison with Paula's travels at certain points. Egeria included Seleucia on her itinerary in order to see the monastery of St.

Thecla.[52] The burial place of St. Thecla, whose spiritual and social resemblance to the Roman monastic women has already been noted, would also have been of keen interest to Paula. Therefore, despite Jerome's silence on the matter, the well-established veneration of Thecla and honoring of her burial site in Seleucia, as revealed by Egeria's travels, must have caught Paula's attention.[53]

Whatever the attraction in Seleucia, Paulinus, who along with Epiphanius had inspired Paula's monastic dream, and, perhaps, Jerome drew her to Antioch. J. N. D. Kelly thinks that Paula and Jerome, waiting discreetly until sufficiently distant from Rome, rejoined in Antioch.[54] Kelly bases his view on the opinion of Cavallera, who points to the compatibility of other references in Jerome's writing with the itinerary and timetable maintained by Paula on her journey.[55] Yet, in view of the absence of any self-references by Jerome (except at Bethlehem) and the fact that our study focuses on Paula, there is no reason to interject Jerome into our survey of Paula's journey.

Jerome tells us little of what Paula did at Antioch and says nothing of what she learned about the Meletian schism, in which Paulinus, a contender for the See of Antioch, was involved. Yet, her contact with Paulinus is hardly surprising given the compatibility of his trinitarian views with the Western resistance to three hypostases voiced by Jerome in Letter XV.[56]

From Antioch, Paula journeyed to the Holy Land to visit the shrines erected in memory of the Lord. While the journey could have been made by sea, Jerome portrays Paula leaving Antioch in suitably humble style riding upon an ass.[57] The conjectured land route of Egeria from Antioch to Caesarea would also argue for the view that Paula traveled by land.[58] Jerome refers to wider travel in the Coele-Syrian and Phoenician areas but makes no explicit references to places until Paula arrives at Berytus (present-day Beirut). Perhaps, Berytus' reputation as a center of learning attracted Paula.[59] Or, perhaps, the existence of an episcopal see there made a welcome reception more likely for her and her entourage. Passing through Zidon (Sidon) and the shore of Zarephath, Paula pressed on to Tyre. The next three stops, all of which are on the coast, suggest a coastal route from Tyre to Ptolemais to Dor to Caesarea. Caesarea may have held particular interest but for its reputation as a place of persevering martyrs.[60]

Paula's stop in Antipater may have been simply a necessary rest before proceeding to Diospolis, for Jerome mentions no mark of Christian distinction in the former. In contrast Diospolis (Lydda) was the site of two New Testament scenes and, therefore, of interest to the Christian pilgrim. While Jerome mentions Joppa and Arimathea as points close to Diospolis, it is not clear that Paula visited either of them.[61] Rather than detouring to such out of the way places, she must have proceeded on to Nicopolis (Emmaus).

From Nicopolis she journeyed to Jerusalem.[62] Jerome tells us little about her stay in Jerusalem. While he mentions the hospitality of the proconsul of Palestine which Paula promptly rejected, he says nothing of overtures from Melania and Rufinus, whose monastery must have held keen interest for Paula.[63] We know only of a dramatic display of emotion prompted by visits to the sacred places but nothing of monastic contacts in Jerusalem.

Bethlehem, the birthplace of the Lord, was Paula's next destination. Jerome implies that he and Paula had social interactions here and quotes a lengthy, rather tangled declaration of praise made by Paula upon seeing the sacred spots of Bethlehem.[64] In view of the fact that Jerome does not attempt to reconstruct Paula's verbal responses to the holy places in other locations, one can assume Jerome heard her exclamations upon viewing the birthplace of the Lord. In judging whether Jerome records her words verbatim, one would hope Paula had more of a gift for clarity. If the quotation bears some degree of authenticity, it demonstrates an ability to recite widely from the Scriptures. Why Paula proceeded further when she pronounced Bethlehem the place she would dwell Jerome does not relate.

If Paula took a reasonably direct route from Bethlehem to her next destination, Gaza, she would have bypassed three monastic establishments, at Eleutheropolis, at Besanduce, and at Bethelia.[65] In that Jerome mentions nothing of them, her reasons for bypassing them would be only conjectural. Jerome mentions two stops on the way from Gaza to Hebron—Bethzur and Eshcol.[66] The location of Bethzur is controversial, while the biblical site of Eshcol is unknown, not appearing in *The Atlas of the Early Christian World*. Paula's swing back to the north at this point is something of a mystery. If she had firmly in mind the plan of visiting the monks of Egypt, it would have made sense to set sail from Gaza, which was closer than a port somewhere East of Capernaum. Either she had definite wishes to see other spots in Palestine such as Nazareth, or her monastic route was charted by the prompting of the Holy Spirit and not the dictates of geography.

From Gaza she journeyed northeast to Hebron, which Jerome calls the "city of the Four Men." He alludes to monuments there to Abraham, Isaac, and Jacob, and to Adam and Caleb, who vied for the spot as the fourth man. Jerome's reference to the "upper springs and the nether springs" may refer to two well-known reservoirs for rain water on the outskirts of town.[67]

Jerome's narrative introduces Paula's return to Jerusalem with quotations from Amos and Luke, cast in the first person, which could be taken as Paula's.[68] The short account of Paula in Jerusalem at this point suggests that her visit was en route to places farther north. Several points of sacred interest caught Paula's attention on the road from Jerusalem to Jericho—the site of the story of the Good Samaritan, the sycamore tree of Zacchaeus, and the place where blind men received sight from the Lord.[69] At Jericho Paula reflected on the religious symbolism presented by the famous fountain of Elisha, which by its water transformed the barren into the fertile.[70]

Passing by the valley of Achor, of indeterminate location, Paula visited Bethel, made famous as the site of Jacob's vision of the ladder.[71] After viewing the tombs of Joshua and Eleazar at Mount Ephraim, she proceeded on to Shiloh (Silo). Paula must have spent little time here, for Jerome's reference to Shiloh is fleeting.[72]

Paula's next stop was Neapolis or Shechem, an important ancient community (and birthplace of Simon Magus and Justin Martyr).[73] Corroborative evidence substantiates the existence of the well associated with Jacob and Jesus, which is mentioned as a highlight of Paula's visit.[74] Paula's encounter with the struggle of demons before the tombs of saints defies modern explanation. According to Jerome, Paula climbed Mount Gerizim, which was called the highest of Samarian mountains by Josephus.[75] No reference is made to ruins of the ancient temple of Sanballat or its successor temple, which would be snatched from the Samarians and given to the Christians in the late fifth century.[76] The other spots on Paula's tour of Galilee receive scant attention. She stopped at Nazareth, Capernaum, the lake of Tiberias, and Nain. At this point Jerome's narrative breaks off with the account of Paula in the Holy Land and resumes with her travels in Egypt. We do not know whether she set sail from somewhere on the coast of Galilee or took a land route. Egeria's route from Bethlehem to Socoth, over the Sinai peninsula, suggests that travel by land was not out of the question.[77] Yet, in Paula's case a land route would have resulted in retracing much of the ground she had already traveled.

Jerome's account of Paula's pilgrimage resumes with her stop in Socoth, which was also on the similar pilgrimage of Egeria. Her next major stop was at Alexandria, though Jerome tells us nothing of what she saw in this major ecclesiastical and intellectual center. Perhaps, she stayed a short time there, drawn away by the allure of the reasonably close centers of monastic heroism—Nitria and Scete. Jerome claims that Paula made quite a splash at Nitria, where the confessor Isidore and such ascetic superstars as the Macarii, Arsenius, and Serapion came to greet her.[78] Surprisingly, Paula did not proceed up the Nile to visit the source of Pachomian cenobitic monasticism which she would imitate in Bethlehem, for Jerome portrays Nitria as her last stop before making ready to return to the Holy Land.

Paula's return from Egypt to the Holy Land was most certainly by sea, for Jerome mentions that she sailed from Pelusium, in the northwest corner of the Sinai peninsula, to Maioma because of the intense heat.[79] This reference could imply that a land route would have been more natural were it not for the heat.

While Paula's pilgrimage to the Holy Land and monastic communities of the East seems unduly risky for a woman possibly unaccompanied by men, she was afforded some protection not only by her entourage but also by provisions of the *Codex Theodosianus*. Jerome portrays Paula as traveling with a group of virgins, among whom was Eustochium.[80] This entourage of Paula, the dedicated widow, and her sanctified virgins would have known of the laws recorded in the *Codex Theodosianus* which called for swift punishment of anyone who raped a virgin or holy widow (*Codex Theodosianus* 9. 25. 1). The law was extended in 364 during the reign of Jovian Augustus to call for capital punishment for anyone who even "solicited" (*attemptare*) consecrated maidens or widows (*Codex Theodosianus* 9. 25. 2). Thus, provisions of the *Codex Theodosianus* would have provided some protection to the personal safety of Paula's wanderings with her sisters in monastic pilgrimage.

By embarking upon this bold, extensive pilgrimage, Paula most certainly defied Jerome's definition of the ideal ascetic woman as one who meekly waits in her chamber for the divine bridegroom to knock. Paula and Eustochium seem to have forgotten this dictate of Letter XXII or, at least, chose to become reclusive according to their own timetable.

Paula's intellectual strides under monastic tutelage were striking. Jerome claims that *"scripturas tenebat memoriter"* and refers to her admiration of the history recounted in the Scriptures in such a way that suggested she had a keen familiarity with it.[81] Jerome notes the persistence of her intellectual curiosity about controverted points of interpretation.[82] Most astonishing is his claim that Paula learned to chant the Psalms in Hebrew without the telltale trace of a Latin tongue.[83] Further assessment of the intellectual attainments of Paula can be made by reference to the accounts of Elizabeth Clark on the significance of education among female monastics.[84]

Paula's organization of a monastery for women alongside Jerome's male monastery in Bethlehem should not be considered an exceptional monastic act. Pachomius had supplied his sister with a female monastery across the Nile from his own cenobium. Other female monastic communities, following the Pachomian model, shot up in Egypt and perhaps reached as many as twelve.[85] Reference has already been made to the communities of virgins in Italy and North Africa under the tutelage of Ambrose and Augustine, respectively. What bears comment is the possibility that this female monastic activity forged a new social order for women, in that they escaped male domination by gathering together as women.[86] The organization of women into all-female communities, under the authority of a woman, should be viewed with reference to current theories of female status which consider female solidarity groups an important element in the attainment of female status.[87] While female monastic communities were not organized for the purpose of improving female status, insofar as they enabled women to escape male domination, these communities for women may have offered a novel alternative to domestic isolation.

Jerome's account of Paula's monastery at Bethlehem portrays her as very much in control of the day-to-day activities. We do not find Jerome interjecting his volatile, controlling personality in the ordering of the monastic life of Paula's followers. Despite monastic disdain for the worldly value system, Paula's monastery appears to have been stratified on the basis of social class.[88] Yet, the passage on which this view is based is not entirely clear. Jerome writes that Paula divided into three groups her followers who were from the upper class, middle class, and lower class.[89] That the division of the virgins was made on the basis of social class is not clearly stated but would hardly be surprising, given Roman attention to the minutiae of differentiating distinctions of rank. However, such a division should not discredit the strides toward egalitarianism evident in Paula's monastery, especially when considered in light of the cruelty between classes common to the secular world. Ammianus Marcellinus reports the harsh intolerance of noble men who visited the public bath with no less than fifty attendants and shouted "in threatening tones" if the attendants were not sufficiently obsequious.[90] Further, if a slave was not sufficiently quick in bringing his master hot water, he was subject to three hundred lashes with the whip.[91] Jerome refers to no slaves in Paula's monastery (only attendants) and to no such cruelty inflicted on the lower class as described by Ammianus. On the contrary, strides were made toward egalitarianism insofar as all were dressed alike, all studied the Scriptures, and all assembled together for the singing of Psalms and the recitation of prayer.[92] The noble virgins were accorded the privilege of having an attendant and may have received better food, in view of the separation of the groups at mealtime.[93] Yet, the stricture against the possession of private property must have been a forceful social leveler of women who in the secular world had been very wealthy.

Paula's monastic experience was marked with severe acts of self-denial. To what extent her behavior may have been pathological, we shall leave to the judgment of psychologists. A description of her ascetic rigors should be sufficient to suggest to the reader the severity of her renunciation not only of patrician comforts but of life-sustaining activity. Jerome's account of Paula's tendency to weep calls to mind Margery Kempe's so-called gift of tears, but it has no parallel among her Roman ascetic contemporaries. According to Jerome, "Her tears welled forth as it were from fountains, and she lamented her slightest faults as if they were signs of the deepest dye."[94] Jerome recounts two instances of Paula's weeping on her monastic pilgrimage—one at the tomb where the resurrection was said to have occurred and one at the sight of the tortured demons who haunted saintly tombs.[95] Paula's defense of this unusual behavior was that her present weeping made amends for her former frivolous laughter.[96] Her reply to Jerome's expression of concern that weeping might damage her eyes demonstrates the same logic. Monastic disregard for the care of one's face makes amends for worldly pampering of it with Roman cosmetics.[97] A student of abnormal psychology might be better able to discern whether there is any link between Jerome's stifling of Paula's grief at the death of Blaesilla and her later tendency toward chronic weeping.

In addition to easily prompted crying, Paula's monastic behavior was marked by other acts of severe self-denial. She rarely bathed, according to Jerome, and slept not on a soft mattress but on the ground with only a mat of goat's hair between her and the earth.[98] Jerome reveals some degree of concern about her immoderate acts of self-denial and alludes to her "frequent sicknesses and infirmities."[99] Reference has already been made to Epiphanius' failure to persuade Paula to take a bit of medicinal wine. Despite the severity of her ascetic disregard for self which prompted both Jerome's admiration and concern, Paula lived to the age of fifty-six years and eight months, hardly a premature death for a Roman matron.[100] According to Jerome's account, Paula's funeral was a monastic extravaganza, attracting every monk and virgin in monastic Palestine not just for a couple of days but for a week.[101] Jerome's images of the chanting of psalms by bishops, monks, and others in unison but in different languages and the grief of the poor who benefited from Paula's largesse create quite a moving scene.[102]

Blaesilla

Evaluating the status of Blaesilla, Paula's oldest child, within the ranks of the senatorial aristocracy is greatly hampered by numerous gaps. Jerome's repeated references to Furia as her sister-in-law establish this relationship but still tell us little about Blaesilla's senatorial rank, for Furia's lineage is also shrouded in missing links. If Furia's lineage were certain, one could determine whether Blaesilla married into the elite ranks of the senatorial class, the so-called "inner aristocracy." Jerome gives us the name of Furia's mother, Titiana, but not that of her father. Jerome's reference to Furia's connection with the ancient house of Camillus, while neglecting to identify her father by name, raises some suspicions. On the basis of a pun in Letter LIV, Jones et al. think that Furia's father may have been Quintilius Laetus 2, who as prefect of the city of Rome would have been among the elite *illustris* rank.[103] Yet, one wonders why Jerome, who relishes elite connections among his protégées, should be so oblique in identifying Furia's father. If the dating of the prefecture of Laetus in A.D. 398/99 is correct (*Prosopography* notes the uncertainty of this dating), further contradictions arise insofar as Jerome, writing in A.D. 394, describes Furia's father as withered by age.[104] One wonders whether a man of such failing vigor would be called upon to oversee a major repair to an aqueduct, apparently carried out by Laetus while PVR (*praefectus urbis Romae*). Further, Jerome is quite indirect in claiming consular status for Furia's father, saying: "Of your father too I speak with respect, not because he is a patrician and of consular rank, but because he is a Christian."[105] Such an oblique claim of consular status raises doubts about its certainty in view of the other missing links. Once again, as in the case of Paula, we are left with Jerome's claim of Furia's links to ancient Republican notables, but no explicit reference to a person of senatorial distinction in her immediate background.

Furia's status within the senatorial aristocracy, and indirectly Blaesilla's, might be established by discerning the rank of her husband, if that of her father lay beyond the historian's grasp. If, as Jerome claims in Letter CXXIII, Furia married one of the sons of Sex. Claudius Petronius Probus 5, her connection with the elite of the Roman aristocracy would be beyond doubt. Probus, holder of a wide array of the highest Roman offices and firmly ranked among the *illustris,* would unquestionably have been a well-placed father-in-law.[106] Yet, the connection of Furia to this paragon of Roman rank as well as his very existence hinges entirely on one reference Jerome makes in writing in A.D. 409 to Ageruchia, a noble woman living in the hinterlands of Gaul. In writing to Furia in A.D. 394 in an attempt to persuade her to the path of celibate widowhood, Jerome makes no reference to any exceptionally prestigious rank of her departed husband or to the promising future snatched away from her. Claudian's panegyric on Probus mentions his two sons, Olybrius and Probinus, who were both consuls in 395 but not another brother snatched away in his prime.[107] While this oversight on Claudian's part might be explained by the Roman preference for success over the failure indicated by death, it further indicates questions about Furia's ties to the upper ranks of the senatorial order.

Whatever Furia's ties to the mighty Probi, Jerome shows none of the ambivalence about her wealth evident in his eulogy on Paula, referring to her riches with no qualifying phraseology.[108] Thus, Blaesilla can be assumed to have married into a family which, even if without certain prestigious rank within the senatorial order, had sufficient resources to provide a life of lavish patrician comfort.

Most of what we know about Blaesilla comes from either Letter XXXVIII or Letter XXXIX. Jerome uses the latter primarily as a forum for rebuking Paula about her public display of grief at her daughter's death. Disregarding the hypothetical dialogue between the departed daughter and Paula which Jerome uses to control Paula's expression of grief, little of a factual nature remains in Letter XXXIX. We do know from Letter XXXVIII that after the death of her husband of only a few months, Blaesilla was struck by a severe fever. This brush with death apparently prompted her ascetic conversion, which once made was extreme.[109] After four months of severe ascetic austerities Blaesilla was dead.[110] Drawing on Jerome's portrait of what he considers Blaesilla's pre-conversion frivolities, one surmises that the woman gaily enjoyed life's comforts and Roman finery: "In days gone by our dear widow was extremely fastidious in her dress, and spent whole days before her mirror to correct its deficiencies."[111] While cast in the language of a rebuke, the portrait unwittingly suggests that the effect of all this attention to self must have been charming, for Paula could not blot Blaesilla's image from her memory.

Jerome makes extravagant claims about Blaesilla's intellectual attainments under monastic tutelage. She spoke Greek without a trace of the accent of a Latin tongue.[112] Her quick mastery of Hebrew rivaled that of Origen.[113] This claim of Blaesilla's mastery of Hebrew, not in a few months but in a few days, seems to be vintage Hieronymian hyperbole. Yet, the underlying claim, i.e., that she was bright, must have had some veracity. In the prefaces to various translations, Jerome remembers the entreaties of Blaesilla for Latin versions, further suggesting her thirst for knowledge.[114]

The effect of Blaesilla's ascetic austerities is suggested by the following description of her physical weakness: "Her steps tottered with weakness, her face was pale and quivering, her slender neck scarcely upheld her head."[115]

Jerome alludes once more to Blaesilla's rank in his description of her funeral, but not in such a way that we can discern with any precision her place among the elite of the senatorial class: "People of rank headed the procession, a pall made of cloth of gold covered her bier."[116] The grumbling by critics of monasticism most certainly came from those who valued life's finery. Yet, the identities of these "people of rank" remain hidden.

Paulina

The status of Paulina, Paula's second daughter, within the ranks of the senatorial aristocracy depended, of course, on the status of her husband Pammachius. Yet, once again crucial missing links make it difficult to determine Pammachius' rank with certainty. None of our sources of information about Pammachius (Jerome, Paulinus of Nola, or Palladius) tell us who his parents were, although Palladius claims Melania the Younger and Pinianus as relatives.[117] Jones et al. in *The Prosopography of the Later Roman Empire* vol. 1 list Pammachius on the stemma of the Ceionii Rufii family but with broken lines, indicating the conjectural nature of the link.[118] While Jerome claims he was descended from the ancient Furia *gens,* he doesn't supply us the name of Pammachius' link to the Furian line.[119]

The one definite piece of evidence which would rank Pammachius within the senatorial aristocracy, despite the missing information about his ancestry, is his holding of the proconsulate (probably of Africa). Proconsuls were classified not as mere *clarissimi* but with the middle ranked *spectabiles.*[120] While Jerome is the only source of the claim of proconsular status for

Pammachius,[121] his straightforward language argues for accepting him at his word. Yet, Jerome, the master of hyperbole, concedes that Pammachius would have been mid-placed among the ranks of the senators: "Still there were many other senators who wore the badges of proconsular rank.... Whilst he took precedence of some, others took precedence of him."[122] Given external evidence of the ranking of a proconsul within the senatorial aristocracy, this would have been an honest assessment.

In a slip which discredits his monastic claim of the glory of ascetic renunciation of senatorial status, Jerome alludes to the cheapening of consular status in his day. No longer is the consulate reserved for the bluest of blue bloods. Despite the possibility of parvenus rising to the highest Roman offices, Jones notes that this was the exception rather than the rule in the Late Empire.[123] On the contrary Jones argues that in the West the highest ranking members of the aristocracy nearly monopolized the highest *illustris* grade offices.[124] This elite group, comprised of the old nobility based on ancient ancestry and the new nobility who had achieved rank earlier in the century, made up what Jones calls "the inner aristocracy" and reserved the highest offices for themselves.[125] Pammachius, who as a proconsul had only the rank of *spectabilis*, had not quite penetrated these elite ranks. Perhaps, one could argue that *illustris* rank lay in his future had it not been for ascetic intervention.

Jerome hints at another deficiency in Pammachius which may have affected his ability to climb the senatorial ladder to illustrious rank. In an apparent attempt to compliment Pammachius, Jerome suggests that he was not skilled in the rhetorical arts: "Your letters in their simplicity are redolent of the prophets and savour strongly of the apostles. You do not affect a stilted eloquence, nor boylike balance shallow sentences in clauses neatly turned."[126] Despite Jerome's flattery of such simplicity of style, his writing makes a lie of his actual admiration of it. Jerome admires a nicely turned phrase as well as any product of a Roman rhetorical education. If, as Jerome suggests, he and Pammachius were comrades in their student days, the rhetorical training took root more successfully in Jerome than in his perhaps duller friend. One further hint at some intellectual deficiency in Pammachius appears in Jerome's reference to current criticism of his friend: "Disregard the remarks which uneducated persons make concerning your ability."[127]

Whatever the information missing about Pammachius' ancestry, his official career, and his rank, evidence from both Jerome and Paulinus of Nola portrays him as quite wealthy. The corroborating evidence of Paulinus on this point lends credibility to Jerome's claims about Pammachius' wealth. Insofar as Paulinus' letter to Pammachius (Letter 13) articulates a Christian perspective on wealth which stresses proper use of it rather than challenging its possession by a Christian, one can assume the recipient is rich. Further,

Paulinus repeatedly classifies his addressee with the rich who through just use of their wealth are acceptable in the eyes of God. [128] Augustine's reference to Pammachius' estate in Numidia further substantiates the view that Paulina's husband was wealthy. [129] Yet, just where on the senatorial scale of wealth Pammachius would have fit is difficult to ascertain. No specific piece of evidence suggests resources quite comparable to that of Symmachus, whom Jones places in the mid-range of senatorial wealth. [130]

On the basis of the preceding assessment one can argue that Paulina married a moderately wealthy senator of some promise, whose ancestry cannot be determined with any degree of certainty and who, though educated, was no rhetorical master.

About Paulina herself we know very little. Jerome tells us that her several efforts at maternity ended in miscarriages. [131] Jerome's language suggests more than one or two pregnancies. Whether her frequent miscarriages contributed to her premature death can only be conjectured. Jerome's reference in Letter LXVI, written in A.D. 397, to Paulina's death two years earlier places her death in A.D. 395. [132]

Eustochium

In Jerome's letters Eustochium lives in the shadow of her mother Paula, a portrayal which may realistically assess her mode of life. Jerome's description of Eustochium as she departs from home as "the partner alike of her [Paula's] vows and of her voyage" hints at the future submergence of Eustochium behind Paula. [133] Eustochium accompanied her mother on the monastic pilgrimage charted earlier but her impressions received none of Jerome's attention. [134] Suggesting little of an independent identity, Jerome describes Eustochium as inseparable from her mother:

> Eustochium... always kept close to her mother's side, obeyed all commands, never slept apart from her, never walked abroad or took a meal without her, never had a penny that she could call her own, rejoiced when her mother gave to the poor her little patrimony, and fully believed that in filial affection she had the best heritage and the truest riches. [135]

Jerome's description of Eustochium's relentless attention to Paula when on her deathbed and of her clinging to her mother's dead body at the funeral further outline this portrayal of Eustochium as submerged in her mother's identity. [136]

Eustochium appears to have taken to heart most of Jerome's monastic advice in Letter XXII about the proper ordering of the ascetic life of a virgin. Rejecting marriage, feminine attention to appearance, and social aspirations, Eustochium along with her mother led the female monastic experiment in Bethlehem. Jerome's advice in Letter XXII to "Read often, learn all that you can"[137] did not fall on deaf ears, for Jerome credits Eustochium with facility at Hebrew equal to her mother's.[138] She lived fifteen years beyond her mother's death in A.D. 404.[139] Yet, we know nothing of her life during this span of time other than that she ran the monastery and brought up her niece, Paula the Younger, in proper monastic fashion.[140]

Rufina

Jerome tells us only that Rufina entreated her mother Paula to wait until she secured a marriage partner to depart from Rome and that she died prematurely.[141]

Toxotius

The status of Toxotius, only son of Paula, within the senatorial aristocracy can be ascertained by reference to the earlier discussion of the rank of his father and by reference to the status of his wife, Laeta. If the Albinus described by Jerome as *"clarissimus et eruditissimus vir"* and father of Laeta is identical with the Publilius Caeionius Caecina Albinus 8, known from numerous inscriptions, Laeta would have definite links to the elite of the Roman aristocracy. Yet, Albinus himself as consularis Numidiae, i.e., a provincial governor, remained in the lower ranks of the senatorial order as a *vir clarissimus*.[142] Perhaps, on the basis of the prestige of his ancestors, Albinus penetrated the inner circles of the pagan blue bloods, and, consequently, received mention in Macrobius' *Saturnalia*. Described by Macrobius as a friend of Praetextatus and Symmachus, both of whom attained *illustris* rank as prefects of the city of Rome, Albinus rubbed shoulders with the elite of the Roman aristocracy.[143] His son, Laeta's brother, Caecina Decius Albinus Iunior 10, acquired senatorial distinction as PVR in A.D. 402.[144] Yet, Albinus himself never attained worldly success comparable to that of his more prestigious comrades, for a provincial governorship pales in comparison to a Roman prefecture.

Despite the connections of Laeta's father with the blue-blooded pagan circles of Symmachus and Praetextatus, her mother was Christian. Jerome alludes to Laeta as a product of a mixed marriage and expresses glee at the prospect of little Paula singing Alleleuias to her well-placed pagan grandfather.[145]

Jerome tells us little else about Toxotius—nothing about any offices he may have held, nothing about his life experiences except that he married Laeta and had a child, Paula the Younger.

In summation, the family of Paula, Jerome's favored protégée, lay on the edges of the elite of the Roman senatorial aristocracy, called by Jones "the inner aristocracy." Coming from a family with maternal derivation of status, Paula married a man with wealth but as far as we know no mark of official distinction. Their eldest daughter, Blaesilla, may have married a man with links to the "inner aristocracy" if, in fact, his sister Furia was the daughter of Quintilius Laetus 2 and the wife of a son of Sex. Claudius Petronius Probus 5. Yet, the evidence which establishes Furia's links to these men of *illustris* grade is scant. Paula's daughter Paulina may have had links to the prestigious Ceionii Rufii family through her husband Pammachius. Yet, Pammachius' ancestry remains highly conjectural, and he himself attained only mid-grade senatorial rank. While Toxotius, Paula's only son, married a woman whose father, Albinus, associated with the so-called "inner aristocracy" in Rome, Albinus himself remained in the lower senatorial ranks, serving no higher office than a provincial governorship. Thus Jerome's portrayal of Paula and her family as the bluest of Roman blue bloods should be considered hyperbole which upon closer scrutiny must be modified. However, the extent to which Jerome's exaggerated claims of prestigious lineage were accepted within the senatorial circles of Rome remains an open question.[146]

Marcella: Originator of Monasticism for Roman Women

Marcella, whom Jerome describes as the first "highborn lady at Rome" to accept the monastic vocation, provided the original impetus for the flowering of Roman female monasticism. Little about her lineage is known with certainty, making it difficult to assess her position within the senatorial class at Rome. Jerome does not provide us with the name or the office of the man who was her husband for seven brief months.[147] While he mentions her mother, Albina, by name, Jerome glosses over Marcella's ancestry by consciously disregarding the rhetorical rules of eulogizing:

> I will not set forth her illustrious (*illustrem*) family and lofty lineage, nor will I trace her pedigree through a line of consuls and praetorian prefects.[148]

Jerome's use of the adjective *illustris* rather than *clarus* may be a play on the double meaning of *illustris,* which can mean both distinguished and of the *illustris* rank. Yet, one wonders if his inversion of the rules of rhetoric has its roots in missing information which makes obedience to the strict rhetorical form awkward. Certainly in the case of Paula, Jerome included a summary of her presumed pedigree, while at the same time disdaining the importance of such worldly concerns.

The station of Marcella's mother, Albina I, which would indirectly establish Marcella's, cannot be determined with any degree of certainty either. Jerome, who is our only source of data about her, tells us little. Jones et al.

conjecture that she may have been the daughter of Ceionius Rufius Albinus 14, prefect of the city of Rome from A.D. 335–37.[149] Presumably, this connection is made on the basis of Jerome's oblique claim of consular status in Marcella's background coupled with the dating of Albina's death in A.D. 388 as well as on the basis of the *cognomen*. Yet, another Albinus, a *vir clarissimus* and vicar of Spain, would also have been in the right generation to be Albina's father.[150]

The only certain evidence which hints at Marcella's actual station is Jerome's references to her ardent suitor, Cerealis. The Freemantle translation of the reference to Cerealis is misleading in that it could suggest Jerome was using the term *illustris* to describe Cerealis and simultaneously to characterize his rank. Actually, Jerome's allusion to the rank of Marcella's suitor is contained in the phrase "cuius clarum inter consules nomen est" (whose name is distinguished among consuls).[151] Despite the use of *clarum* rather than *illustris*, Marcella's Cerealis is most likely Naeratius Cerealis 2, of the *illustris* rank as prefect of the city of Rome from A.D. 352–53 and ordinary consul in 358.[152] Jerome's specific rather than oblique reference to Cerealis suggests he must have known the impressive effect of such an allusion. Given the status of Cerealis as summarized by Jones et al., Albina's pressure on Marcella to marry into the "inner aristocracy" is hardly surprising. Yet, in view of the possible dearth of marriageable women among the aristocracy, one wonders whether the age of her blue-blooded suitor reflects negatively on Marcella's desirability as a marriage partner.[153]

Jerome's reference to Marcella's home on the Aventine might give us a clue about her station.[154] While the Aventine had primarily been a plebian district during the Republic, the presence of Trajan's ancestral home plus the homes of other notables shows a pattern of noble residence on the Aventine during imperial times.[155] Yet, the ample commercial activity which transpired here due to its location along the Tiber may have compromised its residential attractiveness. Jerome notes that Marcella moved her monastic coterie away from the Aventine to the suburbs.[156]

Marcella's possible sibling relationship with Asella provides little aid in assessing Marcella's position within the senatorial order. Several irresolvable inconsistencies arise with regard to Asella, suggesting that little can be said about her with certainty. If in fact Asella was a sibling of Marcella's and embraced ascetic virginity at the age of ten, Jerome cannot be correct in calling Eustochium "the first virgin of noble birth in Rome."[157] Either Jerome is flattering Eustochium or Asella was not of noble birth. While Jerome's two references to Marcella as Asella's sister could be interpreted to mean spiritual sister, his reference to Albina as Asella's mother supports the view that Marcella and Asella were biological as well as spiritual sisters.[158]

While Jerome tells us more of Marcella's ascetic experience than he does of her ancestry, the conclusion to Letter CXXVII, her eulogy, suggests that the preservation of her memory was hardly a serious endeavor in Jerome's estimation: "In one short night I have dictated this letter in honour of you, revered Marcella, and of you, my daughter Principia."[159] Thus, it should be kept in mind that the ascetic struggles of a lifetime have been summarily recorded "in one short night" and, therefore, hardly constitute a comprehensive account for someone as productive at writing as Jerome.

Having been widowed and having rejected a well-placed suitor, Marcella embraced the life of ascetic renunciation as a result of hearing persuasive tales of Egyptian monasticism.[160] Her monastic coterie was already in existence when Jerome made his visit to Rome in A.D. 382 along with Paulinus of Antioch and Epiphanius of Salamis. Jerome portrays Marcella's group as primarily a study group, fostered under Marcella's intelligent guidance. In Jerome she recognized a biblical scholar whose expertise would be of value to her protégées. Therefore, she persistently pursued the reluctant Jerome until he agreed to share some of the fruits of his study with her companions in ascetic renunciation. Letter CXXVII gives several hints which indicate Marcella's intelligence and leadership ability. Jerome notes her intellectual curiosity which refused to accept superficial answers to questions of biblical interpretation.[161] Furthermore, upon Jerome's departure from Rome, Marcella assumed the role of scriptural authority to whom controverted passages were referred.[162] Jerome also claims that Marcella took a leading role in originating charges of heresy against proponents of Origenism in Rome.[163]

Cognizant of human pettiness, Marcella avoided even the appearance of impropriety by keeping her mother, Albina, always at her side. This arrangement must have avoided the problem precipitated by clerical visitation of widows which prompted the decree of the *Codex Theodosianus* (16. 2. 20) which restricts gifts bestowed by widows on clergy.[164] Apparently, intimacy between clergy and widows was threatening patriarchal concern for right ordered dispensation of property.

An assessment of Marcella's wealth seems beyond our grasp, for Jerome makes only one reference to her worldly property. Despite Marcella's wish that her wealth be given to aid the poor, she complied with her mother's wishes that her property be turned over either to an uncle or brother, depending on the referent of Jerome's "her." No further references by Jerome give us clues as to the extent of the wealth Marcella renounced.

Other Roman Women Mentioned by Jerome

Of the other women mentioned in Jerome's letters only Fabiola was part of the Roman monastic circle Jerome fostered. Having been married twice, Fabiola seemed an unlikely convert to Christian asceticism. Yet, upon the death of her second husband, Fabiola humbled herself in public penitence and subsequently dedicated her heart as well as her fortune to the care of the poor.

Jerome provides few clues which would enable us to determine with certainty her place within the Roman senatorial aristocracy. His flouting of rhetorical convention by beginning her eulogy with Fabiola's birth rather than with an account of her prestigious pedigree raises some suspicions. His allusion to her link with the Fabian family lends just the right aura of nobility without having to name actual persons of distinction in her immediate background.[165] Jerome does not tell us the name of Fabiola's first husband whom she divorced for chronic philandering. He only argues Fabiola's case for dissociating her identity from that of an adulterous husband. Nor does he provide the name of her second husband. In an unexpected display of tolerance for second marriage he defends Fabiola's decision to choose remarriage over a fraudulent claim of the status of an *univira*.[166] Thus, no specific evidence about the men who supplied her status according to patriarchal Roman values has been preserved in Jerome's account.

While no specific classificatory data about Fabiola's wealth remains, Jerome describes it as "large and suitable to her rank."[167] His further description of the extent of her ascetic largesse suggests that her resources must have been considerable. Not only did she finance a hospital (presumably at Rome), a shelter house for the homeless at Portus, and monastic aspirations at Rome, she also spread her charitable largesse beyond Rome to the Volscian district (around Campania).[168] Certainly such monastic liberality had its roots in ample pre-conversion wealth.

While the distinguishing feature of her monastic experience was charity as opposed to a focus on intellectual pursuits (Marcella) or monastic organization (Paula), Fabiola had a persistent curiosity with regard to questions of biblical interpretation, and her probing prompted Jerome's investigation of the Book of Numbers.[169] Like Paula before her arrival in Bethlehem, Fabiola was not inclined to take Jerome's case for ascetic seclusion too seriously. She made a pilgrimage to Jerusalem and Bethlehem which was inopportunely cut short by a barbarian threat.

While Jerome describes Fabiola's funeral as a Roman extravaganza in which "Rome saw all her peoples gathered together in one,"[170] he neglects to mention the presence of people of rank or golden decorations for her bier which caught his attention at the funeral of Blaesilla.[171]

Of the other women monastics mentioned by name in Jerome's letters most are relatively obscure persons living in the Roman provinces and, therefore, with no presumed links to the Roman monastic circles of Marcella and Paula. Letter CXXIII is addressed to Ageruchia, about whom we know little other than that she was a recently widowed noble lady of Gaul.[172] All we know of Algasia is that she resided in Gaul and received Letter CXXI. Hedibia, also of Gaul, came from a literary family in that her father and grandfather became professors at Bordeaux.[173] She addressed a series of theological and hermeneutical questions to Jerome and received Letter CXX in reply. Upon being widowed, Theodora received Letter LXXV, which praises the endeavors of her husband, Lucinius, to suppress heresy in Spain and to studiously probe the Scriptures.[174]

With his letter to Salvina, Jerome penetrates closer to the imperial inner circles. Yet it may be a mark of his position vis-à-vis the "inner aristocracy" that he writes as a virtual stranger to the widowed Salvina. Anticipating the suspicions that might arise about his intentions in presuming to write to one close to the imperial court, Jerome concedes that "men may say that I am not so much trying to console a widow in affliction as endeavoring to creep into the imperial court."[175] Despite the apparent prestige of Salvina's position as widow of the emperor's nephew and daughter of the *illustris* grade Gildo, Jerome must have seen the vulnerability of her position. Having been secured by Theodosius not only as a wife for his nephew but as a political bond between Constantinople and Africa, Salvina was left in a vulnerable position when her father, Gildo, was killed in A.D. 398 and she was declared an enemy of the state.[176] Further, the death of her husband deprived her of protective links to the imperial court, suggesting the vulnerability of her position at the time of her ascetic conversion.

The conversion of Demetrias, daughter of Olybrius and granddaughter of Sex. Claudius Petronius Probus, must have been an occasion for monastic exultation. In Demetrias, monastic circles had a convert whose impeccable pedigree included not only ancient Republican connections but persons of consular status in her immediate family. Her grandfather, Probus, as has been mentioned was a paragon of Roman rank, having been the Western praetorian prefect in A.D. 383 and consul in A.D. 371.[177] Her father, Olybrius, also claimed *illustris* grade rank as consul in A.D. 395.[178] Demetrias' connection to the upper echelons of the senatorial aristocracy (the so-called "inner aristocracy") is beyond question. The conversion of this model of noble rank sent shock waves through the Roman world, according to Jerome.[179] Roman astonishment was such that many believed Demetrias' conversion to be a divine sign that the destruction of Rome was over.[180] Yet, it may reflect on Jerome's status vis-à-vis the Roman "inner aristocracy" that he writes to Demetrias as a stranger.[181] While his absence from Rome may account for his failure to have made the acquaintance of Demetrias, he writes as one personally unacquainted with the family.

Insofar as Demetrias was converted to ascetic renunciation around A.D. 414, she was not a part of the female circles in communication with Jerome and led by Marcella. Her significance for our sociological assessment of the ascetic conversion of women lies in the timing of her conversion and her position among the elite of the senatorial class. It may be instructive that

Demetrias, whose pedigree is known, converted to ascetic style Christianity after the sack of Rome in A.D. 410. Jerome portrays her as pondering the advisability of marriage under such inauspicious conditions:

> Your city, once the capital of the world, is now the grave of the Roman people; and will you [Demetrias] on the shores of Libya, yourself an exile, accept an exile for a husband?[182]

Significant for our assessment of the protégées of Jerome are the conclusions that Demetrias' pedigree far outshone Paula's and Marcella's, that Jerome barely knew this offspring of the Probi, and that her conversion, unlike that of the women close to Jerome, occurred in the wake of political disaster in Rome.

The Melania "Gens" of Female Monasticism

Melania the Elder and her granddaughter, Melania the Younger, provide an instructive counterpoint to Jerome's depiction of Roman female monasticism. For our purposes an exposition of the aristocratic status and monastic style of the elder Melania should offer a sufficient balance to Jerome's portrayal of monasticism for women in his letters.

Examination of the aristocratic background of Melania the Elder provides a highly instructive comparison with the protégées of Jerome. The superiority of Melania's pedigree over Paula's somewhat questionable lineage must have been a thorn in the side for ambitious Jerome in his conflict with Rufinus. While Jerome claims links between Paula and the ancient Republican families of the Scipios and the Gracchi, he mentions no person of distinction in her immediate background, but ample evidence links Melania with Antonius Marcellinus 16, consul in A.D. 341. Palladius identifies Melania as "the daughter of Marcellinus, one of the consuls."[183] Paulinus of Nola in Letter 29 claims that the consul Marcellinus was Melania's grandfather.[184] Current opinion favors the view of Paulinus of Nola, who as a relative of Melania would have known the family more intimately.[185] In any case, Melania's link to Marcellinus, whose *illustris* rank is clearly established by his attainment of the Western praetorian prefecture and the consulate, suggests a verifiable pedigree which Jerome must have envied.

Melania's link to Marcellinus gains credibility not only by virtue of the appearance of the claim in three sources (Paulinus, Palladius, and Jerome make this claim whereas Jerome is the only witness of Paula's pedigree) but by virtue of the appearance of the claim not simply as a vehicle for fulfilling rhetorical convention. Palladius, whose simple style stands in striking contrast to the embellishments of Jerome, appears to have no thought of rhetorical convention when he claims a consul in Melania's background.[186] On the other hand, Paulinus of Nola, obviously schooled in the rhetorical arts, introduces Melania with a reference to the grandeur of her heritage. However, Paulinus claims that such a practice has its roots not in pagan rhetorical practices but in the procedure followed by Luke in describing John the Baptist.[187] Therefore, Paulinus' reference to Marcellinus is not an attempt to outdo the rhetoricians but suggests a certain theological understanding of noble lineage, i.e., that distinguished pedigree makes a person even more "suitable to receive God's gifts."[188]

Conclusive evidence identifying the husband of Melania the Elder would further establish her position within the senatorial aristocracy. None of our sources, however, supply us with his name. Palladius says only that she was the "wife of some man of high rank, I forget which."[189] The name of Melania's son, Valerius Publicola, suggests that her husband belonged to the *gens* Valeria.[190] Consequently, it has been conjectured that Melania's husband was Valerius Maximus, prefect of the city of Rome A.D. 361–63.[191] If this claim is valid, Melania certainly would have been among the "inner aristocracy" of the Roman senatorial circles. However, the identity of Melania's husband is highly conjectural. While the memory lapse of Palladius, whose ties to the elite of the city of Rome were tenuous, raises no suspicions, one wonders why Paulinus of Nola would have neglected to mention a person of such high rank as the prefect of the city of Rome, particularly in light of his view that rank resulted in a spiritual *noblesse oblige*. Certainly, if Melania had married someone as distinguished as a Roman prefect, Paulinus, as a relative familiar with her family, would have known it. The nagging question (with regard to the Valerius Maximum connection) is why Paulinus would have failed to mention the name of such a high ranking husband in his account of Melania.

Further clarification of Melania's status within the Roman senatorial aristocracy can be accomplished by reference to the status of her son Publicola. While Palladius claims that he "became great by worldly standards,"[192] no evidence survives of his having held any office higher than consul of Campania.[193] In view of Paulinus' interpretation of Melania's grief at the death of her son, i.e., that her sorrow was less over the loss of her child than over his refusal to denounce senatorial ambitions before dying, one wonders at Publicola's apparent failure to climb the ladder of senatorial distinction.[194] While Constantine had improved the status of the provincial governorship by attaching the title *consularis* to the office, the office of consul of Campania would not have impressed the elite of the Roman aristocracy whom Jones characterizes as disdainful of any but *illustris* grade offices.[195]

Despite the undistinguished career which extant evidence suggests for Publicola, his marriage to Albina 2, who as sister of Rufius Antonius Agrypnius Volusianus had links with the so-called "inner aristocracy,"[196] suggests some compensating claims of status for Publicola. The distinction of Albina's male relatives far overshadowed whatever status claims Jerome could make for the marriage partners of Paula's children. Paula's link to the mighty Ceionii Rufii family hinges on Pammachius' uncertain link as well as Toxotius' link through his marriage to Laeta, daughter of Albinus 8, whose provincial governorship pales in comparison to the political plums won by Albina's brother and father. Both Albina's brother and father, as prefects of the city of Rome, were firmly established among the elite of the senatorial order.[197] Discerning Publicola's claims to status which compensated for his undistinguished public career would only be conjectural.

The details of Melania's life are shrouded in uncertainty. How I wish we had access to "the volumes written about her" to which Paulinus of Nola alludes.[198] However, an overview of her ascetic experience will provide a counterbalancing portrayal of female monasticism from a perspective other than Jerome's. In Jerome's account we have the sense of the women being used as instruments of his monastic ideology and, consequently, must strip away Hieronymian rhetoric to reach our female subjects. The accounts of Melania in *The Lausiac History* and the letters of Paulinus of Nola seem much less controlled by the interests of the authors.

Current opinion favors dating Melania's birth in A.D. 341 or 342, which accords well with Palladius' claim that she was around sixty when she returned to Italy in A.D. 400.[199] Palladius tells us that she was born in Spain; she was, therefore, a provincial rather than a Roman aristocrat. Having married well and fulfilled Roman expectations by bearing three sons, Melania's worldly status was crushed when she lost both her husband and two sons in the same year.[200] After an interlude as a widow in Rome with a small son, Melania flouted senatorial values and set off on a monastic journey to the East. Our sources give us few clues as to the length of this interlude, and scholarly opinion diverges. While Murphy's chronological schema requires some seven years for this pre-monastic interlude as a Roman widow,[201] Moine finds several holes in Murphy's theory.[202] Whatever the age of Publicola at the time of Melania's departure from Rome, he was too young to function independently. Palladius notes that Melania secured a guardian for her son.[203] Paulinus of Nola mysteriously refers to the guardianship arrangement in spiritual terms. The bishop of Nola speaks of "commending him [Publicola] to the Lord" and takes note of Melania's rejection of her "influential and affectionate relatives" as guardians for her son.[204]

Our sources disagree on Melania's destination upon setting sail from Rome. Whereas Palladius designates Alexandria as her destination and recounts her visit among the Nitrian monks, Paulinus and Jerome make no mention of this Egyptian detour prior to her settlement in Jerusalem.[205] However, the historicity of the Nitrian sojourn seems certain despite the oversight of Paulinus and Jerome, given the detail with which Palladius recounts Melania's experiences. He mentions that she spent six months in the

Nitrian desert and befriended noted Egyptian monastics who were exiled by secular Roman authorities.[206] Paula's later visit to the Nitrian monastic establishments would follow Melania's precedent of female intrusion into male monastic enclaves.

Melania's noted clashes with civil authorities are also described somewhat differently by Palladius and Paulinus of Nola. Palladius does not identify the conflict which resulted in the banishment of such notable Nitrian monks as Isidore, Paphnutius, and Pambo to Palestine. Paulinus claims that Melania was caught in the midst of the Arian controversy "during the notorious reign of Valens" and befriended the persecuted orthodox monks.[207] Insofar as Palladius dates Melania's Egyptian sojourn during the reign of Valens, the Palladian account accords well with the known persecution of Egyptian monks by Arian sympathizers immediately after the death of Athanasius.[208] Melania's offense is not clear, although the sources are in harmony in portraying her boldness before the civil authorities, apparently rooted in confidence in the pedigree she had renounced. Palladius implies that Melania's offense had something to do with serving the exiled Nitrian monks who "were not allowed servants."[209] Paulinus of Nola implies that the offense had something to do with harboring fugitives from the law.[210] Palladius recounts that the judge quickly and with some embarrassment dropped his charges against Melania upon being apprised of her status vis-à-vis well-placed Roman men.[211] Paulinus notes that out of respect for Melania, the judge dropped charges against her.[212]

The length of Melania's stay in the monastery she built at Jerusalem is another controverted point. Paulinus of Nola claims that Melania spent twenty-five years in Jerusalem but tells us nothing about these most fruitful years of her life.[213] Palladius reports that his favored female monastic spent twenty-seven years at her Jerusalem monastery and gives more detail about her monastic experience.[214] He reveals that Rufinus practiced monastic retreat "close by," probably forming with Melania a double monastery on the pattern of Pachomius, one which Paula and Jerome subsequently imitated.[215] Palladius' claim that "for twenty-seven years they both [Melania and Rufinus] entertained with their own private funds the bishops, solitaries, and virgins who visited them . . ." has been challenged by Murphy, who can allow twenty years at the most for Rufinus at Jerusalem.[216] Palladius further confuses the question of the number of years Melania spent in monastic retreat in Jerusalem by later referring to the "thirty-seven years she practiced hospitality."[217] Butler has tried to resolve this discrepancy by arguing that the latter figure includes some ten or twelve years that Melania spent in monastic retreat after her return to Rome whereas the earlier figure excludes the post-Rome stint in monastic seclusion.[218]

Palladius portrays Melania as intellectually adept, which accords well with Jerome's portrayal of the persistent intellectual curiosity of his protégées. The prodigious literary effort of Melania seems astonishing:

> She turned night into day going through every writing of the ancient commentators—three million lines of Origen and two and a half million lines of Gregory, Stephen, Pierius, Basil and other worthy men. [219]

However, given Melania's noted ascetic self-discipline, such productivity is not precluded. Paulinus suggests a connection between self-denial and literary progress: "Her hard couch... becomes soft as she studies, for her pleasure in reading reduces the hardship of that stiff bed." [220] Unfortunately, Palladius gives us no hints about the educational grounding which made such intellectual efforts possible. Whether she was schooled in the rhetorical arts and Vergilian criticism, as her male aristocratic peers would have been, can only be guessed. In order to read Origen's works as extensively as Palladius suggests, she might either have been fluent in Greek or have had access to Rufinus' Latin translations.

Nothing has arisen to confute the historicity of the Palladian anecdote regarding Melania's role in the ascetic conversion of Egyptian monasticism's leading philosopher, Evagrius of Pontus. Fleeing a potentially adulterous relationship, Evagrius sought refuge in Jerusalem, where he met Melania. [221] At first resisting ascetic renunciation, Evagrius experienced a spiritual and physical decline precipitated by a fever or, perhaps, by guilt. [222] Melania then secured from Evagrius a confession and a monastic commitment and, thus, launched on the ascetic way one who left behind such monastic treasures as the *Praktikos* and the *Gnostikos*.

The other major event in Melania's life which receives mention in our sources is her departure from Jerusalem and triumphal return (in a monastic sense) to Nola. While Murphy and others place Melania's Italian sojourn in the latter part of A.D. 399 or early 400, Moine points out the tenuous nature of such claims. [223] Whatever the exact date of Melania's return to Italy to attend a family gathering at Nola, Paulinus' account is rich with ascetic contrasts and rhetoric. Melania's arrival on a humble little horse contrasted with the showy transportation of her aristocratic relatives in "swaying coaches, decorated horses, ladies' carriages all gilded, and numerous small vehicles." [224] Melania's rough tunic put to shame those dressed with senatorial splendor in silk and fine wool. [225] Paulinus claims her aristocratic relatives deferred to Melania's spiritual superiority and saw her lowliness as a vehicle for absolving them of the guilt of their worldliness. [226] Housing Melania's ascetic retinue in proximity to the unconverted posed no problems, according to Paulinus, for the holiness of the faithful which emanated from their singing defied criticism. [227]

The stunning impact Melania had on the aristocrats at Nola was repeated when she proceeded to Rome. According to Paulinus: "So Rome admires Melania, as she dwells in the shadow of humility and the light of truth, as she offers incentives to faith among the rich and the consolations of poverty among the poor."[228]

Returning to Jerusalem after a brief detour to North Africa, Melania died shortly thereafter. Most scholars place the date of her death in A.D. 410.[229]

Conclusions

Prosopographical investigation of the Roman ascetic women associated with Jerome and Rufinus in the early stages of the Christian monastic movement suggests that a measure of skepticism is needed to temper Jerome's rhetorical hyperbole about his favored protégées. The evidence linking Melania the Elder with the upper echelons of the senatorial aristocracy (the so-called "inner aristocracy") is less subject to challenge than Jerome's claims for his female allies, in view of the corroborative claim of three sources of a consul in Melania's immediate background. A critical reading of Jerome suggests that Paula's family, while certainly aristocrats, were nevertheless on the periphery of the current aristocratic inner circles. If Paula had links with the aristocratic Gracchi and Scipios of Republican times, her aristocratic credentials had faded greatly in view of the undistinguished position of her husband, Toxotius. If any of Paula's children penetrated into the "inner aristocracy," it would have been the charming Blaesilla; however, the elite status of Blaesilla's husband within the senatorial class hinges on rather tenuous Hieronymian evidence. Paulina's Pammachius, while certainly aristocratic, had some obvious deficiencies in his senatorial status, and the younger Toxotius' father-in-law rubbed shoulders with the elite while attaining only minor office for himself. However, the extent to which Arnheim is correct that these exaggerated claims of links to ancient Republican notables were not viewed with suspicion in Jerome's day but simply expressed the prevailing acceptance of the noble lineage and exalted status of these aristocratic families remains an open question.

In addition to uncovering these surprising deficiencies in status, our prosopographical investigation reveals a portrait of a small group of women in Rome living out a prayerful counterpoint to Roman concerns for wealth, rank, and privilege and of a few bold women who forged a new form of Christian life in monastic retreat in the Holy Land, showing as little concern for the demise of Roman destiny at the hands of Germanic invaders as Roman destiny had shown for Dido's broken heart.

4

The Roman *Matrona* of the Late Empire

By the late fourth century the Roman matron had progressed greatly from the days of early Rome when, according to Cato the Censor (who may be exaggerating), the husband had the right to kill a wife discovered with the telltale smell of alcohol on her breath.[1] Marriage laws and customs had undergone a dramatic change in a way largely favorable to women. While the upper-class women of Rome of the Late Empire had no more political rights than her sister of early Rome, the transformation of her status vis-à-vis her husband and her ability to use her wealth would have shocked a woman married under the ancient form called marriage with *manus*. However, despite advancement in the private sphere the emancipation of the Roman matron has often been exaggerated. The aristocratic women of Rome of the Late Empire who chose monasticism and, consequently, rejected the social milieu of the *matrona* of the day must have experienced the possibilities and contradictions of Roman life as a woman. Insofar as these possibilities and contradictions set the context for their choice of monasticism over the socially accepted path of marriage, an investigation of life as a woman of the Roman aristocracy may provide clues to the interpretive dilemma posed by the study of women of the early monastic movement. Therefore, this chapter will investigate the social, economic, and political status of the Roman matron of the Late Empire, treating such questions as marriage arrangements, children and childbearing, and economic autonomy.

Marriage Arrangements and the Woman's Status

By the Late Empire the institution of marriage had undergone a dramatic transformation from the days when women were married by the rite of *conferreatio* and were transferred from the family of their father to that of their husband. This ancient form of marriage called marriage with *manus* had been largely superceded by the so-called free marriage by the third century B.C.[2] However, free marriage hardly provided freedom for the *matrona* who avoided the *auctoritas* of her husband only by remaining under that of her father. Reflection on the legal precedent for the avoidance of *manus* reveals that the free marriage was a reform achieved without challenge to the hierarchical, patriarchal structure of familial authority.

According to R. W. Leage, the precedent for avoidance of *manus* was provided by the XII Tables, that ancient ground of Roman law.[3] In view of the complete subordination of the wife to the authority of the husband in the marriage with *manus*, it is not surprising that women sought release from this marriage arrangement. Surprising is the discovery of a ground for avoiding *manus* marriages in the Roman traditions themselves. A provision of the XII Tables declares that *manus* shall not occur if the woman in a cohabitating arrangement absents herself from the common home for three consecutive nights.[4] This provision provided women with a legal method of avoiding the *auctoritas* of the husband in a subtle way which did not overtly challenge the patriarchal structure of the family. Male *potestas* was not challenged; only whose *potestas* should prevail over the married woman was at issue in this marriage reform.

A summary of the main features of marriage with *manus* will quickly reveal the vulnerability imposed on Roman women. The Roman family like other institutions was conceived in terms of hierarchical notions of authority; apparently, notions of shared authority evaded the Roman mind. All persons within the Roman family fell under the *patria potestas*, i.e., the power of the *paterfamilias* (the male head of the family) who was the family's oldest living male.[5] In the older form of marriage called marriage with *manus*, the woman broke her relational tie with her family of birth and joined the family of her husband, becoming the legal equivalent of his daughter, *filiafamilias*.[6] Legal impediments to bonds with her natural family must have placed the woman in a highly vulnerable position vis-à-vis her husband from whom she had no recourse.

In the marriage without *manus* the woman did not avoid *patria potestas*, for she remained under the authority of her father which, presumably, was tempered with a measure of paternal sympathy. However, feminine progress was not the only incentive for avoiding *manus* marriage arrangements. The demise of the marriage with *manus* appears to be linked with the unexpected increase in feminine wealth in the third and second centuries B.C. following the Punic Wars.[7] The decrease in the male population, resulting from the wars with Hannibal, enhanced the position of daughters who inherited without competition from brothers. The so-called free marriage which became prevalent about the same time may be interpreted as an attempt on the part of the agnatic line to retain control over wealth of daughters which would accrue to their husbands in the marriage with *manus*.[8]

While the free marriage form gave the woman considerable leverage against the authority of her husband and enhanced her property rights, it did not necessarily make her independent. Theoretically, the woman in a marriage without *manus* remained under the authority of her agnatic *paterfamilias*, i.e., the male head of her family of birth. The extent of the intrusion of the *paterfamilias* into the life of a married daughter in our period is difficult to ascertain. Certainly, the authority of the *paterfamilias* had dwindled considerably from the days when even a son could acquire no independent property which did not accrue to the *paterfamilias*.[9] The *Codex Theodosianus* notes the restrictions placed on a father's right to control his children's maternal inheritance; but this was apparently a consequence of the demise of *manus* marriage in which maternal property was not independent.[10] However, a mark of continued paternal authority is the provision of the *Codex Theodosianus* recognizing the right of the father to control the marriage choice of a widowed daughter under twenty-five even if emancipated, presumably as a way of protecting her property from greedy suitors.[11] Evidence from our fourth century sources of female monasticism reveals no *paterfamilias* poised in the background ready to crush female independence. Paula, Melania the Elder, and Marcella had neither living husbands nor living fathers at the time of their ascetic conversion.

If strides toward independence were not restricted by an intrusive *paterfamilias*, a guardian might perform this function. For a long period in Roman history, women had no independent status before the law. The disability of women before the law gave rise to a form of guardianship known as *perpetua tutela mulierum* which filled the function of the *paterfamilias* in the legal arena in the case of his death. Yet, the strict requirement of guardianship for women, living outside male *potestas*, was evaded by assertive Roman women until it became an empty form. Leage in his study, *Roman Private Law,* notes that the *tutela mulierum* of adult women had little importance by the time Gaius compiled his survey of Roman law (second century A.D.).[12] However, we know that guardianship was enough of a thorn in the side of Roman women in the first century A.D. that Augustus tried to use its abolition to entice women into producing more children for the Roman state. Augustus' famous *Lex Papia Poppaea,* designed to increase the declining Roman birthrate, provided for an exemption from *tutela* for freed women who bore four children and freeborn women who bore three.[13] However, Pomeroy argues that clever Roman women, who had wanted to be free of guardianship, had evaded it long before the manipulative provisions of Augustus.[14] Augustus' successor Claudius further modified the requirement for guardianship by abolishing the automatic guardianship of agnatic males over women.[15]

The changes in the institution of guardianship provide an instructive example of the improved status of the Roman matron by the Late Empire. Whereas in the Republic and Early Empire (until the time of Augustus) a woman was required to have a male buffer (either a *paterfamilias* or its equivalent, a tutor) in order to function in the world of business and legal affairs, the *Codex Theodosianus* contains a law of Valentinian of A.D. 390 which sets guidelines for the appointment of a widowed woman as guardian of her minor children.[16] Because the provisions of the *Codex Theodosianus* dealing with the responsibilities, rights, and appointment of tutors treat the case of the minor almost exclusively, it is difficult to determine to what extent the appointment of a male guardian for widowed, adult women remained customary, if not legally necessary. The relative social disability of women would suggest that the custom or some altered form of male guidance survived for widows in our period. It is interesting to note, however, that Jerome's protégées are not described as having guardians during their long widowhoods. In Letter CVIII, in the section in which Jerome praises Paula for the depth of her generosity with her ample wealth and mentions the zeal with which she depleted her presumed vast fortune, one would expect him to mention a legal guardian objecting to this cavalier attitude toward the senatorial concern for preserving aristocratic wealth.[17] Yet he mentions no interference from a guardian. Likewise, Jerome mentions no guardian when writing of Marcella's administration of her wealth or of the desire of Marcella's mother to transfer her wealth to her brother's family.[18] Jerome's account of the financial generosity of his ascetic protégées certainly suggests that the women had unimpeded control over their property.[19]

While the marriage without *manus* enhanced the status of the Roman matron vis-à-vis her husband, the effect on the institution of marriage was disastrous. Divorce became rampant as a result of the tenuous nature of the legal tie between husband and wife in the free marriage. Originally there was no right of intestate succession or inheritance between them, since the wife for all legal purposes belonged to the family of her father.[20] Also, in the free marriage there was originally no right of succession between a mother and her children for the reason cited above.[21] Among the aristocracy for whom property was the emotional cement tying them together, the estrangement of the woman from the property of her husband and children must have inhibited relational bonds. The disintegration of the institution of marriage became so serious that Augustus saw it as a threat to Roman destiny; his ambitious social policy of the first century A.D. sought to enhance marital dignity and entice Roman citizens, preferably aristocrats, into greater fertility. But while Augustus provided social incentives for marriage partners who embodied the Roman ideal of responsible marriage, his social policy did not go to the heart of the legal basis for the tentativeness of marriage. Not until A.D. 178 was the right of succession between a mother and her children recognized by law.[22] Thus, Sarah Pomeroy in her study of the Roman matron concludes that the second century A.D. marks a decisive transition by identifying the woman with the family of her husband and children instead of that of her father in the free marriage form.[23]

While the Roman matron had made strides in functioning as a person before the law, as indicated by the decline of the institution of *perpetua tutela mulierum,* her moves toward independence must have been greatly hindered by the public and private attitude toward adultery. In view of the fact that the laws on adultery in the Late Empire were largely the legacy of Augustus' major reform, the *Lex Julia de Adulteriis* of 18 B.C., a few comments on the social situation which prompted Augustus' public attack on private morals is in order. Perhaps rooted in the tenuous legal bond between husband and wife in free marriage, divorce and infidelity were so widespread that Augustus felt cause for public alarm. The precipitous decline in the birthrate was becoming more than a private issue of life-style; thus, the social legislative package, of which the *Lex Julia de Adulteriis* was the first, aimed primarily at boosting the Roman birthrate.[24] Thus, Augustus' use of public policy to control private morality had a pragmatic social objective rather than a moralistic one.

Augustan law made adultery by women a public crime for the first time in Roman history,[25] disbanding the faulty private system which was failing to stem the tide of infidelity. Hugh Last attributes the failure of the private familial control of infidelity to the inflexibility of remedies which were the legacy of the Republic.[26] A domestic council could either impose a death penalty on a wayward wife (too severe) or allow her husband to divorce her, in which case she lost part of her dowry (too lenient).[27] Whatever the reasons for the inability of domestic councils to keep their houses in order, the private system was obviously too faulty to trust with the important public task of restoring the Roman family.

In view of the absence of major reforms of the *Lex Julia de Adulteriis* in the *Codex Theodosianus,* we can assume that the main provisions of Augustus' stern approach to adultery remained in force; therefore, a few words about the penalties prescribed by the *Lex Julia* are required. In Augustan legislation there were two moments in the response to adultery— first, the husband must sue for divorce in civil courts, and, second, bring charges for adultery in criminal court.[28] The pragmatic rather than moralistic aims of the *Lex Julia* can be seen in the provision that if the husband chose to ignore the indiscretions of his wife and refused to seek divorce, no one else could charge her with adultery until the husband was convicted of condonance.[29] The penalties for adultery in the *Lex Julia* were severe, when compared with the leniency prevalent among indulgent domestic councils. Exile was required for both the woman and her partner in crime as well as forfeiture of a portion of their property (the woman's to include her dowry).[30] However, the penalty for adultery is the one portion of the legislation for which there is specific evidence of modification. Constantine, who represents the addition of Christian moralistic interests, stiffened the penalty for adultery from banishment to death.[31]

While Augustus' public attack on adultery aimed at restoring the dignity of marriage in order to encourage childbirth, not to repress women, the effect of stringent attitudes towards adultery is often inhibiting for women, not because marital fidelity is problematic, but because the independent woman falls under suspicion. One of the few alterations of the *Lex Julia* in the *Codex Theodosianus* speaks to the inhibiting social milieu created for women in a society which considers adultery a criminal offense. Section 9. 7. 2 of the *Codex Theodosianus* limits the right to accuse a woman of adultery to close kin such as fathers, cousins, or brothers, noting that "some persons use the right of accusation wantonly and ruin marriage by false slander."[32] The ever-present threat of capricious charges of sexual misconduct would unquestionably have limited feminine freedom in the public arena.

Evidence from our period substantiates the claim that the Roman *matrona* had to be extremely circumspect in order to avoid capricious charges of the serious crime of adultery. Ammianus Marcellinus in his history of the Late Empire reports the virtual reign of terror under Maximinus, the cruel prefect of the grain supply at Rome and prefect of the city during the period A.D. 360–72.[33] The senatorial class was not exempt from the carnage carried out by Maximinus. The danger of the times was intensified by the temporary imperial suspension of the legal protection of the senatorial class from torture.[34] Many of the senatorial class, both men and women, were executed for adultery as well as other capital offenses such as practicing magic. Cethegus, Charitas, Flaviana, Rufina and "all who were implicated in, or aware of, the adultery that she had committed," Fausiana, Abienus and Anepsia were put to death for adultery during the Roman prefecture of Maximinus.[35] Whether any or all of these persons were actually guilty of adultery cannot be determined. Ammianus' sympathy is clearly with the accused at a time when "it was not a judicial trial which was to be feared, but a suspension of legal proceedings."[36]

The harsh punishment for adultery coupled with the apparent capricious, if only occasional, suspension of the protection provided by the *Codex Theodosianus* must have had a sobering effect on any longing for independence experienced by the Roman matron of the Late Empire. Jerome refers to the constant threat of slander in rumor-filled Rome as he praises Marcella's excellence in maintaining a faultless reputation:

> In a slander-loving community such as Rome, filled as it formerly was with people from all parts and bearing the palm for wickedness of all kinds, detraction assailed the upright and strove to defile even the pure and the clean. In such an atmosphere it is hard to escape from the breath of calumny.[37]

The inhibiting effect of the threat of slander is indicated in Marcella's practice of keeping her mother constantly by her side to thwart rumors. Jerome relates that upon becoming a widow, Marcella never went anywhere without her mother and conducted no interview with monks or clergy without witnesses present.[38] Personal freedom must have been greatly inhibited by the prudent necessity of having constant female companions while venturing into the city or receiving guests.

Letter I of Jerome provides further evidence of the sobering effect on women of the threat of slanderous charges of adultery.[39] In this earliest extant composition of Jerome, an innocent woman of Vercellae is condemned to death for adultery. While the story fits into the genre of hagiography in its exaggerated claim about the miraculous activity of the holy, surely the main theme of condemnation of the innocent for adultery must have been informed by Jerome's experience. The unbounded cruelty of the authorities in torturing the accused woman in an attempt to elicit a confession was, perhaps, not totally a product of Jerome's imagination.

Divorce and Remarriage

While Roman claims about the extreme rarity of divorce in ancient Republican times were probably a product of a romanticized view of the past, certainly in later Roman history the tenuousness of the legal tie between husband and wife in marriage without *manus* resulted in rampant divorce. By our period when the so-called free marriage was almost universal, divorce customs were largely a legacy of Augustan reform with some later revisions by Christian emperors; therefore, Augustan ordering of nebulous divorce procedures bears some comment. Augustus' legislation included a requirement for public notification of repudiation which, although obviously necessary, had not been required; the tenuous legal tie between man and wife often obscured the status of their relationship, leading to sticky legal problems of estate settlement in cases such as the one mentioned by Cicero of a man who died leaving two families competing over his estate.[40] Such disputes were repugnant to the Roman zeal for order in matters of inheritance as well as authority, and the requirement of the *Lex Julia de Adulteriis* of public notification of divorce functioned to preclude messy inheritance battles. Further, the *Lex Julia,* as stated earlier, required dissolution of marriage by divorce before proceedings on the charge of adultery could begin.[41]

By our period Christian emperors had attempted to thwart the frivolous divorces and pragmatic remarriages common in the Late Republic and Early Empire. The case of Pompey, who divorced his first wife to marry Sulla's stepdaughter, at the time pregnant by her previous husband, would be anathema to the Christian view of marriage.[42] Constantinian legislation appears to be the apex of attempts to restrict the grounds for divorce, imposing stiff penalties on those with a casual view of the durability of a Roman marriage. Subsequent legislation on grounds for divorce in the *Codex Theodosianus* only mollifies the extreme restrictiveness of the laws of Constantine. According to Constantinian legislation, a woman can send notice of divorce only if she proves her husband guilty of a criminal act— homicide or practicing sorcery or destroying tombs.[43] Minor peccadilloes such as philandering or excessive drinking must be overlooked. If the woman proves her husband guilty of any of the above crimes, she recovers her dowry intact;[44] however, if a woman serves a notice of repudiation to a husband on less serious grounds, she loses her dowry and is deported.[45] Constantinian restrictions on the husband's grounds for divorcing his wife were less limiting. The husband likewise had only three legal grounds for serving a notice of divorce—adultery, sorcery, or procuring;[46] however, the husband's punishment for divorcing on minor grounds is much less severe, being required only to restore his wife's dowry and not being permitted to remarry.[47] Thus, preference is accorded the man who could demand fidelity in a wife who must tolerate adulterous conduct in him.

The restrictive Constantinian legislation on divorce remained in force during much of the period covered in this study of Roman monastic women, for attempts to mollify the severe restrictiveness of Constantine's strictures do not enter the *Codex Theodosianus* until A.D. 421. A revision of A.D. 421, which appears in the *Codex Theodosianus,* modifies the severe punishment of women who bring notices of divorce on less than criminal grounds. A sentence of deportation is limited to the woman who sends a notice of divorce without proving any grounds for severing the marriage tie.[48] If the woman proves "merely flaws of character and ordinary faults," her punishment is loss of her dowry, nuptial gifts, and the right to remarry but not deportation.[49] The woman who can prove criminal grounds for divorce receives somewhat better treatment. She retains her property and the right to remarry but must wait five years to re-enter marriage.[50] Once again, the husband's penalties for divorcing on less than the most serious grounds are less severe. If the husband divorces for only character faults, the dowry reverts to the woman and he must wait two years to remarry; however, if he divorces over "a mere disagreement," he not only loses the dowry and nuptial gifts but the right to remarry at all.[51] A law of Theodosius and Valentinian of A.D. 449 found in the Justinian Code further reduces the punishment for divorce.[52] The grounds for divorce are expanded, and the punishment for divorcing without legal grounds is no longer deportation for the woman but only the loss of dowry and nuptial gifts and the loss of the right to remarry for five years.[53]

Roman traditions with regard to remarriage were fraught with ambiguity and contradiction, posing conflict for the Roman *matrona.*[54] The tenacious tradition of the *univira* (the once-married woman) so aptly traced by Marjorie Lightman and William Zeisel in *Church History* (vol. 46, March 1977) suggests Roman esteem for the woman who marries only once. On the other hand, Augustan social policies viewed refusal to remarry after divorce or the death of a spouse an unpatriotic indulgence of individual interests over national ones. In order to thwart the precipitous decline in the birthrate, Augustus passed two stunning pieces of legislation, the *Lex Julia de maritandis ordinibus* and the *Lex Papia Poppaea,* requiring men and women of childbearing age to be perpetually married.[55] In the *Lex Julia,* men between twenty-five and sixty and women between twenty and fifty were required to be married or suffer penalties applied to an aristocrat's most vulnerable spot— his ability to inherit.[56] With the *Lex Julia de maritandis ordinibus* and the *Lex Papia Poppaea,* national interests in halting the trend toward depopulation ran counter to deep-rooted attitudes toward the exclusivity of a Roman marriage.[57] Immediate resistance to Augustus' plan to keep women of childbearing age married occurred, and the subsequent *Lex Papia* at least allowed for a less unseemly period after the death or divorce of a prior husband for contracting a second marriage.[58] Although Augustan legislation penalizing celibacy was repealed by Constantine and had long been void by the late fourth century, it is noteworthy insofar as it reveals the necessity of developing a national policy to discourage the stylish trend away from marriage long before Jerome cast the argument for celibacy in Christian terms.[59]

According to Lightman and Zeisel, the honor accorded a Roman *matrona* who married only once had its origin in the idealized state of marriage of the Republican past.[60] The *matrona* fortunate enough to avoid widowhood and remain an *univira* possessed, according to Roman judgment, cultic power to secure such good fortune for other women, and consequently, assumed a ceremonial role in religious rites.[61] In the Late Republic and Early Empire the decayed state of marriage and pervasive divorce prompted a distinction between the *matrona* who had remarried and those who remained *univirae.*[62] Yet, curiously, in ascriptions of the honored term *univira* on funeral inscriptions of the Early Empire the referent is usually very young, suggesting that death demanded constancy in marriage more effectively than custom.[63] Lightman and Zeisel argue that the epithet *univira* was used in the Early Empire on funeral inscriptions by surviving husbands as a status symbol, presumably because their wives fit the pattern of the idealized Roman woman of the Republic, if only because of an early death.[64]

While the pagan usage of the epithet *univira* in imperial times to refer to a woman who dies having married only once does not suggest a pagan custom of celibate widowhood as Jerome claims, it does suggest the Roman ambivalence toward remarriage. With the imperial policy requiring remarriage for widows during the time of Augustan social reform, the pragmatic interests of the state ran counter to the ancient Roman ideology of womanhood. Certainly the oft-married woman contradicted the image of the ideal *matrona/univira* possessed of cultic powers of the Early Republic. The divided mind of imperial Rome with regard to the remarried woman is aptly illustrated by the fact that Augustus, whose public policies demanded remarriage, erected a bronze statue of Cornelia, mother of the Gracchi and paragon of Roman womanhood who, though prolific, once widowed never remarried.[65] However, the veneration of Cornelia may reveal that fertility rather than marriage was Augustus' main concern.[66] Further, valuation of the *univira* accords with Augustan aims insofar as it has its roots in a vision of the normalcy of marriage for women. The good fortune that conferred cultic power upon the early *univira* was that she remained in marriage, not that she outlived her husband.

By the Late Empire the early Republican usage of the epithet *univira* to refer to a living wife of a living husband (the ideal *matrona*) and the early imperial usage of the term to refer to a woman who died having married once converged in Jerome's appropriation of the term to bolster the case for celibate widowhood by claims of continuity with ancient Roman custom.[67] Jerome's in-depth study of the Roman classics revealed to him the ambivalence of the Roman attitude toward remarriage which informed the Roman social milieu of the aristocracy of the Late Empire. In Letter LIV Jerome attempts to encourage Furia to remain a widow by referring to the pagan custom, long observed in her family, of avoiding second marriages:

> It is a high privilege of your family that from the time of Camillus few or none of your houses are described as contracting second marriages.[68]

Considering that Lucius Furius Camillus was made a consul in 349 B.C.,[69] it is apparent that Jerome is engaging in hyperbole in claiming that second marriages were rare in this ancient family for more than eight centuries. Yet, the passage in Jerome indicates the tenacity and ancient origin of the custom of the *univira* as well as its ripeness for Christian appropriation. Further, it points toward deep-rooted trends among the Roman aristocracy opposing remarriage which so thwarted Augustus.

Maternity

The most striking discovery of an investigation of customs surrounding maternity and childbearing in late antiquity is that one's bourgeois expectations go unfulfilled. Roman girls married very young by modern standards, often dispensed with the bother of nursing by employing wet nurses, and, startlingly, very often avoided pregnancy altogether. The well-documented problem of depopulation beginning in the Late Republic suggests a very curious social phenomenon—the successful limitation of family size in a society with primitive and largely inadequate medical knowledge. A. H. M. Jones in *The Later Roman Empire* argues that the depopulation theory, i.e., that the population declined in the Roman Empire, contributing to its demise, is "very probable, if not certain."[70] Jones further argues that while many factors such as plagues and famines could have led to a decrease in population, one would expect repopulation to have occurred unless the birthrate had been low.

The character of the Augustan social reform, which addressed the problem of depopulation by legislation designed to increase the birthrate, suggests that the low birthrate was becoming a social problem of serious proportions. The *Lex Papia Poppaea* of A.D. 9 was designed primarily with the aim of promoting childbearing.[71] However, earlier provisions of the Augustan social program, perhaps to be found in the *Lex Julia,* underscore the resistance to childbearing. Most instructive for our purposes are the provisions designed to break down resistance to parenthood among the aristocracy. Attaining higher office and consequent higher status was made easier for fathers, who were given precedence on the basis of the number of their children.[72] Last has found a provision recorded in the *Digest* of Ulpian, first century jurist, indicating that men climbing the ladder of senatorial offices were allowed to stand for office before the required age if fathers, and the advantage was calculated on the basis of the number of children.[73] Last notes that women were apparently more tenacious in their antipathy toward parenthood, for the *Lex Julia* swayed them less.[74] Therefore, the *Lex Papia Poppaea* aimed at penalizing or granting privileges to women on the basis of their acquiescence in Roman maternal duty. Control over aristocratic women was exercised by means of manipulating their right to property of manumitted slaves on the basis of the number of children they bore.[75] Likewise, freed women gained release from their obligation to a *patrona* or *patronus* (former owner) in accordance with their fecundity.[76]

Augustus' provisions releasing women from guardianship if they bore three or four children may indicate that three or four offspring was considered a large family at the time, according to John T. Noonan in his study of the history of contraception.[77] Noonan bolsters his view that small families prevailed in the Roman Empire by reference to Pliny's recounting the public attention showered on a humble freedman named Gaius Crispinus Hilarius who made a trek to Rome with his eight children, twenty-seven grandchildren, and eighteen great-grandchildren.[78] The praise heaped on Crispinus suggests the novelty of such fecundity in the Roman Empire of Pliny's day. Balsdon reiterates the view that small families prevailed in the Late Republic and Early

Empire.[79] To what extent the trend toward small families persisted in the Late Roman Empire is difficult to ascertain. Governmental attempts to bolster the birthrate by outlawing celibacy ceased for religious, not social reasons. And a law of Constantine of 315 (*Codex Theodosianus* 11. 27) which provided for governmental subsidy of parents who could not afford to raise their children suggests that the state sought ways to increase the population which would not offend Christian sensibilities. Among the circles of our Roman ascetic women small families certainly prevailed (except for the case of Paula), for fertility was often thwarted by asceticism.

Keith Hopkins agrees that the fertility rate in the Roman Empire is much lower than one would expect given the early age of marriage and consequent length of marriage.[80] Roman girls often married very young. While Augustus established the legal minimum age of marriage for girls at 12, Hopkins argues that the law was lightly enforced and that prepubertal marriage was acceptable if not the most common practice.[81] Hopkins further argues that among the aristocracy the usual age of marriage would have been between 11 and 17.[82] Given this early age for marriage among Roman girls and assuming an average life expectancy of thirty-five, Hopkins concludes that half of most first marriages would have lasted eighteen years.[83] Assuming this span of marriage one would expect that Augustus and subsequent emperors would not have had to manipulate their citizens into producing offspring.

Small families, a low birthrate, depopulation! How does one explain this trend in a society lacking the technological means to control reproduction? One factor was the socially unacceptable but persistent attitude favoring childlessness. Roman historians record a strain of antipathy toward parenthood. Pliny the Younger, writing about A.D. 100, holds up for praise a friend who has fulfilled the Roman duty to produce offspring despite the prevailing popularity of childlessness.[84]

> He [Asinius Rufus] has several children, for here too he has done his duty as a good citizen, and has chosen to enjoy the blessing of a fruitful marriage at a time when the advantages of remaining childless make most people feel a single child a burden.[85]

Tacitus, writing in the second century, dubs Augustus' efforts to increase the birthrate a failure and claims that childlessness is fashionable: "It [the *Lex Papia Poppaea*] failed, however, to make marriage and the family popular— childlessness remained the vogue."[86]

One manifestation of this popular antipathy toward familial responsibilities was that numerous men of the upper class chose to avoid marriage and instead established liaisons with elegant mistresses.[87] Usually the woman was one of a different social class, whom custom, if not law, prevented him from marrying.[88] The love elegists of the first century provide the most striking record of this phenomenon. Propertius had his Cynthia, Ovid his Corenna. One sees the survival of this attitude in the Late Empire in Augustine's resistance to marriage even before his Christian conversion. Preferring the relatively undemanding liaison of concubinage, Augustine put off his mother's persistent efforts to arrange a proper marriage at a stage in his life when Christian considerations were not paramount in his thinking.[89] It is interesting in this regard to note that Augustine's lengthy concubinage produced only one child.

How small families were maintained among those aristocrats who fulfilled their duty to the state and to their class by marrying can only be conjectured. Abortion was practiced, often fatally for the mother. Newborns could have been exposed until late in the fourth century, when exposure was outlawed.[90] And some scholars think that contraceptive information was available in the Roman Empire. Keith Hopkins argues that ample contraceptive advice had currency in the medical sources of the day.[91] Most notably, Soranus, a Greek gynecologist of the second century A.D. who practiced in Rome, articulated quite sophisticated contraceptive advice.[92] Unfortunately, Soranus' contraceptive theories contained both effective and ineffective methods and left the Roman matron unable to distinguish between them.[93] John Noonan agrees that the medical tradition beginning with Aristotle and handed on by Soranus provided the Roman matron with some contraceptive information.[94] Yet, Hopkins argues that in our period (the Late Roman Empire) contraception would have been less likely to have been practiced than in the Late Republic and Early Empire, when the status of women was higher.[95] Further complicating assessment, the lack of distinction between contraception and abortion, resulting from an inability to exactly calculate the gestation period, obscures historical references. Consequently, the existence and use of effective contraceptive means can only be guessed.

Education

That many upper-class women of the Late Roman Empire were educated is indisputable. How they were educated and the content of their education is more difficult to determine. Roman society had long had an ambiguous attitude toward educated women. The woman of culture elegized by the love poets of the first century such as Ovid and Propertius contradicted the ideal of the Roman *matrona* devoted to her husband and family rather than her own accomplishments. The threat that the accomplished woman as defined by Ovid posed to the Roman ideology of wifehood can be seen in Augustus' act of exiling Ovid; however, the woman of Ovid's love poetry wears her education like a necklace, an item useful only insofar as it enhances her erotic attractiveness to men.[96] The thought that education had value in and of itself for the woman apart from its erotic appeal seemed to escape Ovid. This attitude is strikingly illustrated in Ovid's dubbing as coquetishly charming the curious feminine practice of feigning a lisp, which obviously would not have enhanced intelligibility.[97] Yet, despite societal ambiguity, there was a tradition of education among upper-class women which such figures as Marcella, Paula, and Melania of the Late Empire inherited.

The tradition was rooted in the few exceptional women in Roman history who overcame the barriers to feminine intellectual attainment by attaching themselves to the literary circles of their day. Sulpicia, daughter of a friend of Cicero's, became part of the coterie of love elegists which included Ovid and Tibullus.[98] The few extant fragments of her work suggest little originality in her adherence to the form developed by her male elegiac mentors.[99] Yet, her literary activity is a milestone for Roman women. Her successor as an outstanding female intellectual was Julia Domna, the lowborn but bright wife of the emperor Septimius Severus.[100] Julia's acquisition of an education depended on her own initiative and her position at the imperial court. Upon becoming empress, Julia, who had no formal education, was able by virtue of her position to gather around her the leading grammarians, rhetoricians, and sophists of the day.[101] Figures such as Sulpicia, Julia Domna, and Lesbia, made famous by Catullus, suggest that a long tradition of female intrusion into male literary circles stood behind the Roman matron of the Late Empire.

There is ample evidence to glean a fairly clear picture of the character of a late Roman education and some evidence which suggests that girls as well as boys were the beneficiaries of Roman grammatical/literary standards of pedagogy. The *Saturnalia,* in which Macrobius gathers round the intelligensia of the senatorial class of Rome of the Late Empire for the educational benefit of his son, reveals the literary character of the quintessential Roman education which seems quaint and useless by modern scientific standards of teaching. The content of Macrobius' knowledge consists of humorous or catchy anecdotes about the heroes of classical history, particularly Cicero, or characters in the *Aeneid.*[102] Thus, the mark of the educated man of late Roman society was the ability to quote Vergil with ease and engage in flowery rhetoric punctuated with numerous allusions to the great master. Such skill was attained by passing through three educational levels—the primary school, the secondary school, and higher education or school of rhetoric.[103] Roman pedagogy began its focus on the study of the Latin literary masters at the secondary school level which began as early as the age of eleven.[104] The secondary school education focused on two areas of learning—language theory and poetry.[105] Sometime after the first century the study of authors was based on a fixed curriculum which centered around Vergil, Terence, Sallust, and Cicero.[106] Rhetorical training aimed at turning out orators skilled at persuasive argument and, thus, channeled graduates into careers in public office or in law.[107] Therefore, the character of the Roman education, steeped as it was in pagan literature, posed an insoluble contradiction for Christian intellectuals such as Jerome and Augustine. Having cut their intellectual teeth on Vergil and the ancient classical masters and having learned the rhetorical art of composing with quaint Vergilian allusions, as Christians their pagan education implied divided loyalties. For Jerome the contradiction posed by having the roots of his intellect in pagan literature haunted not only his waking consciousness but his dreams.[108]

We may presume that whatever education Roman aristocratic women had would have been grounded in the same standards of pedagogy as that outlined above, i.e., study of the ancient classical masters. Referring to remarks by Ovid and Martial,[109] Marrou concludes that aristocratic girls as well as boys attended the second level of the Roman educational system—the grammar school.[110] How common it was for girls to venture out of the home for grammatical and literary instruction is difficult to ascertain. Quintilian's review of the arguments for and against a private, domestic education for aristocratic boys reveals that education in the home still had its advocates in the Early Empire,[111] and Marrou claims aristocrats "never lost their fondness for it."[112] Claudian's portrayal of Maria studying at the feet of her mother suggests that feminine education in domestic isolation had not been abandoned.[113] However secondary education was acquired by aristocratic women, the mode of higher education reflected in the examples of Jerome and Augustine, who left their towns of birth to venture to prestigious centers of learning, would have been precluded. Matrons such as Marcella, Paula, and Melania who lived at one of the Empire's intellectual centers, Rome, would not have sought a rhetorical education, for not only would it have been useless to them, it would have commenced at the inopportune age of fifteen.[114] However, the intellectually curious woman of late Rome could have gained indirect access to the education offered by professorial lectures, whether at the secondary or rhetorical level. Since state-subsidized chairs at both Rome and Constantinople were supported by the local senates,[115] it is conceivable that among the inbred aristocracy Roman women of the senatorial class would either be related to or at least socially acquainted with professors. Still this informal, unstructured access to higher education would have put them at a decided intellectual disadvantage to their male counterparts.

Whether women attained their education in domestic isolation or ventured into the city to the secondary school, the educational focus would have been on the Latin literary masters of the past. Our sources in the Late Empire reveal some feminine acquaintance with the classical masters. Claudian, called the last of the Roman poets, praises Maria, the fiancée of the emperor Honorius, for ceaselessly poring over "the writers of Rome and Greece, all that old Homer sang, or Thracian Orpheus."[116] Jerome gives us a few hints about education among the Roman matrons of the day in Letter XXII, where he advises Eustochium to avoid the company of the erudite women of Rome and implies by his rhetorical questions that their education fits the pattern discussed above. "How can Horace go with the psalter, Virgil with the gospels, Cicero with the apostles?"[117] he asks in defining the "adultery of the tongue" of which these sophisticated ladies are guilty. In Letter CXXVII, Jerome notes that Marcella often quoted the saying of Plato "that philosophy consists in meditating on death."[118] Whether Marcella had actually read Plato or simply knew the common currency of the day is difficult to ascertain. Yet, Epictetus, who wrote at the end of the first and beginning of the second century, claimed women were seen at Rome carrying copies of Plato's *Republic.*[119] Given this precedent and Marcella's documented intelligence, Jerome's reference may point to an education in the classical masters of Greece and Rome. However, nothing in Jerome's letters explicitly states the character of the education which his protégées received prior to their ascetic conversion. Clark points out that while Jerome embellished his letters to his female protégées with allusions to Cicero, Vergil, and the like, presuming that the allusions would not confuse them, his letters to educated men contain many more classical allusions.[120]

In summary, the scant evidence we have of education among aristocratic women of late Roman society suggests that some attained a classical education parallel to that of their male counterparts, at least at the secondary level. Whether attendance at the numerous secondary schools or private education in domestic isolation was the more common form can only be conjectured. Insofar as education at the secondary level was defined in terms of grammatical and literary skills, we can be assured that whatever intellectual attainments women achieved were grounded in this model.

Conclusions

The Roman *matrona* of the Late Empire had made strides toward independence in terms of marriage arrangements and in terms of control over her property. Avoiding *manus* marriage which had so repressed her counterpart in early Roman history, the *matrona* had some leverage with her husband by virtue of the control she exercised over the property she brought into the marriage. However, legislation which restricted the grounds for divorce and harshened the penalty for adultery probably inadvertently thwarted progress toward independence. Enacted first for pragmatic, political reasons by Augustus, who saw the trend toward depopulation as a serious social problem, and later by Christian emperors for moralistic reasons, restrictive laws on divorce and adultery functioned to create a repressive social climate for the independent woman who lived under the threat of capricious charges of misconduct.

Behind the Roman *matrona* of the Late Empire stood a long, if somewhat limited, tradition of education in women. The biting satire of Juvenal about the tedious nature of mental accomplishments in women and the erotic slant put on feminine education by Ovid reveal the Roman ambiguity toward education for women. But some actual women appeared to break through the possible social stigma by attaining at least a secondary level education, characterized by the study of Latin literature.

Behind the Roman *matrona* of the Late Empire there also stood an ambiguous tradition with regard to remarriage and parenthood. The social reform of Augustus, revealed most dramatically in the *Leges Juliae,* suggests that Jerome didn't invent Roman antipathy to marriage and childbearing. The resistance of aristocrats to the social duty of producing the next Roman generation created a social problem long before Jerome's eminent friends rejected maternal responsibilities in order to pursue the monastic call.

5

Parsons' Theory of Action and the Analysis of Asceticism

Historical investigation of Roman ascetic women of the early Christian monastic movement points toward various hypotheses about the cause of their break with aristocratic, worldly standards. The constancy of the barbarian threat may have called into question the maternal commitment to preserve the family line. Paula's somewhat tangential relationship to the bluest of the Roman blue bloods may have encouraged her to opt out of the senatorial class milieu with its obsession for the minutiae of status differentiations. Despite the plausibility of many theses which might be derived from the historical investigation, there is a sense of groping in this kind of analysis. There is the sense that if only one had better conceptual and theoretical tools, one could move beyond speculation to a more refined hypothesis based upon the historical investigation, of course, but articulated by means of an integrated theoretical framework.

It is my view that the interaction model of social structure and social dynamics provides a very revealing theoretical tool for analyzing the ascetic choice of the women in question. Therefore, I shall draw upon the conceptualization of the social process in terms of Talcott Parsons' theory of action, especially as set forth in *The Social System,* to analyze the social and relational contexts out of which the ascetic choice emerged for such figures as Paula, Marcella, and the Melanias.[1] While challenges to the theoretical validity of Parsons' model of the social order continue to be raised by theorists who charge that it emphasizes the normalcy of stability to the neglect of conflict, it is not within the scope of this study to address the current state of sociological theory. Rather, I have chosen to apply one particular model of the social process to the historical phenomenon under study here in order to press further the interpretive analysis of asceticism. This is not to claim that the Parsonian theory of action is without flaw in its description of the social process nor to claim that the interpretive insights it provides are the definitive explanation of ascetic renunciation of late antiquity. Rather, reference to

Parsons' theory of action provides a theoretical model of the social process which serves as a tool to highlight certain aspects of the historical situation which otherwise might be overlooked, specifically the significance of the closeness of paganism and Christianity within the senatorial aristocracy and the significance of ambiguous cultural norms for the monastic choice. The purpose of the model is to illuminate fresh aspects of the historical situation in an effort to discern possible sources of motivation, not to characterize the social order of late antiquity or to characterize monasticism from a sociological perspective.

Parsons' theory of action and its model of a stable interaction system prove to be useful tools by illustrating the importance of the conflictual relational context of Roman monastic women whose families were in the painful process of shedding ancient pagan roots. Prosopographical study presses further Peter Brown's portrayal of the aristocracy of late Rome as experiencing a "sea change."[2] As paganism's hold on Rome's elite finally gave way to Christian pressure, the skewing of socialization, resulting from the co-existence of conflicting value standards among Roman aristocratic families, created a situation ripe for social deviance, defined in interaction terms.

Of striking applicability to ascetic dynamics is Parsons' analysis of the genesis of deviance in interactionist terms. While the origin of deviance may not be central to Parsons' theoretical system, it should be kept in mind that my purpose is not to do a Parsonian analysis of monasticism but to find a theoretical tool in sociological theory which fits the historical data. With the historical data as the controlling category rather than Parsons' system as the controlling category, his analysis of the genesis of deviance proved to be most enlightening. While Jerome and company would have bristled at being designated deviates rather than embodiments of pure Christian sentiment, suggesting that perspective is a factor in the classification of any behavior as deviance, asceticism, insofar as it placed the women under study here in conflict with the social expectations of the Roman aristocracy of which they were a part, can be identified with Parsonian categories of deviance. This suggests nothing perjorative about ascetic spirituality, only its relationship to the wider aristocratic value system. Thus, the congruence of certain monastic behavior with patterns of social deviance suggests the applicability of sources of motivation to deviance to an analysis of the source of motivation to ascetic renunciation.

While the conflictual relational context of the Roman aristocracy in the late fourth century as it extricated itself from its pagan origins provides sufficient explanation for the monastic choice in terms of the interaction model, further refinement in identifying dimensions of this unstable relational context as possible sources of motivation to asceticism can be gained by referring to the ambiguous cultural norms for women which were a by-product of this clash of cultures, or as Brown says the "sea change." The historical study in chapter 4 pointed toward highly ambiguous expectations for the Roman woman; however, I believe this can be demonstrated more dramatically to the reader by reference to sources of cultural images. In order to demonstrate the highly contradictory nature of the expectational structure for the *matrona* of late Roman aristocratic society which moves beyond the clues revealed in chapter 4, I will in the next chapter construct a typology of images of women current in late Roman society, using feminine images found in classical and ecclesiastical literature. Further explanation of the methodological basis for this typology will be deferred to the introduction of the typological section of this study. At this point I introduce the notion of the typology of images in order to explain that it is an extension of the unstable relational context which will be investigated here and, as such, is the source of stress which I shall argue prompted the monastic choice.

The Action Frame of Reference and the Relational Context of the Senatorial Aristocracy of Late Rome

While the clash of pagan and Christian cultures in late antiquity is a commonplace of early Christian scholarship, application of this notion on the individual level often focuses on the intellectual dilemma of bridging two cultures.[3] The intrusion of guilt over his love for Plautus and Terence into Jerome's dream is a psychological and intellectual problem but not at this level a social one. However, the interaction model of social structure enables us to analyze the effect of conflicting cultures on the individual's relationship to society. The following application of Parsons' action frame of reference to the ascetic choice of Christian women of late Roman antiquity will be the basis for my thesis that the closeness of Christianity and paganism among the aristocracy and the consequent malintegration of cultural norms for women prompted their rejection of aristocratic values by means of monastic renunciation.

   While role theory/interaction theory has spawned writing from various perspectives, the basic interaction paradigm articulated by Talcott Parsons in *The Social System* provides an adequate theoretical framework for our analysis.[4] The interaction model of social structure centers on the relational aspect of a person's orientation to society. In other words, an individual's identity and social orientation, other than that aspect grounded in physiology, is in large measure a product of his/her interaction with the social order and significant others. The rudimentary notion on which the interaction model of social structure is based is summarized in the following statement of Talcott Parsons:

> An established state of a social system is a process of complementary interaction of two or
> more individual actors in which each conforms with the expectations of the other(s) in such
> a way that alter's reactions to ego's actions are positive sanctions which serve to reinforce
> his given need-dispositions and thus to fulfill his given expectations.[5]

This quotation points to what Parsons considers the three foci for analyzing a social system in interaction terms—the individual, the interactive system, i.e., the relational pattern or patterns in which the individual has his/her social existence, and the cultural standard.[6] The basic unit of the interaction system is the individual's (ego's) relation to significant others (alters) and their mutual relation to the normative patterns of the social order. Culture building results from the fact that ego and alter orient themselves to each other in light of cultural norms. Theorists call this interdependency "complementarity of expectations." Ego expects alter to conform to ego's expectations which have their source in the common value pattern of the social order. Likewise, alter expects ego to meet alter's expectations. If ego and alter share the same values and norms, they engage in mutually reinforcing behavior which not only upholds the common value pattern but keeps their relationship on a positive keel. In terms of relationship to alter, ego experiences the value pattern as an expectation requiring fulfillment. In terms of his or her self-identity, ego experiences a need to conform to the value pattern, if (as will be further explained) the value is sufficiently institutionalized and, consequently, internalized by ego. Alter likewise is reinforced in his or her attachment to the value pattern in question by the threat of ego's sanction for non-conformity. Thus, the mutual relatedness of ego and alter serves to reinforce the dominant values of the culture. The stability of the interactive system requires a certain compatibility between ego's needs and alter's expectations.

The social system itself relies for its stability on the institutionalization of value standards which function for its continuation.[7] Insofar as a value pattern is institutionalized it becomes internalized, primarily through the process of socialization, by the constituent members of the social system in question.[8] The socializing adults interact with the child to reinforce their own value standards, which generally are compatible with the dominant standards in a stable system. The importance of internalization of value patterns for the stability of the social order is that the values are transformed from external demands into internal needs. For example, Parsons points out that the dictum "to do a good day's work" functions positively not only for an employer but provides gratification to the employee if productivity is an internalized value. Parsons argues that the stability of any social system depends upon compatibility between the personal, internal needs of the constituent actors and the functionally important expectations of the larger order.[9]

In summary, a stable interaction unit, which is the building block of a stable social system, relies on mutual conformity to common social value patterns. In a complex social order the individual mediates between the expectations of innumerable others in a variety of contexts. However, the basic unit for analysis, on the basis of which a complex interaction pattern would be disassembled, is ego and alter in their mutual relation to each other with reference to the dominant value patterns of the social order.[10] Insofar as the value patterns are institutionalized and internalized, ego and alter experience the social expectations of the larger order as internal needs requiring fulfillment and as possible sanctions vis-à-vis the other. As long as ego and alter interact in such a way as to mutually reinforce the value patterns of the larger society their relationship to each other and to the social order is stable. This summary of the primary insight of the interaction model into the relational context of social orientation provides the basic paradigm for further analysis of the social context of the ascetic choice of Roman Christian women of the early monastic movement.

Certain aspects of the historical context of ascetic women of late Roman antiquity who broke with the social order are incompatible with Parsons' model of a stable interaction system. The syncretistic pagan/Christian milieu so aptly described by Peter Brown in "Aspects of the Christianization of the Roman Aristocracy," exposed the first generation of Roman monastic women to a clash of cultures in which pagan, worldly values existed in the same aristocratic families alongside Christian, otherworldly ones. Socialization and internalization of uniform value patterns would have been skewed by this disharmony of perspective. The co-existence of conflicting value patterns was a product of the Christianization of the aristocracy, as families with strong pagan roots adapted themselves to the political and religious demise of paganism.[11] The struggle took on a personal character in the families of Melania and Paula and must have disturbed familial equilibrium over several generations. If Brown is correct, both sides won. Christianity asserted its religious ascendancy over paganism, while the montage of ancient Roman traditions so dear to the Roman elite survived behind outward Christian trappings.[12]

However, the pagan/Christian conflict does not fully define the disharmony of values in the Roman society in which Melania, Marcella, and Paula found their social existence. Divisions were more nuanced than that. Paganism was hardly of one mind, particularly with regard to the ideal woman which will be the focus for our definition of norms. Was the *univira,* the once-married woman who remained faithful to the memory of her dead husband, or the prolific woman the pagan ideal? Likewise, Christianity suffered serious divisions between non-ascetic, worldly oriented believers and the otherworldly, ascetic faction. An obvious example of Christianity's divided mind is provided by the heated debate between Jerome and Jovinianus, who in typical Roman fashion felt it necessary to decide precedence, in this instance between virginity and marriage. It mattered not to Jerome whether the silk dress and strung pearls were on a pagan or a Christian, they still smacked of worldly decadence. His chastisement of Christian women who, in imitation of the worldly, painted their faces indicates such indulgence was not uncommon.[13] Jerome's portrait of the city of Rome reveals that there were Christians whose mien and behavior were indistinguishable from the pagan aristocracy. Thus, the conflict between Christian and pagan, in which was rooted the disparity of value standards in Rome of the late fourth century, has to be qualified by recognition of the Christian faction whose value system had been largely subsumed into the pagan. Christian widows dashed about in ostentatious litters (Jerome, Letter XXII); Blaesilla, daughter of Paula, gaily indulged her girlish fantasies of acquiring incomparable beauty (Jerome, Letter XXXVIII).

The clash of cultures which created the conflictual value standards among the aristocracy of late fourth century Rome might be politically symbolized by the ejection of the Altar of Victory from the Senate in A.D. 383.[14] To the casual student of early Christian history it is surprising that the ejection from the Senate of a symbol of Roman paganism would have been necessary at this late date in view of Constantine's ostensible Christianization of the empire in the early fourth century. The incident over the removal of the Altar of Victory from the Senate and Symmachus' defense of paganism in his famous Relatio III reveal that paganism survived quite well among the senatorial class in Rome until the early fifth century.[15] Jones notes that not until the latter part of the fifth century did the upper class in the Western part of the Roman Empire fully extricate itself from its pagan roots.[16]

A curious aspect of this tenacious paganism among the senatorial class in the West was its apparent retention of entry into the highest political offices.[17] The fasti of the prefects of the city of Rome (*Praefecti Urbis Romae* or PVR) contain the names of eminent pagans through the 390s. Quintus Aurelius Symmachus was PVR from A.D. 384 to 385; Ceionius Rufius Albinus, noted pagan of the *Saturnalia,* was PVR from A.D. 389 to 391.[18] Nicomachus Flavianus, PVR from A.D. 392 to 394, was the son of a pagan mother and father.[19] Pinianus I (PVR A.D. 385 to 387), the uncle of Melania the Younger's husband, and Faltonius Probus Alypius (PVR A.D. 391) may have been Christian; certainly Christians attained the urban prefecture. However, many of the favorite sons of the ancient senatorial families, whose prestige was cemented by their official roles, clung tenaciously to the pagan traditions of Rome in which their preeminence was rooted.[20]

The clash of pagan and Christian within the senatorial aristocracy suggests competing value systems and points toward the lack of integration of cultural norms for women. While a value system can encompass a wide range of norms regarding social behavior, this study shall focus on the implications of conflicting value patterns on the normative expectations for women. Fortunately, our primary Christian source for life at Rome during this period, Jerome, concerns himself with the minutiae of feminine behavior as it reflects values. While we cannot always trust his hagiographical perspective on his protégées, he aptly illustrates conflicting expectations of the feminine ideal which informed life in Rome of late antiquity for the senatorial class.

Before we look at the unintegrated normative structure for women which I will argue was a product of the clash of cultures in Rome of the Late Empire, it is helpful to take a closer look at some of the prosopographical evidence which supports the claim that our subjects found their social existence in families characterized by pagan/Christian intermingling. [21]

Insofar as Melania the Elder was closer than Paula and Marcella to the elite of the Roman aristocracy, the so-called "inner aristocracy," her familial ties aptly illustrate the co-existence of pagan and Christian among the senatorial families of Rome of the Late Empire. Whether Melania's illustrious grandfather, Antonius Marcellinus 16 (PPO A.D. 340–41 and consul A.D. 341), was pagan or Christian is difficult to ascertain. We know that he was active in the conspiracy to oust Constans as emperor of the West, although this need not imply paganism, since Christian scruples hardly precluded intrigue even among Christian emperors during this turbulent time. [22] As Constans, who appointed Marcellinus PPO (*Praefecti Praetorio*) of Italy in A.D. 340, favored the old aristocratic families for the office of praetorian prefect of Italy, [23] Marcellinus' aristocratic status suggests, at this early stage of Christianization among the nobility, a nearness to paganism.

If, as Jones et al. conjecture in *The Prosopography of the Later Roman Empire*, Melania the Elder's husband was Valerius Maximus 17 (PVR A.D. 361–62), her marriage would have placed Melania very close to a pagan milieu. While this writer has questioned the identification of Melania's husband with Valerius Maximus 17, his closeness to paganism might explain the reticence of Paulinus of Nola in naming the husband of his cousin and spiritual compatriot. As prefect of the city of Rome appointed by Julian the apostate during his attempted pagan revival, [24] Maximus 17 almost certainly was a pagan. His father or grandfather, Valerius Maximus 48, was indeed a pagan, according to the *Codex Theodosianus*. [25] While Maximus 17 had two uncles, Vulcacius Rufinus and Neratius Cerealis, the first of whom was pagan and the second Christian, Ammianus implies a closeness between Maximus and Rufinus which suggests similar religious sentiments. [26]

However, even if the connection between Melania and Valerius Maximus 17 is not genuine, the syncretism in the families of the next generation suggests syncretism in the previous generation where gaps in evidence prevent firm conclusions. Publicola, Melania's only surviving son, who emulated the worldly ambitions of his pagan counterparts, married the daughter of a mixed marriage, Albina. Albina's father mingled with the pagan blue bloods, according to Macrobius' *Saturnalia*.[27] Her brother, Rufius Antonius Agrypnius Volusianus, receives mention in Christian sources not for attaining the urban prefecture but for tenaciously clinging to his paganism until a deathbed conversion by Melania the Younger.[28]

Melania the Elder's niece, Avita, exemplifies the syncretistic milieu of the senatorial aristocracy of her generation and, thus, by implication the previous generation in her marriage to a pagan named Turcius Apronianus. We know that Apronianus was pagan, because Palladius credited his conversion to Christianity to Melania the Elder (*The Lausiac History* 54) and because his father was appointed PVR by Julian during the pagan revival.[29] Paulinus of Nola likewise refers to Apronianus as newly Christian.[30]

The generation of Melania the Younger, who was the daughter of two Christian parents, and of her husband, Pinianus, who had an eminent Christian father, was more thoroughly Christianized. However, Melania the Elder and Publicola found their social existence in a family in transition in which pagan and Christian co-existed in an implicit disharmony.

Paula, favored protégée of Jerome, must also have experienced the stress of pagan/Christian clashes. Identifying any pagan connections in Paula's family of origin is hindered by missing evidence. However, if Jerome's claim that Paula's mother, Blaesilla, was a descendant of Republican families has any shred of truth to it, paganism lay in the background. Just how far back cannot be determined. However, the nearness of Paula's husband to pagan circles placed her in the midst of conflictual values. As Jerome's scant evidence about Julius Toxotius is our only source, any claims about the religious preferences of Paula's husband would be highly conjectural. Jerome writes nothing disparaging about Toxotius which would imply unchristian sentiments. Nevertheless, in view of the pattern of pagan male solidarity in late Rome the pagan connections of Toxotius' brother, Hymetius, raises questions about the former and certainly must have involved Paula in the syncretism of late fourth century senatorial families. Ammianus Marcellinus reports that Hymetius incurred imperial wrath for attempting to carry out a sacrifice to the pagan deities, whose aid he sought in a dispute with the emperor.[31]

If Praetextata, wife of Hymetius, is, as some scholars suppose,[32] the sister of Praetextatus, Paula's family is linked to the intellectual and political center of late Roman paganism. Praetextatus stands second in eminence only to Symmachus as champion of Roman pagan dreams in our period. Sepulchral inscriptions reveal that he held the following pagan offices—"augur, priest of Vesta, priest of the Sun, quindecemvir, curial of Hercules, consecrated to Liber and the Eleusian mysteries, high priest, temple overseer (*neocorus*), initiate of the taurobolium, Father of the Fathers [priest of Mithras]."[33] Macrobius' portrayal of Praetextatus as well-versed in the esoterica of pagan traditions also speaks for his position among the pagan movement of late fourth century Rome.[34] Jerome's account of Praetextata's interference in the ascetic choice of her niece Eustochium reveals that the families, if conflictual, were nonetheless in contact with each other.[35]

Julius Toxotius' nearness to paganism is repeated by his son, Toxotius, with the latter's marriage to a daughter of a mixed marriage, Laeta. Jerome even hints that Toxotius may not have been Christian from birth. While this claim is conjectural, it is one possible interpretation of Jerome's analogy between Paula's son, Toxotius, and Laeta's father, Albinus. Comforting Laeta about her father's tenacious paganism, Jerome argues that all is not lost, for the Christianization of her family makes conversion probable.[36] Even if Albinus laughs at Jerome and calls him a madman, conversion is not precluded, for "his son-in-law did the same before he came to believe. Christians are not born but made."[37]

Whatever the original religious sentiments of Paula's only son, Toxotius, his wife's family unquestionably linked his family with paganism. Jerome refers to Laeta's father as a *pontifex* ("heathen pontiff"),[38] and Macrobius mentions him as a member of the pagan coterie chronicled in the *Saturnalia*. Furthermore, Laeta's eminent brother, Albinus 10, carried on the paganism of his father, according to the Roman fashion.[39] Thus, Toxotius with a pagan uncle, an intrusive pagan aunt, and a pagan father-in-law but a zealously Christian mother and wife illustrates the religious mixture of the late Roman senatorial families.

Evidence for religious syncretism in the lives of Paula's other children is less certain. Eustochium was dedicated to virginity at an early age (cf. Jerome's Letter XXII). Rufina's premature death precluded marriage, which would have linked her with the larger society. Paulina married the properly Christian Pammachius, and the identity of Blaesilla's husband is quite hypothetical. However, the one certain piece of evidence about Blaesilla's husband (that he was Furia's brother) establishes the Christian context of his parental home. While Jerome is oblique about the name of Furia's father, he writes explicitly that both her parents were Christian.[40] Thus, in Paula's family the clash of pagan and Christian occurred primarily through her husband's family and through the family of her son's wife. It is interesting to note that links with paganism came through male members of Paula's family.

Evaluating the pagan intrusion into the social existence of Jerome's less favored protégée, Marcella, poses some difficulty in view of the uncertainty of her genealogy. If, as her name suggests, Albina, Marcella's mother, was the daughter of Albinus 14 and sister of C. Ceionius Rufius Volusianus (not to be confused with the uncle of Melania II), Marcella would be firmly placed near ongoing paganism. Yet, as noted in the prosopographical section of this study, Albina's link with the illustrious Ceionii Rufii is conjectural. That Marcella's rejected suitor Cerealis was Christian seems likely in that he served on Constantius' council at Sirmium which condemned Photius for unorthodox trinitarian views.[41] However, Cerealis' brother, Vulcacius Rufinus, who matched Cerealis in achieved eminence, was indeed pagan.[42] Yet, Marcella's speedy rebuff of Cerealis makes it doubtful that she had much contact with his pagan and, therefore even less desirable, brother.

The nearness of Christianity to the pagan roots of the senatorial class must have resulted in a clash of values in the families of Melania and Paula. While the focus of this study is on the conflicting cluster of expectations for women resulting from this collision of value systems in the senatorial families, one further word at this point about the anxiety produced by a disparity of values helps establish the context for the analysis of the interaction system which follows. Jerome in his letters chronicled the Christian aristocrats of Rome whose behavior was indistinguishable from their pagan counterparts: the fashion conscious ladies who changed "their gowns from day to day" or feigned frugality by wearing the same dress repeatedly, while their closet bulged with others,[43] and the beauty conscious women who painted their faces chalky white "like those of idols."[44] While, as usual, Jerome's attention seems to be riveted on feminine foibles which are only the material manifestation of a larger social problem, his satire points toward the incompatibility of senatorial indulgence and Christianity which posed an agonizing contradiction. For someone as religiously sensitive as Pammachius, the contradiction was a serious issue on which the fate of his soul might hinge. Letter 13 of Paulinus of Nola reveals Pammachius' agony over the fate of the rich man in Scripture whose disdain for the suffering of Lazarus gains for him eternal damnation. Paulinus notes that Pammachius was "fearful of that rich man's punishment" and reassures his wealthy friend of senatorial rank "that it is not riches but men's use of them which is blameworthy or acceptable to God."[45] Paulinus tries to salve Pammachius' worried conscience with the claim that he is "rich in God's spirit" and that "God loves rich men of this kind in company with His poor."[46] Letter 13 provides compelling evidence that some in the senatorial class felt the stress posed by the clash of their aristocratic status with Christian spiritual values.

Pammachius may not have been responding just to an internal pang of conscience. Recent studies (cf. John Morris, "Pelagian Literature," *Journal of Theological Studies,* n.s., vol. 16, pt. 1, April 1965) have uncovered the presence about this time of a powerful social critique of the disparity between the rich and the poor in the writings of a Briton living in Sicily. The so-called Caspari Corpus (*Migne, Patrologia Latina,* supplement 1)[47] of six documents centers thematically on the claim that Christianity and wealth are incompatible.[48] The unsubtle, radical nature of such charges was, according to Hilarius' letter to Augustine, disturbing the Christians of Roman Sicily.[49]

The obvious social disparity between the rich and poor in his society is contrary to the will of God, according to this relentless social critic. A further barb at the Roman rich was his view that such disparity is not the result of chance fortune but caused by the avarice of the rich whose greed grinds down the poor:[50]

> Would that they really cared for the poor, and not for wealth, which they try to defend on the pretext of being forced to have some means of showing pity to the poor, not realising that some are poor simply because others have too much. Remove the rich man and you will not discover the poor man. Let no one have more than he needs, and then all will have as much as they need. The few rich are the cause of the many poor.[51] (*De Divitiis*)

Such charges were bound to have been a prick to the consciences of aristocratic Christians. How widely read were the angry tracts of this anonymous critic of late Roman inequities? One could not say for sure that Pammachius or anyone of the senatorial families under study here had read them. However, Pelagius certainly provides a link between the aristocratic circles around Melania the Elder in Rome[52] and the social critic in Sicily whose tracts contain literary links to Pelagian literature.[53] We know that Pelagius endeared himself to Melania and her aristocratic, ascetic circles at Rome who kept the Augustinian wolves at bay for some time.[54] And we know that one called the "Sicilian Briton" by John Morris got the kernel of his ideas from Pelagius' writings. Whether "the patrons of Pelagius" (Brown's term) had read the unanticipated social consequences of Pelagian thought cannot be determined. However, it would not have been necessary to have read such tracts as the "De Divitiis" in order to have heard that the inherent contradiction in their lives as senatorial Christians was not going unnoticed. The "Sicilian Briton" articulated the clash of senatorial norms and Christian norms regarding wealth which the more religiously sensitive would already have felt. Pammachius' agony over the stumbling block to salvation posed by his wealth is symptomatic of the anxiety resulting from this clash of norms. Thus, the conflict illustrated by Pammachius' anxiety over his riches and the "Sicilian Briton's" anger at the wealthy becomes transposed in feminine terms to issues of silk dresses, precious jewels, and fawning servants.

In summary, reference to the interaction model brings to light the disharmonious relational context of the senatorial families of the early monastic renunciants whose lives encompassed the final, painful extrication of the aristocracy from its pagan roots which reached back centuries in the past. Paula, Melania the Elder, and Marcella must have found their familial existence characterized by clashes between pagan, worldly values and Christian, otherworldly ones. Socialization to a particular value orientation would have been disturbed by this disharmony of familial perspective. One aspect of this disharmony of value (with which we will deal later) would have been conflicting expectations about and for women, which posed serious problems of self-integration for the woman whose relational context was centered in the midst of this religious and social conflict.

Parsons' Interaction Model of Social Deviance and Its Implications for the Analysis of Asceticism

We have seen from further prosopographical analysis that the relational context of Roman aristocratic women, as the senatorial class shed its pagan roots, was the obverse of Parsons' description of a stable interaction system. The skewing of socialization by the presence of conflictual value standards within the same families would have created a situation ripe for the emergence of social deviance as described in interaction terms by Parsons. While "deviate" would not have been a self-designation by those engaging in the monastic quest for wholeness, the congruence between some monastic behavior patterns and the deviant behavior patterns which emerge from the interaction framework argue for the legitimacy of applying the interaction categorization for analytic purposes. This section will demonstrate the interpretive value of Parsons' categorization of deviant behavior patterns, on the basis of the interaction framework, for monastic analysis. Having established the similarity of certain monastic behavior patterns with social deviance, the next chapter will demonstrate the stress in norms which (as a by-product of the conflictual relational context of Christian women of the senatorial class of late antiquity) precipitated this deviance.

While Jerome and his protégées would have bristled at the designation "social deviates," evidence indicates that many non-ascetic Roman aristocrats would have found the epithet quite apt. Jerome's paraphrasing of Roman anomosities toward monastic behavior illustrates the point: "How long must we refrain from driving these detestable monks out of Rome? Why do we not stone them or hurl them into the Tiber?"[55] And we know that Jerome was virtually run out of Rome, the lure of desert monasticism providing the ostensible motive for his departure. Conceding that perspective is unquestionably a factor in the designation of asceticism rather than aristocratic values as deviance, I think the fact that Jerome rather than his detractors left Rome indicates which perspective had dominance in the city. In sociological terms deviance and conformity are not words which describe the essence of a social phenomenon but rather its relation to the norms of the larger order; thus, nothing perjorative is implied in the term, deviance. Furthermore, Parsons' definition of deviance in interaction terms (with respect to the actor) indicates the suitability of applying this designation for analytical purposes to asceticism: "deviance is a motivated tendency for an actor to behave in contravention of one or more institutionalized normative patterns."[56] Unquestionably, monastic mores contravened many norms of the social order of the Roman senatorial class. While the aristocracy valued the preservation of wealth, monastics had no qualms about depleting aristocratic wealth by aiding the poor and financing monasteries. While the Roman aristocracy valued the production of the right number of heirs, monastic valuation centered on virginity or at least newly found continence. While Roman aristocrats valued having precedence over their neighbors in rank and possessions, monastics valued precedence only in holiness and humility. Monastic contravention of senatorial norms could be further elaborated, but this explanation in broad strokes sufficiently notes the similarity of monasticism to Parsons' definition of social deviance insofar as it contravened institutionalized aristocratic values.

According to Parsons' interaction analysis, social deviance is a product of an ambivalent motivational structure which contains an element desiring conformity to the norms in question and an element desiring non-conformity. The internal conflict, resulting from these incompatible elements in the motivation of the individual, can result in deviant behavior if sanctions thwarting non-conformity are insufficient. The relational dynamics which create ambivalence of motivation coincide with the conflictual relational context of our monastic women in whose families senatorial, pagan values and Christian, spiritual values vied for ascendancy.

A brief description of the paradigm for the emergence of an ambivalent motivational structure should be sufficient to reveal its congruence with the unstable relational context of our subjects whose families' equilibrium was disturbed by the Christianization of a pagan aristocracy. According to Parsons, ego and alter, who are affectively attached, remain stably oriented to each other and the social order as long as they mutually conform to each other's expectations. One or the other can introduce a strain into this stable interactive system by refusing to conform with a norm the other values and, consequently, thwart the fulfillment of the other's expectations.[57] As long as ego cannot or will not break the relationship with alter, he/she will be motivated both to conform to alter's expectations so that the relationship remains stable and to defy alter's expectations in order to fulfill his/her own need. As long as ego and alter mutually fulfill each other's expectations with reference to a common value system, there is no reservation about their attachment to each other or the shared norms. A disharmony of value between an affectively attached ego and alter causes them to be divided against themselves, desiring to express both the need to conform to the other's expectations and the need to deviate from them in some way.

In the case of Melania the Elder and Paula, the disharmony of values, demonstrated by the prosopographical evidence, would have been sufficient to create an ambivalence of motivation toward affectively attached people. If

Melania's husband was (as Jones et al. speculate) Valerius Maximus 17, a serious conflict of perspective would have occurred in her marital relationship in view of Melania's Christianity and Maximus' paganism. While pagan roots are possible but certainly conjectural for Paula's husband, Toxotius, the certain paganism of his brother would have put Paula in a conflictual familial situation. Whatever ambivalence of motivation was prompted by this disharmony of value in their families, Melania and Paula, according to all available evidence, suppressed their alienative needs as long as their husbands lived; expression of their alienation from senatorial class values by means of ascetic renunciation occurred after the death of husbands who would have functioned as sanctions on this bold activity.

Further analytic aid is provided by Parsons' classification of the directions of deviant orientation on the basis of an interaction model. If, in fact, the disharmony of values in the senatorial families of late Rome created the kind of ambivalence of motivation Parsons views as a prerequisite for social deviance, one would expect that the behavior of Paula, Melania the Elder, and Marcella would have points of compatibility with Parsons' classification of deviant orientation. And, not surprisingly, Parsons' categorization of deviant behavior has considerable illuminative value when applied to the first generation of monastic women. Thus, the congruence of many monastic behavior patterns with patterns of social deviance and the congruence of the unstable relational context of late Roman aristocratic families with an unstable interaction system point toward the applicability of motivation to deviance in interaction terms to questions of monastic motivation. In order to make comparison of monastic behavior to Parsons' classification of deviant orientation more apparent to the reader, I have included a copy of his chart for reference (see fig. 1).

Some prefacing remarks by way of explanation are necessary before the applicability of the chart of directions of deviant orientation becomes apparent. According to Parsons, the ambivalence introduced into the motivational structure by the disharmony of ego with alter or alter's norm results in the co-existence of mutually exclusive elements in the personality, a conforming element and an alienative element.[58] Ego can maintain equilibrium by suppressing the alienative element, in which case the conformative element is dominant; Parsons calls this posture "compulsive conformity," presumably to indicate the compulsion necessary to repress the opposing element.[59] Conversely, ego can suppress the conformative element, allowing the alienative element of mixed motivation to gain the upper hand, which case Parsons calls "compulsive alienation."[60]

Distinctions in these two postures are made by Parsons first on the basis of whether the personality is basically actively oriented or passive. The source of this distinction according to Parsons may be external; however, it can be thought of as deriving from the interaction framework itself, being a

Figure 1.   Parsons' Classification of Deviant Orientation

	ACTIVITY		PASSIVITY	
	Compulsive Performance Orientation		Compulsive Acquiescence	
	Focus on Social Objects	Focus on Norms	Focus on Social Objects	Focus on Norms
Conformative Dominance	Dominance	Compulsive Enforce-ment	Submission	Perfectionistic Observance (Merton's Ritualism)
	Rebelliousness		Withdrawal	
Alienative Dominance	Aggressive-ness toward Social Ob-jects	Incorrigi-bility	Compulsive Independ-ence	Evasion

Reprinted with permission of The Free Press, a division of Macmillan, Inc. from *The Social System* by Talcott Parsons. Copyright 1951 by The Free Press, renewed 1978 by Talcott Parsons.

description of ego's attempt to control or consent to be controlled by the other.[61] Further distinctions in the two basic modes of handling an ambivalent motivational structure, i.e., conformative dominance and alienative dominance, are made by Parsons on the basis of whether the object of ego's orientation is a social object, i.e., a person, or a norm.

Paula's behavior as recorded by Jerome fits most clearly the directions predicted by Parsons' analysis of deviant orientation; it will, therefore, be the primary object of comparison between monastic renunciation and Parsonian social deviance. If, as the disharmony of value among the senatorial aristocracy of late antiquity would suggest, Paula's socialization was disturbed by conflicting values and an ambivalence of motivation was created, Paula would have had both a conformative and alienative dimension to her motivational structure. While her familial roots would have created a conformative element in terms of aristocratic pagan values, her Christian sentiments would have qualified her commitment in this direction and created an alienative element toward these same values. The co-existence of these opposing elements would have created the kind of internal conflict which according to Parsons results in an ambivalent motivation and consequent social deviance.

If, as my argument goes, Paula's socialization was skewed by the disharmony of familial perspective present among the Roman aristocracy as it became Christianized, one would expect (on the basis of interaction theory) an ambivalence of motivation both toward pagan, worldly values and toward Christian, spiritual ones. Unreserved commitment to either would be hindered by ambivalence of socialization. Therefore, the form of deviant behavior predicted by Parsons' categorization of deviant orientation would vary, depending upon which element of the internal ambivalence had ascendancy. Prior to ascetic conversion, when in interaction terms her alienation from aristocratic values was repressed and the conformative element had dominance, one would expect Paula's behavior to fit Parsons' category of "compulsive acquiescence." This presumes that Paula was basically more passive in orientation than active, a presumption that is consistent with the evidence. Unfortunately, however, Jerome's record of Paula's life contains insufficient reference to her life prior to ascetic conversion to engage in a comparison with Parsonian categories.

After ascetic conversion, when in interaction terms Paula's alienation from aristocratic values was dominant and the conformative element suppressed, one would expect Parsons' categories of deviant orientation to have some congruence with Paula's behavior as we know it from Jerome. While Paula's ascetic experience is not circumscribed by the Parsonian categories, there is sufficient contiguity between what we know about Paula's behavior and patterns of deviant orientation to provide a compelling argument for the applicability of interaction analysis of deviance to ascetic renunciation. The basic pattern of orientation in the case of a predominantly passive personality in which alienative needs are in the ascendancy is "withdrawal."[62] Avoidance of conflictual situations in which the conformative need toward the values in question will disturb internal equilibrium becomes the pattern. Certainly in the case of Paula "withdrawal" took on a dramatic form as she cut ties with aristocratic Rome and set up her own like-minded community in Bethlehem.

The basic behavior mode of "withdrawal" of the passively oriented whose alienative needs are dominant is further differentiated with respect to the object of orientation, whether social such as persons or norms. With respect to social objects who represent the opposing value pattern, an ambivalent ego in whom alienation is dominant will show signs of "compulsive independence."[63] In other words, ego will avoid intimacy with persons of a conflicting persuasion and repress any need to be dependent on them. Paula shows some signs of this deviant pattern. She abandoned four young children in Rome to follow her monastic dream in the Holy Land. Jerome reports the displeasure Paula found in the social obligations required of her in aristocratic circles.[64] Certainly "compulsive independence" (or in ascetic terms, monastic detachment) was part of Jerome's monastic ideology. In Letter XXII he repeatedly advises Eustochium to be reclusive and avoid contact with highborn ladies of a different persuasion.[65] In Letter CVIII our definer of monastic mores speaks hopefully of Paula's maternal disengagement as she leaves her children in Rome.[66] However, in contrast to his vision, Jerome's evidence indicates Paula's continued, if unmonastic attachment to her children, suggesting that with regard to social objects Paula retained more ambivalence than fully alienative expression. The following observation of Jerome suggests an internal conflict with regard to her feelings for her children rather than clearly alienative "compulsive independence."

> While thus unyielding in her contempt for food Paula was easily moved to sorrow and felt crushed by the deaths of her kinsfolk, especially those of her children. When one after another her husband and her daughters fell asleep, on each occasion the shock of their loss endangered her life.[67]

Continued ambivalence with respect to the expression of alienative needs with regard to social objects in Paula's case suggests that the strain in the interactive pattern was focused more on norms than social objects; fully alienative orientation toward her children who remained in Rome does not occur.

According to Parsonian analysis, the basically passive person, whose ambivalent motivation is controlled by the dominance of the alienative element, would be oriented toward "evasion" with regard to the norms from which he/she is alienated. In the case of Paula, withdrawal to the desert was a striking way to evade aristocratic expectations attendant upon her at Rome. Had she stayed in Rome she would have had to confront the offensive expectational pattern of kin and associates by refusing to comply; withdrawal to the desert was a convenient form of evasion of confrontation as well as sanctions. At Bethlehem her ascetic style was certainly in conflict with the prevailing expectational structure of the Roman aristocracy. Rather than hoarding and preserving wealth, Paula cast it to the wind so to speak. Rather than feasting in the grand style of aristocrats reported by Ammianus, Paula ate a meager diet, avoiding meat and wine altogether. Rather than affirming the Roman infatuation with public baths, Paula never bathed. Rather than concerning herself with the Roman obsession with precedence and protocol, Paula's humility was such that "when she was surrounded by companies of virgins she was always the least remarkable in dress, in speech, in gesture, and in gait."[68] Had Paula remained in Rome this contravention of the expectational structure of the aristocracy of which she was a part would have led to confrontation and sanctions. Monastic withdrawal provided for evasion of norms without confrontation which Parsonian analysis indicate is a predictable pattern of deviant behavior when alienation prevails over the conformative element in an ambivalently motivated (passive) person.

With respect to the alternative normative standard of Christian asceticism, Paula's behavior after ascetic conversion has some compelling points of congruence with Parsonian patterns of deviant orientation. In this case ambivalence of motivation toward certain norms and their social representatives is resolved by the dominance of the conformative element. In other words, with respect to ascetic norms, Paula, after monastic conversion, was predominantly conformatively oriented. Parsons' interaction schema suggests that in this case the ambivalently motivated (basically passive) person will demonstrate deviance characterized by "submission" with respect to social objects and "perfectionistic observance" with respect to norms.[69] While Jerome's evidence doesn't present a conclusive case for labeling Paula's behavior as "submissive," there are some indications of this. Jerome recounts Paula's handling of an anonymous foe who tried to undermine her at the monastery in Bethlehem. Citing the precedent of Jacob and David who fled before intimate enemies, Jerome advised her to leave Bethlehem.[70] Paula, however, chose to submit to persecution and wear down her opponent with patience:

> Why may I not by my patience conquer this ill will? Why may I not by my humility break down this pride, and when I am smitten on the one cheek offer to the smiter the other?[71]

Jerome's evidence about Paula contains striking indications of "perfectionistic observance" of monastic mores. No tenet of monastic spirituality received less than full compliance if Jerome's account of Paula is at all accurate. If monastic mores called for generous charity, Paula not only gave away all that she had, she "borrowed money at interest and often contracted new loans to pay off old ones."[72] If monastic norms called for fasting, Paula's "fasts and labours were so severe as almost to weaken her constitution."[73] No exception was made to this monastic rigor even when she was ill; in fact, she redoubled her ardor for self-denial when sick.[74] If monastic mores called for disdain of worldly comforts, Paula was most disdainful, resting only on a mat placed on the ground rather than a soft bed. Jerome summarizes the rigidity of her compliance with monastic norms. "No young girl of sound and vigorous constitution could have delivered herself up to a regimen so rigid as that imposed upon herself by Paula whose physical powers age had impaired and enfeebled."[75] "Compulsive observation" is an apt characterization of Paula's rigorous compliance with ascetic mores.

One other observation of Parsons furthers our insight into possible monastic motivation. Whereas, according to Parsons' interaction analysis, alienation from social objects tends to result from questions of security, alienation from norms tends to focus on questions of adequacy.[76] This observation is particularly applicable to Paula in view of the questions which have emerged in the prosopographical investigation about her status within the senatorial aristocracy. Her links with the bluest of the Roman bluebloods may have been tenuous, and her wealth may not have been vast compared to that of the richest senatorial families. A faded aristocrat might indeed be plagued with a sense of inadequacy in living up to aristocratic norms.

Conclusions: The Implications of the Interaction Model for the Analysis of Asceticism in Late Antiquity

The preceding application of the interaction framework to the context of the Roman senatorial aristocracy of late Rome, as Christianity displaced paganism among the elite, reveals a context ripe for social deviance, as defined by Talcott Parsons. Christian, otherworldly values vied with pagan, worldly values for the hearts of the Roman aristocracy and must have disturbed socialization to a particular value pattern as well as created a climate of conflict. The clash of values among the aristocracy, which Parsons considers a situation conducive to the genesis of ambivalent motivation and consequent social deviance, must have disturbed familial equilibrium in the families of Melania, Paula, and, perhaps, Marcella. The interaction model illuminates the instability of the relational context of the senatorial class protégées of Jerome and Rufinus whose families, according to further prosopographical investigation, were in the process of shedding ancient pagan roots. Furthermore, certain monastic behavior patterns as we know them from Jerome show striking similarity to the patterns of deviant orientation which are predicted in an unstable relational context. Thus, one can argue for the legitimacy of applying sources of motivation to deviance, defined by sociological theory, to the monastic choice.

The source of motivation to deviance discussed by Talcott Parsons in *The Social System* which has the most congruence with what we know about the senatorial aristocracy of late Rome is ambiguity or malintegration of expectations, in this instance in terms of the cultural norms for women. This malintegration, which shall be explained in the next chapter by means of a typology of images of women, is a dimension of the clash of aristocratic, quasi-pagan culture with Christian, otherworldly culture. Whereas in a general sense aristocratic valuation centered around compliant wife, prolific mother, and well-coiffured lady, Christian valuation in a general sense centered around virgin, martyr, and celibate widow. While the malintegration was more nuanced than that, this provides in broad strokes an idea of the ambiguity of the expectational structure for women of the senatorial class of Rome which was a by-product of the social and religious conflict of late antiquity.

6

Images of Women Current in Late Roman Antiquity

Introduction on Methodology

While the historical investigation of the Roman *matrona* (chapter 4) points toward the ambiguity of expectations for upper-class women of late antiquity, a clearer demonstration of this claim substantiates my thesis that the lack of integration in the normative structure for women may explain the ascetic choice of aristocratic Roman women of the early monastic movement. The conflictual Roman expectations for the matron can be more dramatically demonstrated by the construction of a typology of feminine images (which would have been current in the Late Empire) gleaned from classical and ecclesiastical literature.[1] It is my view that by the Late Empire the clash of cultures, pagan and Christian, created irresovably incompatible images of women, affecting particularly those women whose aristocratic families spanned both cultures. Whereas in a general sense the pagan aristocratic culture held up images of woman as compliant wife, devoted mother, and vehicle for preserving property, Christianity in a general sense clustered its praise around woman as martyr, ascetic, and benefactress. Of course, divisions were more nuanced than this characterization. Roman pagan culture was hardly of one mind, holding up for emulation the often mutually exclusive ideals of the prolific mother and the *univira* (one-man woman). Just as Jerome agonized over the contradictions posed by his intellectual delight in pagan literature, senatorial women of the Late Empire whose families were shedding their pagan roots must have agonized over the contradictions raised by the diversity and incompatibility of images of women which defined cultural expectations. To forge an authentic self-image would have invariably put them at odds with one aspect of the disharmonious culture. Balancing between aristocratic expectations which were in themselves unintegrated and Christian ideals would have posed a severe problem of self-integration. I believe the following typology will be a more dramatic presentation of the malintegration of Roman expectations for the matron than the historical account in chapter 4 and will further my thesis that conflicting expectations prompted the ascetic choice.[2]

The following typology of images of women has its source largely in the educational curriculum Jerome followed as a young man seeking the best education Rome could offer in late antiquity. While we do not know for sure that the women subjects of this study read the literature on which Jerome cut his intellectual teeth (see chapter 4), we do know that the curriculum followed by Jerome at Rome had formed the basis of Roman pedagogy among both pagans and Christians for centuries.[3] Thus, despite the fact that authors such as Terence, Juvenal, Ovid, Vergil, and Plautus had written in an earlier age, their enduring presence in the Roman educational curriculum made their writings part of the common cultural tradition for the educated class of the Late Empire.[4] Therefore, even if such figures as Paula, Marcella, Melania et al. had not read Vergil or Ovid, their husbands, who as senators were certainly educated, would have passed through the standard literary curriculum consisting of the Latin masters of the past.[5] Thus, the images of women in these sources would have informed the common cultural tradition of the day, of which our subjects as ladies of the noble, leisure class, among whom antiquarian interest was valued, would have been aware.

The use of Juvenal as a source of images of women in my typology requires some comment in view of the relative absence of references to Juvenal in Jerome. While Jerome quotes a phrase from Satire I three times, he does not mention Juvenal by name and the borrowed phrase was, apparently, common currency of the day.[6] However, other evidence suggests that Juvenal was read in our period and, therefore, can legitimately be used as a source for reconstructing the cultural ambience with regard to women in the Late Empire. I refer to the criticism of Ammianus Marcellinus of the intellectually lazy senators who read only Juvenal and Marius Maximus.[7] Further, Gilbert Highet in his study of Juvenal argues that Juvenal was rediscovered about this time after a long period of obscurity, when a pagan scholar (likely a student of Servius in Rome) edited an old text of Juvenal's satires.[8] While Juvenal wasn't a "school-author," and, thus, part of the Roman educational curriculum, Highet argues that he was read in the Late Empire, soon to become a "school-author," and that Jerome apparently knew the Sixth Satire (which contains the scathing commentary on women and marriage).[9] It may be that Jerome knew Juvenal's work but neglected to mention him by name because of his questionable status as author worthy of study at the academies. Certainly, Juvenal and Jerome were kindred spirits with regard to the intolerable foibles of the aristocratic Roman woman. And even if Jerome were only acquainted with Juvenal in a limited way, the evidence in Ammianus, coupled with the evidence of an ardent editor of Juvenalia at an academy in Rome, argues for including his portrayal of women in our reconstruction of the cultural milieu by means of a typology of feminine images.

A few words about including Ovid as a source for reconstructing the cultural milieu with regard to women in the Late Empire are in order. One stumbling block to using Ovid (born 43 B.C.) as a reflection of the cultural milieu of late Roman society is that the women subjects of his elegies probably were not upper-class matrons and, therefore, may not have been viewed as role models by the aristocratic women of Rome who are the focal point of this study. However, the social position of the women immortalized by the Roman elegists of the first century is a highly controverted issue. While the prevailing view has been that the elegiac women were freed women, usually of Greek origin, who assumed the position of high-class Roman courtesans, the unanimity of that view has been shattered. [10] Some scholars now think that the women of elegy were freeborn Roman women, with Saara Lilja in her detailed study of the elegiac women concluding that they may have been "freeborn Roman matrons who had conformed to freed women's manner of living." [11] The apparent license of the Roman matron in Ovid's day, which prompted Augustus' policy of social reform, functioned to obscure the social position of the women subjects of Ovid's as well as Propertius' and Tibullus' elegies. However, recent investigations reveal that the disparity between their social position and that of the aristocratic woman may not be as great as once thought, and "De Medicamine Faciei Femineae" was specifically directed to the respectable matron. [12]

While Ovid doesn't rank with Vergil as the quintessential Latin poet of the Roman schools, inclusion of his images of women in my reconstruction of the cultural milieu of the Late Roman Empire is justified by evidence that he was indeed read by the educated class. In Macrobius' *Saturnalia,* an account of the antiquarian discussion of the pagan intelligensia of late Rome, there are twelve allusions to Ovid, one of which is from the amatory poetry. [13] While scholarship has not conclusively established that Jerome had read Ovid's amatory poetry, [14] there is a reference to the *Amores* in Letter CXXIII which suggests that Ovidian images could function as interpretive models of female behavior. In his Letter CXXIII to Ageruchia, Jerome is explaining I Timothy 9 and 10 in order to mollify Paul's approval of remarriage for young widows. In explicating what Paul means by the phrase that remarriage will prevent any "occasion for the adversary to speak reproachfully," Jerome writes that the behavior of the professed widow must be such that: "she must give no ground for the application to herself of the *well known* (*uulgatus*) line 'She gave a meaning look and slyly smiled.'" [15] Jerome implies that this line from Ovid's

Amores was common currency and could function as an interpretive image applied to the silent behavior of the Roman widow.

The inclusion of Vergilian images as a source of the cultural milieu of the Late Empire hardly needs explanation in view of the place of Vergil not only in the educational curriculum of the academies but in the hearts of upper-class Romans who believed in Roman destiny. In the *Saturnalia,* which provides a paradigm of dialogue of late Roman literati, there are seven hundred and nine allusions to Vergil, five hundred and eighty of which come from the *Aeneid.* [16] Jerome, despite his Christian sentiments, was not immune to the Roman love affair with Vergil. Hagendahl, in his detailed identification of classical allusions in much of Jerome's writing from the commentaries to the letters, notes that "no poet, no classic author came nearer to Jerome's heart than Vergil." [17] Hagendahl cites an early study by Aemilius Luebeck in which one hundred and twenty-eight allusions to Vergil were found in Jerome's work and himself uncovers forty additional Vergilian allusions. [18] Thus without question Vergilian images pervaded the consciousness of the erudite of late Roman society, both pagan and Christian, and require inclusion in any reconstruction of the cultural milieu. The fate of Dido would not have been inconsequential for the self-consciousness of the Roman matron of late antiquity.

Inclusion of images from Terence, one of the leading poets of the Republic, bears some comment. Insofar as Terence was among what Jones calls "the standard four" authors (along with Vergil, Sallust, and Cicero) which comprised the basis of the Roman educational curriculum, his writing was definitely widely read in the Late Empire. [19] The richness of Terentian images of women along with the evidence that his comedies had a special place in Jerome's heart also argues for inclusion of Terence in reconstructing the cultural climate of late Roman society. Donatus, Jerome's professor at Rome in his schoolboy days, wrote commentaries on Terence and may have kindled Jerome's interest in this master of the past. [20] While Jerome only names two of Terence's comedies, *The Self-Tormentor* (*Heauton Timorumenos*) and *The Mother-in-law* (*Hecyra*), allusions to all the comedies appear in Jerome's writing, particularly in the prefaces. [21] Furthermore, in view of the close parallel between Jerome's allusions and their source, Hagendahl concludes that Jerome read Terence intermittently well into old age. [22] Rufinus' reference to Terence as part of Jerome's curriculum for his students at the Bethlehem school furthers the evidence for Jerome's continued familiarity with Terence beyond his days as a student in Rome. [23]

Ecclesiastical writers whose feminine images will form the basis for a reconstruction of the cultural milieu of late Roman society will be Jerome, of course, and Tertullian.

The Conflicting Images

The Ideal Matrona/Univira: *Consummate Womanhood, Tedious Virtue, or Spiritual Vacuity*

Images of the married woman current in late antiquity, which emerge from Latin literature, pose conflicting perceptions of the Roman *matrona* and, thus, would have presented a problem of integration for such figures as Paula, Marcella, and Melania. Describing a composite of the ideal *matrona* of Roman culture is relatively easy given a degree of unanimity about the ideal wife. However, the embodiment of such an ideal was at once valued and devalued in the literature which provides our basis for a cultural reconstruction of late antiquity. A brief description of a composite ideal *matrona* will provide a reference point for literary perceptions of her which must have posed conflicts for the subjects of this inquiry.

An essential element in the character of the ideal Roman *matrona* would have been to embody in some fashion the traditionally valued concept of the *univira*, i.e., the woman who remained loyal to one husband. Lightman and Zeisel have traced the persistent presence of this epithet as a term of praise from Republican times through its Christian reappropriation in the Late Empire, filtering down from the aristocratic classes to the lower ones.[24] Further, Gordon Williams points to the *univira* concept as one of three distinctively Roman ideals of marriage.[25] The ideal *matrona* would marry only once, retaining constancy to her first husband either through good fortune, steadfast character, or death. The most striking literary paradigm of the centrality of remaining faithful either to one's husband or at least his memory is Vergil's tragic Dido.[26] Dido's unexpected strength of character in forging a new state in Carthage despite memories of the murder of her husband, Sychaeus, by her brother is ultimately of no value to her when she strikes a blow at Roman esteem for the *univira*. Dido's initial resolve to remain faithful to the memory of Sychaeus (*The Aeneid* 4. 15–20)[27] gives way to the passion kindled by the aura of Aeneas. Under the veil of legitimacy provided by a mock wedding ceremony, Dido gave her heart and, presumably, her body to Aeneas.[28] However, Roman destiny as described by Vergil and socially embodied by Augustus shall not be subject to the erotic whims of a woman, particularly a Carthagian queen. Aeneas' role in establishing a Roman state shall not be thwarted, and he abandons Dido to set sail for Italy. The significant aspect of this tragically dramatic account of Aeneas' abandonment of frantic Dido is the Vergilian treatment of Dido's final fate. Having lost her right to be called *univira* as a result of her liaison with Aeneas without at least gaining the respectability of a *matrona* through an authentic marriage, Dido, according to Roman values, forfeits her right to live; events unfold in the only possible way consistent with Roman valuation—death to Dido.[29] Vergil disposed of Dido not only as one who tried to undermine Roman destiny but as one who played fast and loose with the time-honored tradition of loyalty to one husband.[30]

Another essential element in the character of the ideal Roman *matrona* would have been a properly subservient relationship to her husband. Gordon Williams describes this quality of the *matrona* by reference to the term *morigera* and traces this term's appearance in the comedies of Plautus and Terence. Speculating that the term implies roots in an earlier marriage ritual, Williams argues that the feminine subservience it expressed remains a constant element in Roman ideals of marriage even when the word itself falls into disuse.[31] The meaning of *morigera* can be seen in the self-application of the term in Plautus' *Amphitryo* by Alcumena, whom Williams regards as a portrayal of the ideal *matrona*. Defending herself against her husband's charges, Alcumena describes her unimpeachable behavior as a wife as *"morigera,"* "conforming in my likings to your own."[32] While Williams cites a list of epitaphal inscriptions which demonstrate the tenacious presence of high valuation of subservience and obedience in wives,[33] I would like to add a reference from our period among our Roman senatorial circles which furthers the claim that the ideal of *morigera* persisted into the fourth century. Praetextatus, eminent blue-blooded pagan of late fourth century Rome, dedicated a funeral monument to the memory of his wife with the following approbation which reveals the character of the ideal *matrona*:

> Vettius Agorius Praetextatus to his wife Paulina: Paulina, associate of truth and chastity, dedicated in temples and friend of the divine powers, *putting her husband before herself,* Rome before her man, modest, faithful, pure in mind and body, kind to all, a blessing to her household.[34]

The persistent worth of wifely subordination can be seen in the congruence of praiseworthy behavior in Paulina of the fourth century with the wifely virtue of Terence's Philumena, whose selflessness had the power to lure her husband away from a mistress. Philumena's subordination of self is described as follows: "She [Philumena] as became her breeding, was modest and retiring, endured all the wrongs and slights which she received from her husband, and tried to conceal his affronts to her."[35]

Another element in the character of the ideal *matrona* would be devotion to family, preferably demonstrated by lovingly spinning wool to make cloth for the family garments. The Roman *matrona* was not expected to fulfill the role of the modern American housewife, described so painfully in *The Feminine Mystique*; slaves and servants performed the maintenance chores which consume the modern bourgeois mother. Yet, a sentimental attachment to the wifely devotion implied in the act of spinning preserved this as an element in the character of the ideal *matrona* beyond the days when it was actually integral to her role.[36] Pomeroy refers to a public relations stunt by Augustus, in his attempt to restore traditional Roman virtues, whereby he paraded the homespun cloth made by his wife.[37] Further demonstration of wifely devotion would occur by bearing many children, preferably sons.

While the ideal *matrona* as described by the preceding composite remained the sentimental favorite, literary treatments of her indicate that she was at once valued sentimentally but devalued as well.[38] Juvenal's famous Sixth Satire seems to have the composite ideal *matrona* as the reference point for his scathing criticism of his women contemporaries of late first century Rome, suggesting his esteem for the former. What of wifely fidelity? "If you marry a wife, it will be that the lyrist Echion or Glaphyrus, or the flute player Ambrosius, may become a father," writes Juvenal.[39] What of motherly devotion to family? Our satirist answers by asking "how often does a gilded bed contain a woman that is lying in? So great is the skill, so powerful the drugs, of the abortionist, paid to murder mankind within the womb."[40] With these bitter comments about departures from traditional matronly honor, one would expect Juvenal to praise the virtuous woman. However, even if one ideal wife could be found in all of Rome, Juvenal would find her virtues tedious:

> I would rather have a Venusian wench for my wife than you, O Cornelia, mother of the Gracchi, if, with all your virtues, you bring me a haughty brow, and reckon up triumphs as part of your marriage portion.[41]

The wifely virtues of the *matrona* find little favor in Ovid's controversial *Ars Amatoriae* in which the sophisticated woman of culture is extolled. Without addressing the controverted issue of the social status of the woman subjects of elegiac poetry,[42] one can note the contrast between Ovid's sophisticated lady and the traditionally subservient *matrona*. The uncultivated matron is identified with "the Sabine dames of old ... who have wished to cultivate their paternal acres rather than themselves"[43] and holds no appeal for this most famous elegiac poet. Contrary to Augustan aims to restore the dignity of marriage,[44] Ovid devalues marriage as an impediment to sensual love. Marriage is a breeding ground only of quarrels and erotic boredom: "With quarrels let wives pursue husbands and husbands wives, and deem that they are ever at issue with each other; this befits wives; the dowry of a wife is quarreling."[45] And further "'tis this which prevents wives from being loved: to them their husbands come whenever they will."[46]

The woman of *Ars Amatoriae* 3 does not (like Terence's Philumena) win her husband's love by the subordination of self; rather she wins masculine approval by enhancing her erotic appeal. She knows the hairstyle most becoming to her face: "An oval face prefers a parting upon the head left unadorned.... Round faces would fain have a small knot left on top of the head."[47] She is well-versed in the exotic ancient art of makeup: "You know, too, how to gain a bright hue by applying powder."[48] And she knows how to obscure her physical deficiencies: "Let her that is too slender choose garments of full texture.... Let a pale woman adorn her person with purple stripes."[49] Yet, the new woman of Ovid's ideology, like the virtuous *matrona,* is conceptualized by men as oriented toward being pleasing.

Despite the disdain for the traditional wifely virtues implied in Ovid's adulation of the *matrona*'s rival, the sophisticated woman of culture, Saara Lilja points out a strange paradox of elegiac poetry—the casting of erotic love in metaphors congruent with the traditional marital relationship.[50] Lilja argues that, despite Ovid's occasional indiscretion, the ideal of monogamous love is transferred from the marriage relationship to the free love relationship.[51] Lightman and Zeisel, as well as Williams, refer to Propertius' description of Cornelia as *uni nupta,* which is a derivative of *univira.*[52] Further, Lilja points out that Tibullus even fantasizes Delia in the traditional matronly posture of spinning wool.[53] In another inversion Ovid seems to put the hopeful paramour in the position of being *morigera* to the woman:

> Only play the part she bids you play. Blame if she blames, approve whatever she approves. Affirm what she affirms and deny what she denies.... let her impose her laws upon your countenance.[54]

Thus, while the ideal *matrona* as described in the previous composite is devalued as provincial by Ovid, some of the deep-rooted ideals of marriage inform the elegiac conception of sensual love, according to Lilja's study. The reappropriation of Roman marital ideals in terms of extramarital relationships does not, however, diminish the devaluation of the traditional *matrona* and her motherly devotion.

The ideal *matrona* of our composite is devalued not only by Juvenal and Ovid but is often denied deserving accolades by persistent Roman misogyny. In Terence's *The Mother-in-law,* feminine virtue is received not with husbandly gratitude but with misogynist disdain. We have seen in Plautus' Alcemena of *The Amphitryon* and in Terence's Philumena of *The Mother-in-law* that the ideal *matrona* image often informs the portrayal of the respectable Roman matron in New Comedy. In *The Mother-in-law* we see, further, that exemplary behavior doesn't always prompt masculine approval. When Laches returns home to find the marriage he had arranged for his son in a state of estrangement, he immediately blames his wife Sostrata for alienating the daughter-in-law. Feminine virtue does not preclude male stereotyping of woman's behavior. Laches' speech is instructive in this regard:

> Gods and men! What a set women are! How they conspire together! How exactly the same all their likes and dislikes are, and you never find one of them differing the least in character from the rest. [55]

Highly interesting is Terence's portrayal of the women characters as more noble than the men in the drama think them to be. However, husbandly misogyny appears to be blind to feminine virtue. Bacchis, former courtesan of the young husband, agrees to the highly degrading act of appearing before Philumena and Myrinna, the young bride and her mother, to swear she has had no dealing with the young man since his marriage. [56] Sostrata, mother of the groom, agrees to leave Athens in order not to come between the estranged young couple. [57] Myrinna, the bride's mother, allows her husband to blame her for the estrangement rather than compromise her daughter by revealing the truth. [58] However, feminine virtue does not insure approval from husbands whose misogyny colors their interpretation of events.

The ideal *matrona/univira* of our composite is also devalued by Jerome who disdains marriage as an impediment to spiritual wholeness. He portrays the devoted mother as sacrificing her spiritual commitment for attention to the comfort and well-being of her family:

> Then come the prattling of infants, the noisy household, children, watching for her word and waiting for her kiss, the reckoning up of expenses, the preparation to meet the outlay.... can any fear of God be found? [59]

Jerome's disparagement of marriage figures so prominently in all his writing that further citations would be redundant. However, Jerome does pluck out one aspect of the traditional *matrona* for affirmation—the *univira* concept, but as a way of devaluing marriage rather than honoring it. [60] While Jerome's ascetic ideology would prefer that Christians avoid marriage altogether, his Roman pragmatism allows the argument against marriage to be directed toward those freed from the wedded state by the death of a spouse. While Jerome uses the term *univira* (Letter LXXVII,3: *PL* vol. 22, p. 692) and a variation of it, *unius viri uxor* (Letter LXXIX,7; *PL* vol. 22, p. 727 and Letter CXXIII,6; *PL* vol. 22, p. 1050), he more often casts the argument against remarriage in terms of *monogamia,* monogamy. [61] Jerome's preference for the term *monogamia* suggests that ascetic scorn for remarriage applies equally to men and women, whereas the traditional Roman idea of the exclusivity of marriage applied the *univira* concept only to women. Not only must a widow refrain from remarriage in order to be worthy of ecclesiastical charity, a

Christian priest should likewise remain a "monogamist," according to Jerome's Christian reappropriation of single marriage.[62]

While Jerome's defense of the *univira* departs dramatically from the original intention of the ideal, insofar as he uses it as a vehicle for devaluing marriage rather than exalting it, this propagandist for Christian chastity argues that celibate widowhood is congruent with ancient Roman traditions. Lightman and Zeisel, alluding to Jerome's use of a dialogue in Seneca's *De Matrimonia* in making his case against remarriage, conclude that he unwittingly projected Christian motives into the past.[63] However, I wonder if Jerome's reappropriation of pagan traditions deserves such a benign assessment. Jerome obviously knows of the heathen tradition of the *univira,* referring to it repeatedly, perhaps most clearly in Letter LIV,1, and in "Against Jovinianus," Book 1,43. Yet, his treatment of Dido in "Against Jovinianus" is decidedly curious for such a devotee of Vergil. Here Jerome claims that Dido exemplifies the heathen rejection of remarriage, for she chose to die on a funeral pyre rather than face remarriage, to "burn rather than to marry," so to speak.[64] Jerome radically distorts the sense of the *Aeneid,* in which Dido throws herself on the funeral pyre because her remarriage to Aeneas fell through, not because she wished to avoid a second marriage.[65] This distortion probably reflects Jerome's preference for the chaste Dido of the classical example literature tradition (a part of the rhetorical tradition) over against the Dido of the Aeneid who betrayed chastity.[66] A further distortion of his inherited legacy is that he only values the *univira* whose husband is dead rather than the one whose good fortune has continued her in the married state.

In addition to claiming the pagan ideal of *univira,* severing it from its connections with marriage, Jerome reappropriates another aspect of the ideal *matrona* of our composite—the ideal of *pudicitia* as an aspect of feminine virtue. Jerome's argument for chastity cast in the language of *"pudicitia"* would have had connotations far beyond our narrow idea of sexual continence.

Pudicitia and *castitas* were terms long-associated with the ideal, virtuous Roman woman of old, the former appearing more often in the literature I examined. Alcumena, singled out by Williams as a model of the ideal wife, in addition to being *morigera* defines the dowry of a virtuous wife not as money but as *"pudicitiam et pudorem et sedatum cupidinem"* ("purity and honor and self-control").[67] This ideal may have had ancient Roman roots. According to Livy, whose connection with Augustus may have colored his recounting of the ancient honor for *pudicitia,* there was in the 3rd century B.C. a pagan cult of *Pudicitia Patricia,* comprised of aristocratic matrons, and a cult of *Pudicitia Plebeia,* comprised of plebian matrons.[68] Livy's account of the foundation of the *Pudicitia Plebeia* is notable on two accounts. First, *pudicitia* in women is paralleled to valor in Roman men, indicating its importance.[69] Further, only matrons of proven *pudicitia,* evidenced by having been married to only one man, could offer sacrifices at the temple of this Goddess.[70] In these passages, in which *pudicitia* is linked with the virtuous married woman, its meaning implies virtue in a much broader sense than Jerome's use of it to argue for sexual continence.

Further, Juvenal, in satirizing the allegedly decadent ways of Roman women in the early second century, invoked the Goddess *Pudicitia* who guarded over women of old but had fled from wives such as Cynthia and Lesbia, immortalized in elegiac poetry.[71] Juvenal invoked the Goddess *Pudicitia* three times in Satire Six (lines 1, 14, and 308), preferring other words such as *castas, pudicam* and *pudorem* when referring to the qualities desired in virtuous human women. All of these terms are used to contrast the allegedly decadent, lusty women of his day with the women of old who worshipped *Pudicitia* and conformed to her likeness. Many additional references could be cited which reveal the pagan usage of *pudicitia* and its derivatives to refer to the virtuous married woman. However, I will mention only two more in order to establish this point without belaboring it. Ovid in *Fasti* 2. 794 referred to Lucretia, that ancient virtuous woman whose rape prompted willing suicide, as *"nupta pudica."* Pliny in Book 7. 25 referred to a woman chosen by other matrons to dedicate a statue of Venus as *pudicissima femina.*

In addition to giving new meaning to the *univira* concept, Jerome claimed for monastic purposes the ideal of *pudicitia,* likewise severing it from its connections with marriage. While it is not within the scope of this study to examine every reference Jerome makes to chastity in order to see whether he uses *pudicitia* or *castitas,* a closer look at Letter CXXX, which is addressed to Demetrias whose impeccable aristocratic roots insure awareness of the pagan traditions, might reveal something about Jerome's concept of chastity in women. In this letter Jerome uses the word chastity seventeen times, employing *castitas* six times and *pudicitia* eleven times. While Jerome most often uses the words to mean sexual continence, some references imply the broader, ancient meaning of *pudicitia.* In Section 12 Jerome advises Demetrias to obey her grandmother and mother in a suitably obsequious gesture to those scions of aristocratic position. They by their honorable marriages have "communicated their chastity (*pudicitiam*)" to their descendant, Demetrias.[72] Further, Jerome notes the cultic power attributed to Demetrias' *pudicitia* by her mother and grandmother whose attitude is reminiscent of pagan beliefs in the political importance of virtue: "She [Demetrias] had found, they said, a way to benefit her family and to lessen the calamity of the ruin of Rome."[73] One can imagine the connotations of those of the senatorial class, schooled intellectually and emotionally in paganism, of Jerome's image of consecration of Demetrias to eternal *pudicitia* alongside the image of the pontifex's dedication of a "virginem castam."[74]

Despite Jerome's devaluing of the maternal aspect of our composite of the ideal *matrona/univira,* he retains attachment to the image of the woman spinning wool. While the spinning of cloth for garments was certainly a practical necessity in the monastic economy, Jerome alludes to it as a symbol of contrast with indulgent, worldly standards. In Letter CVII, Jerome advises Paula the Younger to shun silk and elegant fabrics and instead "learn too how to spin wool, to hold the distaff,"[75] suggesting an association of the task of wool spinning with the old virtues.

In summary, the images of women which informed the cultural milieu of late antiquity would have at once valued and devalued the ideal *matrona* of our composite. Aristocratic notions of the respectable woman would have been rooted in the concept of the *univira,* who was devoted to husband and children and *pudica* in marriage, but would have been challenged on the pagan side by sophisticated notions of womanhood portrayed by Ovid and on the Christian side by ascetic disdain for marriage and maternity. Thus, the devaluation of the traditional *matrona* would have occurred in pagan as well as Christian literature.

The Educated Woman: The Accomplished Seductress, the Erudite Shrew, or the Spiritual Pilgrim

Positive images of the educated woman occur in both the pagan and Christian sources which form the basis of our cultural reconstruction; however, the object of feminine education differs dramatically in sources such as Ovid and Jerome. In Ovid education is one more alluring accoutrement, whereas in Jerome education is a necessary skill for a serious spiritual pilgrim.

Though Ovid complains of the rarity of accomplished women,[76] he advises the woman who seeks to enhance her sensual appeal to be able to read and write. He alludes to the spoiling effect of ill-written letters on a blossoming relationship which even beauty cannot overcome:

> Dainty, O women, be the words you write, but customary and in common use: ordinary speech gives pleasure; ah, how often has a message inflamed a doubting lover, or some barbaric phrase done harm to beauteous shape.[77]

In addition to singing and dancing, the accomplished woman who holds appeal to Ovid and his kind should be able to read enough poetry at least to flatter the poet:

> And you should be able to read a poem of tender Propertius or something of Gallus or of you, Tibullus,... and Aeneas, the wanderer, origin of lofty Rome.[78]

If she can read Ovid's poetry, her status would be even higher:

> [Perhaps] someone will say, "Read the elegant poems of our master [Ovid], wherein he instructs the rival parties... or let some Letter be read by you with practiced utterance.[79]

Despite these reference to the importance of a cultivated mind as well as a cultivated appearance, Ovid's reference to the flirtatious custom of feigning a lisp provides a clue to the object of education in the poet's eyes. In *Ars Amatoriae* 3, Ovid speaks of the charm of misspoken speech:

> What, when they defraud others of their rightful utterance, and the tongue is compelled to lisp at their command? The defect has charm—this uttering some words amiss; they learn the power to mar their power of speech.[80]

In Ovid's ideology of the new woman, education enhances erotic appeal but has no higher aim. This disparity between the male and female social contexts may account for the stronger emphasis on mental qualities in the first two books of the *Ars Amatoriae,* which are addressed to men. Lilja alludes to the difference in emphasis in Ovid's directives to men who seek to enhance their appeal and those to women, the former containing many more references to mental accomplishments. Some commentators explain this difference by arguing that Ovid grew tired of the theme of mental accomplishment when he reached Book III, which coincidentally was written for women; others think that the lower social class of the women prompted a different emphasis on the value of their mental accomplishments.[81] Lilja on the other hand argues that Ovid did indeed emphasize intellectual abilities in women.[82] However, I think that the stronger emphasis on mental ability in Ovid's advice to men may be accounted for by the difference in the social utility of education for men and women in antiquity.[83] In the case of men, Ovid is advising them of the erotic appeal of a skill they already have or would acquire for pragmatic reasons. The following quotation in Ovid points to the double purpose of eloquence in men:

> Learn noble arts, I counsel you, young men of Rome, not only that you may defend trembling clients: a woman, no less than populace, grave judge or chosen senate, will surrender, defeated, to eloquence.[84]

On the other hand, in Book 3 of *Ars Amatoriae,* in which women are advised to cultivate their minds in order to be more charming, the social utility drops out. Further, despite Ovid's advice to girls that mental qualities are important in love, Lilja notes that the accomplishments of the poet's inspiration, Corinna, receive scant mention in comparison to references to her physical beauty.[85]

It may be the absence of any social utility of education in women as well as the Greek character of a Roman education in Juvenal's day that accounts for his disdain for the erudite woman. Juvenal finds the woman well-versed in the grammatical arts insufferable and not a little threatening:

> She lays down definitions, and discourses on morals, like a philosopher; thirsting to be deemed both wise and eloquent.... Let her not know all history; let there be something in her reading which she does not understand.[86]

Further, female adherence to the fashion favoring the Greek influence on educational standards particularly rankles Juvenal's Roman sensibilities: "They [the women] talk nothing but Greek, though it is a greater shame for our people to be ignorant of Latin."[87]

Jerome alludes to the only purpose of education for the worldly Roman matron who is unconcerned with acquiring erudition in order to be charming—the fostering of mental accomplishment in one's children. In Letter CVII, in which he outlines the proper educational program for an aspiring holy virgin, Paula the Younger, Jerome notes the importance of picking a tutor with care so that deficiences aren't transferred from teacher to pupil. He refers to the conventional wisdom that the "eloquence of the Gracchi is said to have been largely due to the way in which from their earliest years their mother spoke to them."[88] Quintilian in his comprehensive account of a Roman rhetorical education also alludes to this purpose of a feminine education in one of his few references to women:

> In parents I would wish that there should be as much learning as possible. Nor do I speak, indeed, merely of fathers; for we have heard that Cornelia, the mother of the Gracchi...contributed greatly to their eloquence.[89]

E. E. Best in "Cicero, Livy and Educated Roman Women" points to this function of education in women by reference not only to Cornelia but to Aurelia (mother of Julius Caesar), Rhea (mother of Sertorius), and Atia (mother of Augustus).[90] Yet, even this respectable purpose for mental accomplishment offers only vicarious value to the mother.

In Jerome the educated ascetic woman is depicted very positively, for education becomes a prerequisite for spiritual striving. Within the monastic milieu mental accomplishment takes on a purpose for the woman as spiritual pilgrim. The following in Letter CVII seems to summarize the basis for Jerome's positive view of the educated woman: "Thus must a soul be educated which is to be a temple of God."[91] Jerome retains continuity in his belief in the value of education for the spiritual pilgrim from his early Letter XXII to Eustochium to his outline of the ascetic program for Demetrias in Letter CXXX. He refers to the value of education in Letter CVII (written to Laeta on the ascetic upbringing of Paula the Younger) and in Letter CXXVIII (written to Gaudentius on the proper monastic tutelage of Pacatula).

In Letter XXII Jerome advises Eustochium to "Read often, learn all that you can. Let sleep overcome you, the roll still in your hands. When your head falls, let it be on the sacred page."[92] This positive attitude toward the value of education in fashioning an ideal monastic continues to inform the images of women in Jerome's letters throughout his years of seeking ascetic converts.

Two negative images of the educated women in Jerome's letters disturb his otherwise positive portrayal of education for women. Clark deals with the pretentious women who seem to fit Ovid's pattern of displaying eloquence in order to enhance their charm.[93] Another negative image occurs in Letter CVII in which Jerome disparages the deficiences of speech displayed by some women whom he feels would be unsuitable tutors for Paula the Younger: "You must see that the child is not led away by the silly coaxing of women to form a habit of shortening long words."[94] However, this negative image occurs in the context of Jerome's attempt to secure the best possible education for little Paula. Thus, in the monastic world of disdain for concerns of the world, such as romantic liaisons and senatorial precedence, education at last takes on a pragmatic end for women—the nurturing of the spiritual pilgrim on the manna of biblical literature.

The Woman of Beauty: The Simple Woman of Charm, the Cultivated Seductress and the Self-Indulgent Narcissist

Beauty in women as beauty in all things natural or humanly created has been valued from time immemorial. Since Plato associated beauty with the divine forms and viewed it as a manifestation of the divine, Western culture has placed value on that which is beautiful. However, the radical dualism, which pervaded the consciousness of late antiquity not only in marginally Christian groups such as the gnostics but in groups with roots in paganism such as the Neo-Platonists and Neo-pythagoreans, disparaged the body and by inference beauty of form. Likewise, monastic spirituality was informed by the body-soul dualism of its philosophical predecessor, Neo-platonism. That monastic disdain for sexuality and its consequent childbearing pervaded the religious consciousness of late antiquity can be seen in the extent to which it influenced Augustinian notions of sin as concupiscence. A radical reconsideration of the value of beauty in women was an obvious consequence of notions of the body as impediment to spiritual wholeness.

While paganism had its anti-body sources such as Plotinus who simply tolerates the body as the home of the soul, most of the pagan sources under consideration here depict the woman of beauty positively. However, there is a disparity in views of the priority of virtue over beauty, particularly in the dutiful wife. Christian ascetic sources find little spiritual value in beauty—no spiritual noblesse oblige for the beautiful as for the wealthy.

To what extent beauty was valued in the respectable woman of the Republic or Early Empire is not apparent from our sources. While Ovid criticizes the inattention to self of "the Sabine dames of old," the attitude to beauty in the *Octavia* attributed (but with dispute) to Seneca probably captures more closely the traditional view.[95] Based on historical events of the imperial rule of Nero, the play treats the controversial divorce of Octavia and Nero, when the latter put away his wife for the more appealing Poppaea. In the drama Seneca tries to persuade Nero not to abandon Octavia, with the following attitude to the comparative value of matronly virtue and beauty:

> But honour, wifely faith, and modesty—These should the husband seek, for these alone, the priceless treasures of the heart and soul, remain perpetual; but beauty's flower Doth fade and languish with each passing day.[96]

Surprisingly, a very similar attitude is found in Ovid's "De Medicamine Faciei Liber" despite the theme of the essay—exotic makeup techniques for the enhancement of sensual appeal. The endurance of character and the impermancence of beauty is an unexpected sentiment in one whose ideology of love in the *Ars Amatoriae* focuses on the essential nature of beauty in women. Perhaps because the intended reader of this essay is the respectable matron,[97] Ovid pays homage to this traditional sentiment which has little place in his *Ars Amatoriae* 3: "Think first, ye women, to look to your behavior.... Love of character is lasting: beauty will be ravaged by age."[98]

Beauty is valued in the woman of Ovid's *Ars Amatoriae* 3 but not as some reflection of divine perfection. Rather, beauty is the basis for attracting illicit loves. That Ovid's program for enhancing feminine appeal is not designed to foster marital love is clear.[99] Yet, the image of the woman of beauty bears comment not only because of the positive valuation of feminine charms but because of the congruence of Ovid's sophisticated lady with the presumably respectable matrons of late Rome disparaged by Jerome.

As Lilja points out, the beautiful woman for Ovid had not a natural beauty of simple charm but a cultivated beauty, what we might call manufactured or made-up.[100] Ovid notes that "beauty is heaven's gift: how few can boast of beauty!" and proceeds to advise the imperfect how to make the most of what endowments they have. Borrowed tresses are a possibility for those with deficient hair.[101] Or a tint to color the gray or brighten the sheen was as much the order of the day in first century Rome as it is now.[102] Dental hygiene was advised: "I enjoin that no laziness leave the teeth to darken"; attention to the enhancements of cosmetics is also recommended. Cosmetics include some type of powder, rouge, "powdery ash" and "saffron" for eyeshadow, [103] as well as an exotic facial composed of such bizarre ingredients as "the first horns that fall from a nimble stag," ground to a pulp. [104] Yet, the cultivation of one's beauty should take place behind closed doors so that only the finished product is apparent, lest preparations spoil the mystery. [105]

The extent to which a woman schooled in Ovid's ideology of beauty would go is revealed by the poet in an anecdote in the *Amores* about his love's scorched hair, which fell out after abuse with some sort of curling iron. Despite Ovid's protests his mistress continued to subject her finely textured hair "to iron and fire to form the close-curling ringlet with its winding orb." [106] Over-cultivation of beauty resulted in baldness, and wigs were the woman's only recourse. [107] Yet, the emphasis on cultivated beauty is not a uniform characteristic of the elegiac poets. Lilja points out that, in contrast to Ovid, Propertius and Tibullus prefer a more natural fairness. [108]

While Ovid depicts the woman of beauty positively as a mark of Roman sophistication, Juvenal finds feminine attention to appearance a mark of Roman decadence. Foreshadowing Christian attitudes Juvenal satirizes ancient facials designed to improve complexion: "Meanwhile she ridiculously puffs out and disfigures her face with lumps of dough; she reeks of rich Poppaean unguents which stick to the lips of her unfortunate husband." [109] While Ovid recommends borrowed tresses, Juvenal finds them ridiculous and an occasion for satirizing the woman whose wigs or curls make her appear tall from the front but short from behind. [110]

By Jerome's day the respectable Roman matron as portrayed in Jerome's letters appears to have conformed to the standards of beauty of the cultivated woman of Ovid's poetry. Not only pagan Praetextata, who attempted to style Eustochium's unkempt, ascetic hairdo, but our Christian monastics, before conversion to the ascetic spiritual mode, bear striking similarity to Ovid's sophisticated ladies in terms of attention to feminine adornment. Jerome's portrait of Blaesilla before the mirror in Letter XXXVIII, as "maids arranged her hair, and her head, which had done no harm, was forced into a waving head-dress," [111] reveals the customary conformity to Ovid's cultivated standards of beauty. Likewise in Letter CVIII Jerome recounts that Paula prior to ascetic conversion had used the cosmetic arts to enhance her appearance. [112] Jerome, of course, finds feminine efforts at beautification scandalous. In the context of a veiled reference to criticism of Blaesilla's newfound monastic ardor, Jerome claims that not ascetic renunciation but worldly attention to self ought to be cause for criticism:

> The women who ought to scandalize Christians are those who paint their eyes and lips with rouge and cosmetics; whose chalked faces, unnaturally white, are like those of idols. [113]

Grounded in ascetic disdain for the body as impediment to spiritual wholeness, Jerome characterizes beauty in women as narcissistic indulgence and inappropriate for the Christian spiritual pilgrim. Jerome's image of the proper posture with respect to feminine appearance might be characterized as disinterested inattention. The monastic objective is not to provoke attention by one's shabbiness. A contrived, unkempt look suggests unnecessary attention to self as much as cultivated beauty: "Neither an affected shabbiness nor a stylish smartness becomes a Christian."[114] And further, "Let your dress be neither too neat nor too slovenly; neither let it be so remarkable as to draw attention of passersby."[115] Thus, Jerome's monastic attitude requires renunciants to focus their attention on God and their spiritual pilgrimage, not on their appearance, whether by design slovenly or stylish.

A very similar attitude toward beauty in women is found in Tertullian's "On the Apparel of Women," written about 202 A.D. in the rigorous Christian milieu of North Africa. Tertullian was as scandalized by the standards of cultivated beauty (Ovid's legacy to Roman women) as Jerome would be in the late fourth century. Tertullian characterizes the customary cosmetic arts as having their source in the devil insofar as they alter what God has created: "Whatever is *born* is the work of God. Whatever, then, is *plastered on* (*infingitur*) is the devil's work."[116] Tertullian recounts the same overattention to hair which resulted in baldness for Ovid's mistress and prompted Jerome's criticism of pagan and Christian women alike.[117] Tertullian criticizes the bleaching of hair with saffron to make it light: "I see some (women) turn (the color of) their hair with saffron. They are ashamed even of their own nation, (ashamed) that their procreation did not assign them to Germany and to Gaul."[118] This practice isn't surprising given the recurrent attention to blonde beauty in our literature. Lilja notes that Tibullus and Propertius prefer blonde hair and remarks on the curiosity of this preference given the rarity of fair-headedness in Southern Europe.[119]

While arguing that his position is not a plea for slovenliness, Tertullian claims that grooming is acceptable but within limits which his readers were apparently surpassing.[120] Despite this concession to conservative grooming, Tertullian advises the Christian woman of beauty to "obscure" her charms rather than enhance them, for the only object of beauty is "voluptuousness."[121] Tertullian finds no positive value for feminine loveliness, criticizing the cultivated kind and repressing the natural kind. In any event, Christian responsibility is such that women of faith have no occasion for flaunting their endowments in public; a Christian woman visits the sick, not the theatre.[122]

The preceding typology reveals that the legacy of pagan culture to the woman of late antiquity was considerable ambiguity about marriage, education, and the value of beauty in women. Our monastic women, insofar as their elite families retained a nearness to paganism with its tenacious hold on the senatorial class, would have been affected by these ambiguities. While many women of the senatorial class in late Rome largely conformed to Ovidian images of the value of cultivated femininity, the image of the self-sacrificing *matrona* lay somewhere in the background for those who had cut their literary teeth on Plautus and Terence. Praetextatus's funeral epitaph for his wife and Claudian's praise of *prisca pudicitiae* ("old-fashioned virtue") point to the survival of esteem for the virtuous woman dedicated to hearth and home. While education was valued in the upper-class woman as a vehicle for producing erudite sons, the legacy of pagan culture included negative images of the educated woman as the tedious authority figure and as the seductive woman devoted to her own accomplishments rather than to a husband. The legacy of pagan culture with regard to marriage was equally ambiguous, maintaining the normalcy of marriage for women and the image of Dido whose remarriage was ill-fated by its challenge of Roman destiny.

The influx of Christian, otherworldly values into the senatorial aristocracy of Rome, where Christians often remained close to their pagan roots by virtue of the religious syncretism in their families, would have further compounded the already present ambiguity of the expectational structure for the women monastics. Christian images of women, surprisingly, seem to raise some of the old questions such as the priority of virtue over self-interest and the value of beauty in women. The conflict was already there in the Roman traditions in the opposition of Ovid's new woman with the ideal *matrona* dedicated to her husband, her children and Rome. In Jerome, the argument for the priority of virtue takes on a spiritual, God-directed slant rather than a nationalistic, family-directed slant.

In the same vein the typology of images reveals that Jerome's monastic ideology of womanhood can be read as a critique of the image of woman in Ovid's *Ars Amatoriae,* to which many senatorial women of late antiquity appear largely to have conformed, according to Jerome's portrait of late Rome. Whereas Ovid recommends makeup to enhance natural endowments and even provides exotic recipes, cosmetics are the bane of Jerome's existence. Whereas Ovid advises the woman to display her beauty in public ("Let the beautiful woman also offer herself to the people to be seen."),[123] Jerome repeatedly entreats the monastic woman to remain secluded: "Do not seek the Bridegroom in the streets; do not go round the corners of the city."[124] Ovid's sophisticated woman knows how to sing and dance; Jerome advises against this aspect of feminine accomplishment: "Do not...trifle with verse, nor make yourself gay with lyric songs."[125] Ovid recommends hygiene, Jerome's protégée, Paula, refused to bathe. This parallel between Ovid's image of womanhood and the woman of Jerome's satire has, however, some limits. The sexual license of the woman of elegiac poetry would have been dangerous for even the most sophisticated given the stiff penalties for adultery and frivolous divorce in the late fourth century. Nonetheless, the similarity of Ovid's new woman to the portrait painted by Jerome of aristocratic women of late Rome is striking.

Thus, the otherworldly, spiritual values of Christianity which questioned marriage, the value of beauty in women, and the value of motherhood and put the priority on virtue rather than self-interest, raised some of the old questions which informed the ambiguous pagan tradition with respect to feminine norms. The woman of monastic ideology is, in a sense, a reconstruction of the ideal *matrona* of our composite but on a spiritual rather than nationalistic basis. Granted, the maternal role had no place in the eschatological community, where Christian destiny replaced Roman destiny. Yet, if one considers that in monastic ideology as well as in old-world nationalism, maternity served higher aims than personal ones, the woman of Jerome's monastic ideology has many points of congruence with the virtuous woman of old. We find her at the distaff, spinning and weaving, but not for her family, rather for compatriots in monastic pilgrimage. We find her shunning the garrish crowds, humbly going about her duty. She recognizes the superiority of virtue over beauty, disdaining the indulgence of cosmetic arts. She is *univira* as widow, *morigera* to God, and above all, *pudica*.

7

Conclusions

Fresh Historical Insights

While the primary intention of this study has been to press further interpretive insights rather than historical ones, some fresh points of historical interest have emerged which bear comment. Further prosopographical investigation has raised questions about the elite status of Jerome's favored protégée, Paula, within the senatorial aristocracy. Despite missing evidence about Melania the Elder which would further our understanding of her (such as precisely who her husband was), evidence is sufficient to firmly establish her place among the so-called "inner aristocracy." Paula, by contrast, seems to be on the periphery of the elite of the senatorial class of late Rome. She has no consul or PVR in her immediate background, although Jerome claims she is a descendent of ancient Republican notables. While her husband's pagan brother attained senatorial distinction, Toxotius himself has left no record of eminence based on prestigious office. Just how well-placed within the aristocracy the marriage partners of Paula's children were is also questionable. The evidence establishing the status of Blaesilla's husband within the senatorial aristocracy rests entirely on a few tenuous references in the letters of Jerome. The identification of Blaesilla's father-in-law with Laetus 2, PVR in A.D. 398/99, hinges on a play on words in Jerome's Letter LIV. The identification of Blaesilla's brother-in-law as an anonymous fourth son of eminent Sex. Claudius Petronius Probus relies entirely on one reference in a letter written by Jerome to Ageruchia in Gaul. Paulina's Pammachius attained mid-grade senatorial distinction and apparently had some deficiencies which Jerome unwittingly exposed. While Jerome would have us believe that Paula's monastic commitment was made in the context of a social existence among the most elite of Rome, this attempt to throw ascetic renunciation into sharp relief must be tempered with a bit of realism about the actual status of the Paula *gens* of female monasticism within the Roman senatorial aristocracy. While Arnheim must receive credit for questioning Jerome's linking of his protégées with families of the Republic, I wonder if the contemporary acceptance of such exalted status for which Arnheim argues would have been the case for Paula whose immediate background had some deficiencies.

Interpretive Insights

The thesis of this study is that the ascetic choice of women of the senatorial class of late Rome was in part prompted by the ambiguous cultural norms for the Roman matron, which was exacerbated by the collision of pagan and Christian in the same aristocratic families. I have arrived at this thesis by applying the insights of Talcott Parsons' interaction model of social dynamics to the social context of aristocratic women of late Rome. While the close mingling of pagan and Christian among the inbred aristocracy, as it finally shed its pagan roots, is well known by historians,[1] scholars have not applied a social science model to this context of social and religious conflict which might uncover its effect on the individual's relationship to the wider social order.

Action theory provides a model of social dynamics which highlights the effect of such conflicts in value with significant others on the individual. According to Talcott Parsons' discussion of social deviance in interaction terms, the stress introduced into an interaction unit by a serious conflict of value or norms can precipitate social deviance. Prosopographical investigation reveals that the first generation of Roman monastic women lived in a relational context which in interaction terms would be ripe for social deviance. It may be that Melania the Elder and Paula were married to pagans, although missing evidence prevents the conclusive establishment of this claim.[2] Whatever the religious preferences of their husbands, Melania and Paula lived on the borderline between Christianity and paganism in senatorial families in which certain pagan roots lay behind the Christianization taking place in their lifetimes.

If the social context of Roman senatorial families of the Late Empire can, on the basis of interaction analysis, be characterized as ripe for social deviance, one might go a step further and compare patterns of deviant orientation with what we know of monastic behavior patterns in order to discern points of congruence. While monastic behavior patterns were quite diverse, ranging from the rigorism at Scete and Nitria to modified desert monasticism in the Holy Land to intellectual retreats à la Seneca at Rome,[3] I think certain patterns of Paula's have enough congruence with Parsonian patterns of deviance to argue for the applicability of the interaction model of deviance without appearing facile. In view of the congruence of certain monastic behavior patterns and patterns of social deviance as described by Parsons, I think one can argue that sources of motivation to deviance might then be reasonably applied to the question of monastic motivation. This does not necessarily imply that I am characterizing monasticism as social deviance, although it may be that. My purpose is to apply the interaction framework to the monastic framework in order to uncover sources of motivation, not to argue for a particular characterization of monasticism.

The motivation to social deviance discussed by Parsons in *The Social System* which most clearly fits the historical situation of the Roman *matrona* as uncovered in chapter 4 and further refined in chapter 6 of this study is an ambiguous, malintegrated expectational structure. As Parsons points out, malintegration of an expectational system is an extension of the malintegration of the interaction system which gives rise to ambivalent motivation and its consequent social deviance.[4] In the case of Roman women the malintegration of expectations for the Roman matron was an aspect of the unstable interaction framework created by the collision of paganism and Christianity among the inbred aristocracy of late Rome. However, the typology of images gleaned from the literary curriculum of the educated class (which functions as a reconstruction of the cultural norms) reveals that Christianity didn't create this ambiguity about the Roman matron; it merely raised many of the old questions about feminine norms—the value of remarriage and maternity and the relative worth of beauty and virtue. Christianity exacerbated the malintegrated expectations for the Roman matron, adding spiritual, Christian dimensions to those already existing.

The congruence of Jerome's ideology of womanhood and ancient ideals of the self-sacrificing, virtuous Roman woman is quite surprising, particularly in view of current theorists who characterize monasticism as social advancement for women (Clark) or an exception to the pagan/Christian synthesis of late antiquity (Yarbrough). As stated in chapter 4, Jerome's monastic woman as *univira,* living a simple life characterized by spinning wool, and committed to virtue defined as *pudicitia* rather than her own accomplishments and elegance is highly congruent with ancient images of the self-sacrificing women who made Rome great. Instead of being an exception to the pagan/Christian synthesis, which was taking place in the senatorial aristocracy, Jerome's monastic ideology of womanhood may be another dimension of this synthesis. Of course, the severing of these images from their connection with marriage and family was a radical departure from Roman traditions, conceived by Jerome's monastic genius.

Interaction theory provides a theoretical explanation for these surprising elements of congruence between monastic feminine images and ancient, pagan ones. According to Parsons, in situations where alienative patterns seek legitimation by the larger social order rather than only confrontation, rhetoric about these patterns will seek "'bridge' elements," between the competing value systems.[5] Thus, it may be that Jerome's claiming of the *univira* concept and the broad meaning of *pudicitia* for monastic purposes is simply monastic rhetoric designed to make monastic renunciation more palatable to his aristocratic converts schooled in these traditions. If the linking of monastic ideals of womanhood with ancient traditions was conscious on Jerome's part, it may have been a brilliant propaganda stroke. If it was not by design, it reveals an unexpected conservative element in monasticism. While monastic ideology contravened most norms of the Roman aristocracy, such as those concerning preservation of wealth and worldly eminence, in the case of norms for women it was social deviance with a conservative slant. The interpretation of these so-called bridge elements would be very important for a characterization of monasticism as social advancement for women (Clark) or liberation (Ruether). It may be that the bridge elements are superficial, outward characterizations pasted on to a radically changed concept of womanhood to make it palatable to a tradition-conscious aristocracy. Or the bridge elements may require that we qualify our hopeful characterization of monasticism as a step toward feminine progress, viewing it rather as a Christian extension of Roman efforts to circumscribe female experience.

The reconstruction of the social context and cultural milieu of the Roman matron of late antiquity provides some clues for their choice of monasticism despite its misogynist, anti-maternal *Weltanschauung.* For someone such as Paula or Melania the Elder the so-called bridge elements between monasticism and traditional feminine norms would have blurred the anti-maternal dimension of monastic values. Further, anti-maternal sentiment had a long and eminent place in Roman history, confounding worried emperors at least since Augustus. Misogyny was not a monastic novelty either. Certainly, Augustus' embrace of the Roman family and motherhood was not an effort to promote in woman an authentic experience of maternity. Further, anyone whose education contained a bit of Terence or Plautus knew that misogyny lay just below the surface of most any Roman man, schooled as he was in hierarchical notions of authority and Roman nationalism. Thus, for breaking out of misogynist value patterns the choices for the woman of late Rome weren't much better than Dido's. One could choose monasticism which devalued the maternal aspect of one's person but which offered compensatory social benefits, or one could choose conventional, aristocratic values which were ambiguous toward the mother and no less misogynist.

Without regard to the question of whether monasticism was social progress (Clark) or a Christian extension of Roman repression, reference to our basic precept of interaction analysis, i.e., that ambiguity of normative expectations can prompt social deviance, suggests a benefit in terms of social dynamics. At least within the monastic context, the expectational structure for the woman was clearly defined with respect to the foci of our analysis of cultural expectations. Jerome raised many of the old questions regarding feminine norms; however, he clearly answered most of them for the monastic. Jerome's monastic attitude toward maternity may have been negative, but it was not ambiguous. Maternity was to be avoided for those schooled in monastic precedence in which virginity was the pinnacle. Maternity may be useful insofar as it produces virgins; however, the newly continent widow might be comparable in monastic precedence to the level of Pammachius in senatorial precedence—"While he took precedence of some, others took precedence of him" (Letter LXVI,7). Yet, at least the monastic attitude toward maternity was clear, providing the matron with the opportunity to be valued for conformity by significant monastic associates.

Likewise the monastic attitude toward beauty in women was well-defined. Feminine attention to self, exemplified by concern with makeup, wigs, and luxurious finery, was unnecessary for the spiritual pilgrim and a sinful impediment to the spiritual progress of men. The worldly counterpart of our monastic pilgrim might be encouraged to enhance her beauty in order to climb the senatorial ladder of success but at the same time satirized her vanity. Feminine conformity to monastic disregard for beauty enhancing aids at least met with ascetic approval. An example of this esteem is that within monastic lore ascetic denial of the body is met not only with human approval but puts one in right relationship with the animal kingdom, according to monastic rhetoric. Palladius' anecdote about noted anchorite, Macarius, and his healing of a blind hyena pup may not be historical, but it expresses the common monastic theme of reconciliation with nature and all of God's creation, resulting, at least in part, from the taming of one's body. Thus, according to monastic ideology, conformity to the ascetic disregard for feminine beauty and the body met with approval of the whole creation, so to speak (with the exception of a few disgruntled aristocrats in Rome).

Likewise Jerome's attitude toward education in women becomes a clearly articulated norm. While in general the monastic attitude toward education varies from the anti-intellectual milieu in Nitria and Scete to the intellectually lively milieu at Jerome's monastery, the expectational structure for our women subjects, who were linked to leading monastic intellectuals, was clear. Education had value for the spiritual pilgrim, whether male or female. As such, feminine conformity to this norm would have met with monastic approval. While Jerome may have satirized the aristocratic matron, absorbed in herself, he never satirized the serious spiritual pilgrim for her intellectual efforts, remaining, in contrast to Juvenal, unthreatened by feminine intellect.

In summary, the interaction framework of social dynamics has proven to be a highly suggestive basis for analyzing the monastic choice, pointing toward fresh aspects of the question. First of all, Parsons' action frame of reference has highlighted the unnoticed significance of the closeness to paganism of such figures as Melania the Elder and Paula for their motivation to monasticism. The unstable relational context of senatorial families of late antiquity as the aristocracy was finally Christianized may hold a key to monastic motivation. Further, the interaction model has pointed toward the importance of examining the cultural expectations or norms, in this instance of the feminine ideal, in order to complete our picture of the interaction system. The cultural reconstruction, grounded in the typology of images in chapter 6, has revealed a highly ambiguous expectational structure for the Roman matron which Christianity exacerbated by raising anew many of the old questions about feminine norms, such as the priority of virtue over beauty and the value of maternity. On the basis of the action frame of reference, I have argued that this malintegration in the expectational structure insofar as it can be a cause for social deviance might reasonably be considered a sociological cause for the monastic choice.

In addressing the original problematic which provided the inspiration for this study, the interaction analysis suggests a compensatory benefit in terms of social dynamics which augments the social benefits of monasticism highlighted by Clark and Yarbrough. In terms of social dynamics, the monastic definition of feminine norms provided a clear expectational structure (although at times subject to a characterization as misogynist), conformity to which would have been assured of monastic approval.

This study began with a suspension of the theological and spiritual motivations to monasticism in order to focus on the sociological dimensions of motivation. It might, therefore, rightly conclude by returning to theological reflection on the sociological discoveries. One must not lose sight of the fact that the sociological and cultural dimensions of motivation explained in this study are but one aspect of very rich and complex motivational possibilities. Thus, in a Weberian mode, this study has abstracted one aspect of the motivational dynamics in order to fully explore it. However, in so doing one should not overlook the spiritual power of the monastic embodiment of liminal-like inferiority. The, perhaps, transformative spiritual power of the ascetic counterpoint to aristocratic values may have provided a chilling critique on social disparities in a society under seige. The sociological and cultural perspective of this study on the ascetic choice of aristocratic women of late Rome in no way denies the significance of a powerful spirituality embodied by the monastic.

Abbreviations

ACW	*Ancient Christian Writers*
ANF	*The Ante-Nicene Fathers*
CSEL	*Corpus Scriptorum Ecclesiasticorum Latinorum*
LCL	*The Loeb Classical Library*
NPNF	*A Select Library of Nicene and Post-Nicene Fathers*
PL	Migne's *Patrologia Latina*

Jerome's letters, which are a major source for this study, can be found in Migne's *Patrologia Latina* vol. 22 or the more recently published *Corpus Scriptorum Ecclesiasticorum Latinorum* (CSEL), volumes 54–56. An English translation by Freemantle appears in *A Select Library of Nicene and Post-Nicene Fathers,* second series, vol. 6 (New York: The Christian Literature Co., 1893) with a reprint in the Eerdmans 1979 edition. Citations of Jerome's letters contain volume and page number of the CSEL edition as well as page number of the NPNF (1893) edition. English translations are those of the NPNF edition.

Notes

Chapter 1

1. F. Van Der Meer, *Augustine the Bishop,* trans. Brian Battershaw and G. R. Lamb (New York: Sheed and Ward), p. 217.

2. Anne Yarbrough, "Christianization in the Fourth Century: The Example of Roman Women," *Church History* 45 (1976):149.

3. Ibid., p. 149.

4. Ibid., p. 162.

5. Elizabeth Clark, "Ascetic Renunciation and Feminine Advancement: a Paradox of Late Ancient Christianity," *Anglican Theological Review* 63 (July 1981):243.

6. Cf. Jonathan Z. Smith, "The Social Description of Early Christianity," *Religious Studies Review,* vol. 1, no. 1, September 1975.

7. Harnack agrees that the prevalence of women in the Apocryphal Acts has significance despite the challenges to the historicity of the stories. "[A]lthough the details of these stories [The Apocryphal Acts of the Apostles] are untrustworthy, they express correctly enough in general the truth that Christianity was laid hold of by women in particular, and also that the percentage of Christian women, especially among the upper classes, was larger than that of Christian men" (Harnack, *The Mission and Expansion of Christianity in the First Three Centuries,* 2 vols., trans. and ed. James Moffatt, 2d ed. [London: Williams and Norgate; New York: G. P. Putnam's Sons, 1908], 2:73).

8. Kraemer's dissertation entitled "Ecstatics and Ascetics: Studies in the Functions of Religious Activities for Women in the Greco-Roman World" was completed in January 1976. It uses theoretical models from the social sciences to evaluate the function of religious activities for women.

9. Cf. Elisabeth Fiorenza, "Word, Spirit and Power," *Women of Spirit,* ed. Rosemary Ruether and Eleanor McLaughlin (New York: Simon and Schuster, 1979).

10. Cf. Carol Christ, "Heretics and Outsiders: The Struggle Over Female Power in Western Religion," *Soundings,* vol. 61, fall (1978) and Elaine Pagels, "What Became of God the Mother? Conflicting Images of God in Early Christianity," *Signs: Journal of Women in Culture and Society,* vol. 2, no. 21 (1976) and the reworking of this essay in Pagels' *The Gnostic Gospels* (New York: Random House, 1979).

11. Adolph Harnack, *The Mission and Expansion of Christianity in the First Three Centuries,* 2:75. "Among the gnostics especially women played a great role, for the gnostics looked not to sex but to the Spirit."

12. Cf. Elisabeth Fiorenza, "Word, Spirit, and Power," *Women of Spirit* for further comments on the role of women in gnostic circles.

13. Tertullian, *De Praescriptione Haereticorum,* 41, trans. The Rev. Peter Holmes, *The Ante-Nicene Fathers* vol. 3, eds. The Rev. Alexander Roberts and James Donaldson (New York: Charles Scribner's Sons, 1908), American reprint of the Edinburgh edition, p. 263. James Donaldson in *Woman: Her Position and Influence in Ancient Greece and Rome, and Among the Early Christians* (New York: Longmans, Green, and Co., 1907), p. 165, thinks this statement refers to a Montanist sect.

14. Tertullian, 6:6, 30 (ANF 3).

15. Irenaeus *Adversus Haereses* 1. 25. 6, *The Ante-Nicene Fathers* vol. 1, The Rev. Alexander Roberts and James Donaldson, eds. (New York: Charles Scribner's Sons, 1908), American reprint of Edinburgh edition (1885), p. 351.

16. Ibid., 1. 13. 3 (ANF 1:334–36).

17. *The Gospel of Mary, The Nag Hammadi Library in English,* trans. by members of the Coptic Gnostic Library Project (San Francisco: Harper & Row Publishers, 1977), p. 473.

18. Fiorenza, "Word, Spirit, and Power," p. 51f, esp. p. 54.

19. Ibid., p. 51f.

20. Harnack, *The Mission and Expansion of Christianity in the First Three Centuries,* 2:76.

21. Pagels, "What Became of God the Mother? Conflicting Images of God in Early Christianity," *Signs,* p. 301.

22. Pagels, *The Gnostic Gospels,* p. 60.

23. Refer to the chapter on "virgins" in the western monastic movement at the time of Augustine by Van Der Meer in *Augustine the Bishop,* p. 217f., and to an assessment of the dates of the earliest communities of women in Rome, Milan, Vercelli, and Aquileia by John Kevin Coyle in "Augustine's 'De Moribus Ecclesiae Catholicae'," *Paradosis* 25 (Fribourg, Switzerland: The University Press, 1978).

24. Ambrose, "Concerning Virgins," trans. The Rev. H. DeRomestin, *The Nicene and Post-Nicene Fathers,* 2d ser., vol. 10 (New York: The Christian Literature Company; Oxford: Parker and Company, 1896).

25. Joseph T. Lienhard, *Paulinus of Nola and Early Western Monasticism* (Koln-Bonn, 1977), p. 72.

26. Refer to the following essay for a summary of the activity of women in the early monastic movement: "Asceticism and the Monastic Life among Women," chap. 2 of *The Way of the Mystics* (New York: Oxford University Press, 1978) by Margaret Smith.

27. Palladius, *The Lausiac History,* 33, Ancient Christian Writers Series, no. 34, trans. Robert T. Meyer and ed. Quasten, Burghardt, and Lawler (Westminster, Md.: The Newman Press; London: Longmans, Green and Co., 1965), p. 95.

28. Ibid., 59 (ACW 34:140).

29. John Chrysostom, "Homilies on the Gospel of Saint Matthew," Homily viii (NPNF) 1st ser., vol. 10, *Saint Chrysostom* (1969), p. 54. "For the war against the devil and his powers is common to them [the women] and to the men, and in no respect doth the delicacy of their nature become an impediment in such conflicts."

30. *The Lausiac History*, 5 (ACW 34:36).

31. Refer to C. Butler's discussion in *Texts and Studies*, vol. 6, *The Lausiac History of Palladius*, section 15, ed. J. A. Robinson (Cambridge, England: The University Press, 1898–1904), p. 178f.

32. *The Gospel of Thomas* (II,2), *The Nag Hammadi Library in English* (1977), p. 130.

33. The Greek *Gospel of the Egyptians* is not to be confused with the *Gospel of the Egyptians* found at Nag Hammadi. Evidence suggests that the former was used by a gnostic group known as the Naassenes (*The New Testament Apocrypha*, ed. Wilhelm Schneemelcher and Edgar Hennecke and trans. A. J. B. Higgins et al. [Philadelphia: Westminster Press, 1963–64], 1:166 and 167). Thanks to Fiorenza for pointing me toward this quotation.

34. *The Dialogue of the Savior* (III,5), *The Nag Hammadi Library in English* (1977), p. 237. Brackets are present in the reconstructed text.

35. Pagels, *The Gnostic Gospels*, p. 66, and "What Became of God the Mother?," *Signs*, vol. 2, no. 21, p. 293f.

36. Fiorenza, "Word, Spirit, and Power," p. 50.

37. *The Lausiac History*, 71 (ACE 34:153).

38. Palladius mentions in *The Lausiac History*, 46 that Melania "served them [Pisimus, Pambo, and others] from her own private treasury" (ACW 34:124).

39. Jerome, Letter CVIII,14 (CSEL 55:325; NPNF 6:202).

40. Jerome, "Against Jovinianus," NPNF, 2d ser., 6 (1979): 385.

41. Jerome, Letter LIV,4 (CSEL 54:469; NPNF 6:103).

42. Jerome, Letter XLV,2 (CSEL 54:324; NPNF 6:59). The ambiguity of Jerome's attitude toward women has been an object of attention in an essay by J. K. Campbell entitled "St. Jerome's Attitude Toward Marriage and Women," *The American Ecclesiastical Review* 143 (July-December 1960): 384f.

43. Cf. Clark, "Ascetic Renunciation and Feminine Advancement: a Paradox of Late Ancient Christianity," for the thesis that asceticism constituted social improvement for the Roman matron.

Chapter 2

1. While the monasteries of Rufinus and Melania in Jerusalem may have been modeled on the Rule of Basil (Ruether, "Mothers of the Church: Ascetic Women in the Late Patristic Age," *Women of Spirit*, p. 84), it is fair to characterize them as "Egyptian" given the degree of separation from community required of converts and their similarity to the Pachomian style.

2. Anne Yarbrough in "Christianization in the Fourth Century: The Example of Roman Women," p. 157, aptly compares the monastic style of the study groups in Rome like that of Marcella's to the philosophical *otium* at that time popular among pagan dilettantes such as

Symmachus. Clark in "Ascetic Renunciation and Feminine Advancement: A Paradox of Late Ancient Christianity," (p. 246) terms Latin monasticism a "genteel form of asceticism."

3. See *St. Gregory of Nyssa: The Life of St. Macrina,* trans. W. K. Lowther Clarke (London: Society for Promoting Christian Knowledge, 1916).

4. For comments on the other women's monastic communities in Italy, cf. John Kevin Coyle's "Augustine's 'De Moribus Ecclesiae Catholicae'," *Paradosis* 25 (Fribourg, Switzerland: The University Press, 1978).

5. For familial stemmae cf. Yarbrough, "Christianization in the Fourth Century," p. 150, A. H. M. Jones, J. R. Martindale, and J. Morris, *The Prosopography of the Later Roman Empire,* vol. 1 (Cambridge: Cambridge University Press, (1971): Stemma 13, p. 1138, and M. T. W. Arnheim, *The Senatorial Aristocracy in the Later Roman Empire* (Oxford: Clarendon Press), appendix a–e.

6. Jones, Martindale, and Morris, *The Prosopography of the Later Roman Empire* 1: Stemma 13 and 20, pp. 1138 and 1143.

7. Ibid., 1: Stemma 13 and 20, pp. 1138 and 1143.

8. Francis X. Murphy, "Melania the Elder: A Biographical Note," *Traditio* 5 (1947): 59.

9. Murphy, "Melania the Elder," p. 59. Cf. Cardinal Rampolla del Tindaro, *Santa Melania giuniore, senatrice Romana: documenti contemporanei e note* (Rome, 1905).

10. Murphy cites the following studies: G. Goyau, *Melanie la jeune* (Paris, 1908); E. Da Persico, *Die hl. Melania die Jungere* (Berlin, 1912); and an English translation of Rampolla's own version of the *Vita,* the *Life of St. Melania,* edited by H. Thurston (London, 1908).

11. Yarbrough, "Christianization in the Fourth Century," p. 153.

12. Ibid., p. 161.

13. Refer to Jonathan Turner's discussion of the history of functionalist theory beginning with Durkheim in *The Structure of Sociological Theory* (Homewood, Ill.: The Dorsey Press, 1974).

14. Yarbrough, "Christianization in the Fourth Century," p. 162.

15. Rosemary Ruether, "Misogynism and Virginal Feminism in the Fathers of the Church," *Religion and Sexism: Images of Woman in the Jewish and Christian traditions,* ed. Rosemary Radford Ruether (New York: Simon and Schuster, 1974).

16. Ruether, "Mother of the Church: Ascetic Women of the Late Patristic Age," *Women of Spirit,* Rosemary Ruether and Eleanor McLaughlin, eds. (New York: Simon and Schuster, 1979), p. 73.

17. Jerome's strictures regarding the proper life of a maiden written in the famous Letter XXII, as well as the repressive ascetic upbringing outlined for Paula the Younger in Letter CVII, call into question the universal legitimacy of interpreting the ascetic choice as self-definition.

18. Cf. Jerome's Letter XXXIX for an account of the scandal caused by the premature death of Blaesilla.

19. Clark, *Jerome, Chrysostom, and Friends,* essays and translations (New York: The Edwin Mellen Press, 1979), chapter 2, "Friendship between the Sexes: Classical Theory and Christian Practice," pp. 48–59.

20. Ibid., p. 49.

21. Refer to Phillip Rousseau's "Blood-Relationship among Early Eastern Ascetics," *Journal of Theological Studies,* vol. 23, n.s. (1972), p. 235f. for another account of abrogation of kinship ties in monasticism.

22. Clark, *Jerome, Chrysostom, and Friends,* p. 51.

23. Ibid., pp. 48–59.

24. Elizabeth Clark, "Ascetic Renunciation and Feminine Advancement: a Paradox of Late Ancient Christianity," *Anglican Theological Review* 63 (July 1981): 243.

25. Ibid., pp. 245, 246, and 247.

26. Ibid., p. 251.

27. Ibid., p. 251.

28. For further comments on the intellectual attainments of Jerome's ascetic followers, cf. *Jerome, Chrysostom, and Friends,* pt. II, section V.

29. Cf. "Misogynism and Virginal Feminism in the Fathers of the Church."

Chapter 3

1. Cf. Jones, *The Later Roman Empire* vol. I (pp. 523 and 524) for a similar pattern in Symmachus' speeches, introducing aspirants to the Senate of Rome, in which the ancestry of the applicant was praised where possible. Also, cf. Jerome, Letter CXXX,3: "It is the practice of the rhetoricians to exalt him who is the subject of their praises by referring to his forefathers and the past nobility of his race, so that a fertile root may make up for barren branches" (CSEL 56:177; NPNF 6:261). Cf. Quintilian, *Institutes of Oratory,* 3. 7. 10.

2. Jerome, Letter CVIII,1 (CSEL 55:306; NPNF 6:195).

3. Ibid., 3 (CSEL 55:308; NPNF 6:196).

4. A. H. M. Jones, J. R. Martindale and J. Morris, *The Prosopography of the Later Roman Empire,* 1:767.

5. Cf. "Fasti" at the conclusion of *The Prosopography of the Later Roman Empire,* vol. 1.

6. Jones, *The Later Roman Empire,* 1:528.

7. Ibid.

8. Cf. Jones' stemma, *The Prosopography of the Later Roman Empire,* 1:1143.

9. M. T. W. Arnheim, *The Senatorial Aristocracy in the Later Roman Empire* (Oxford: Clarendon Press, 1972), p. 107.

10. Ibid.

11. Jerome, Letter CXXX,13 (CSEL 56:177; NPNF 6:261).

12. Cf. the *Fasti Consulares, The Prosopography of the Later Roman Empire,* 1:1045.

13. Jones, Martindale and Morris, *The Prosopography of the Later Roman Empire,* 1:447.

14. Ibid., pp. 721 and 722. Where confusion may arise over multiple persons bearing the same name, names will be cited with numerals as they appear in *The Prosopography of the Later Roman Empire.*

15. Jerome, Letter XXII,16 (CSEL 54:163; NPNF 6:28). Yarbrough, using a phrase of M. K. Hopkins, calls this the "competitive salon culture" ("Christianization in the Fourth Century: The Example of Roman Women," p. 153).

16. Jones, Martindale and Morris, *The Prosopography of the Later Roman Empire,* 1:663.

17. Jerome, Letter CVIII,5 (CSEL 55:310; NPNF 6:197).

18. Jones, *The Later Roman Empire,* 1:554. For Olympiodorus' comments, cf. Olympiodorus, frag. 44 as found in Photius, Migne PG 103:279 and 280.

19. Jerome, Letter CVIII,16 (CSEL 55:327; NPNF 6:203).

20. Ibid., 6 (CSEL 55:312; NPNF 6:197).

21. Ibid., 15 (CSEL 55:326; NPNF 6:203).

22. Ibid., 7 (CSEL 55:312; NPNF 6:198).

23. Ibid., 10 (CSEL 55:316; NPNF 6:199).

24. Ibid., 14 (CSEL 55:324; NPNF 6:202).

25. Ibid., 15 (CSEL 55:327; NPNF 6:203).

26. Ibid., 15 (CSEL 55:327; NPNF 6:203).

27. Ibid., 27 (CSEL 55:346; NPNF 6:210).

28. Cf. Keith Hopkins, "Contraception in the Roman Empire," *Comparative Studies in Society and History* 8 (1965): 126 and 127.

29. Jerome notes that Paula had four daughters before she had a son, presuming that she would have put a check on her fertility if a son had been born sooner (Jerome, Letter CVIII,4 (CSEL 55:310; NPNF 6:197).

30. Jerome, Letter CVIII,6 (CSEL 55:311; NPNF 6:197).

31. J. N. D. Kelly, *Jerome: His Life, Writings, and Controversies* (New York: Harper & Row Publishers, 1975), p. 114.

32. P. G. Walsh, "Paulinus of Nola and the Conflict of Ideologies in the Fourth Century," *Kyriakon: Festschrift Johannes Quasten,* ed. Patrick Granfield and Josef A. Jungmann, vol. II (Munster Westf.: Verlag Aschendorff, 1970), p. 569.

33. Jerome, Letter CVIII,6 (CSEL 55:311; NPNF 6:197).

34. Ibid., 21 (CSEL 55:337; NPNF 6:207).

35. Ibid., (CSEL 55:338; NPNF 6:207).

36. Ibid., (CSEL 55:338; NPNF 6:207).

37. Ibid., (CSEL 55:338; NPNF 6:207).

38. Jerome, Letter XXXIX,5 (CSEL 54:304; NPNF 6:52).

39. Ibid., 6 (CSEL 54:306; NPNF 6:53).

40. Jerome, Letter XXII,17 (CSEL 54:165; NPNF 6:28).

41. For more extensive background giving the context and comparison of pilgrimages at this time, see E. D. Hunt, *Holy Land Pilgrimage in the Later Roman Empire A.D. 312–460* (Oxford: Clarendon Press, 1982).

42. Kelly, *Jerome*, p. 113.

43. Ibid., p. 116.

44. Jerome set sail for the Holy Land from Ostia. Cf. Letter XLV.

45. Jerome, Letter CVIII,7 (CSEL 55:312; NPNF 6:197).

46. *A Dictionary of Greek and Roman Geography*, vol. 2, ed. William Smith (London: John Murray, 1873; New York: AMS Press, Inc., 1966), p. 658.

47. Jerome, Letter CVIII,7 (CSEL 55:312; NPNF 6:198).

48. Ibid.

49. Cf. Letter CVIII,6 (CSEL 55:310 and 311; NPNF 6:197). Jerome records that Epiphanius, Bishop of Salamis, was Paula's house guest in Rome.

50. Cf. *New Catholic Encyclopedia*, vol. 5 for an account of Epiphanius, Bishop of Constantia/Salamis.

51. Jerome, Letter CVIII,21 (CSEL 55:327; NPNF 6:207).

52. Cf. *Egeria: Diary of a Pilgrimage*, trans. George E. Gingrass Ancient Christian Writers (New York: The Newman Press, 1970), p. 86f. The dating of Egeria's pilgrimage is disputed. The ACW translation dates the pilgrimage between A.D. 404 and 417. John Wilkinson in a slightly later translation dates the pilgrimage between A.D. 381 and 384. E. D. Hunt agrees with Wilkinson. If Hunt's dating of the pilgrimage is correct, Egeria's pilgrimages in 381 through 384 immediately preceded Paula's and Jerome's. Thus, one would expect that the monastery of St. Thecla viewed by Egeria remained an attraction in Seleucia at the time of Paula's journey.

53. Cf. "Thecla," *The Catholic Encyclopedia*, vol. 14, ed. Herbermann et al. (New York: Robert Appleton Company, 1912), p. 564.

54. Kelly, Jerome, p. 117.

55. Ibid.

56. Jerome, Letter XV,4 (CSEL 54:65; NPNF 6:19).

57. Jerome, Letter CVIII,7 (CSEL 55:313; NPNF 6:198).

58. *Atlas of the Early Christian World*, trans. and ed. Mary F. Hedlund and H. H. Rowley (Nelson, 1958), map 32.

59. Cf. *Dictionary of Greek and Roman Geography*, 1:394.

60. Ibid., 470.

61. Jerome, Letter CVIII,8 (CSEL 55:313; NPNF 6:198).

62. Ibid., (CSEL 55:314; NPNF 6:198).

63. Ibid., 9 (CSEL 55:314 and 315; NPNF 6:198).

64. Ibid., 10 (CSEL 55:316 and 317; NPNF 6:199).

65. Cf. map 15a, *Atlas of the Early Christian World*, p. 18.

66. Jerome, Letter CVIII,11 (CSEL 55:319; NPNF 6:200).

67. Cf. *Dictionary of Greek and Roman Geography*, 1:1033.

68. Jerome, Letter CVIII,12 (CSEL 55:320; NPNF 6:200).

69. Ibid., (CSEL 55:321; NPNF 6:201).

70. Ibid.

71. Ibid., 13 (CSEL 55:322; NPNF 6:201).

72. Ibid.

73. *Dictionary of Greek and Roman Geography*, 2:412.

74. Ibid.

75. Ibid., 1:991.

76. Ibid.

77. *Atlas of the Early Christian World*, map 32.

78. Jerome, Letter CVIII,14 (CSEL 55:324; NPNF 6:202).

79. Ibid., (CSEL55:315) and (NPNF6:202).

80. "She . . . warned the virgins *her companions* to beware of 'wine wherein is excess' " (Letter CVIII,11 [CSEL 55:320; NPNF 6:200]); "together with the girls who accompanied her" (Letter CVIII,14 [CSEL 55:325; NPNF 6:202]); and "At this point I conclude my narrative of the journeys that she made accompanied by Eustochium and many other virgins" (Letter CVIII,14 [CSEL 55:325; NPNF 6:202]).

81. Jerome, Letter CVIII,26 (CSEL 55:344; 27 NPNF 6:209).

82. Ibid.

83. Ibid. (CSEL 55:344 and 345; 27 NPNF 6:210).

84. Cf. Clark, "Friendship between the Sexes" Section II, *Jerome, Chrysostom, and Friends*, pp. 41–48 and "Ascetic Renunciation and Feminine Advancement: a Paradox of Late Ancient Christianity."

85. Margaret Smith, *The Way of the Mystics: The Early Christian Mystics and the Rise of the Sufis* (New York: Oxford University Press, 1978), p. 36.

86. The autonomy suggested by these "female-directed communities" is highlighted by Ruether in "Mothers of the Church," *Women of Spirit*, p. 73.

87. Peggy Sanday, "Toward a Theory of the Status of Women," *American Anthropologist* 75 (1973): 1694.

88. Ruether makes this claim in "Mothers of the Church," *Women of Spirit*, p. 81.

89. Jerome, Letter CVIII,20 (CSEL 55:335; NPNF 6:206). "Plures uirgines, quas e diversis prouinciis congregarat, tam nobiles quam medii et infimi generis, in tres turmas monasteriaque diuisit."

90. Ammianus Marcellinus 28.4.9, *Ammianus Marcellinus,* trans. John C. Rolfe, The Loeb Classical Library, ed. E. H. Warmington (Cambridge, Mass.: Harvard University Press; London: William Heinemann, 1971), 3:131.

91. Ibid., 28.4.16 (LCL 3:147).

92. Jerome, Letter CVIII,20 (CSEL 55:335; NPNF 6:206).

93. Ibid.

94. Ibid., 15 (CSEL 55:326; NPNF 6:203).

95. Ibid., 19 (CSEL 55:315; NPNF 6:199 and 200).

96. Ibid., 15 (CSEL 55:326; NPNF 6:203).

97. Ibid.

98. Ibid.

99. Ibid., 19 (CSEL 55:332; NPNF 6:205).

100. Cf. Jones, Martindale and Morris, *The Prosopography of the Later Roman Empire,* 1:674.

101. Jerome, Letter CVIII,29 (CSEL 55:348; NPNF 6:211).

102. Jerome must be exaggerating with the following claim: "The whole population of the cities of Palestine came to her funeral. Not a single monk lurked in the desert or lingered in his cell" (Jerome, Letter CVIII,29 [CSEL 55:348; 30 NPNF 6:211]).

103. Jones, Martindale and Morris, *The Prosopography of the Later Roman Empire,* 1:493. Jerome writes that Furia's father should fulfill his name and be happy [*impleat nomen suum et laetetur*].

104. "His hair is already gray, his knees tremble, his teeth fall out, his brow is furrowed through years, death is nigh even at the doors" (Jerome, Letter LIV,14 [CSEL 54:481; NPNF 6:107]).

105. Jerome, Letter LIV,6 (CSEL 54:472; NPNF 6:104).

106. Cf. *The Prosopography of the Later Roman Empire,* 1:736.

107. Claudian, "Panegyric on the Consuls Probinus and Olybrius," *Claudian* vol. 1 (LCL) (London: William Heinemann; Cambridge, Mass.: Harvard University Press, 1963), p. 19. Jerome himself neglects to mention this anonymous brother of the Probi consuls: "That Proba...who has made nothing of the regular consulships enjoyed by her three sons, Probinus, Olybrius, and Probus" (Jerome, Letter CXXX,7 [CSEL 56:183; NPNF 6:264]).

108. "To whom then are you to leave your great riches?" and "You have wealth and can easily therefore supply food to those who want it?" (Jerome, Letter LIV,4 and 14 [CSEL 54:469 and 481; NPNF 6:103 and 107]).

109. Jerome, Letter XXXVIII,2 (CSEL 54:290; NPNF 6:48).

110. Jerome, Letter XXXIX,3 (CSEL 54:299; NPNF 6:51).

111. Jerome, Letter XXXVIII,4 (CSEL 54:291; NPNF 6:48).

112. Jerome, Letter XXXIX,1 (CSEL 54:294; NPNF 6:49).

113. Ibid.

114. Cf. preface to the Commentary on Ecclesiastes and the preface to Translation of Origen on St. Luke.

115. Jerome, Letter XXXIX,1 (CSEL 54:294; NPNF 6:49).

116. Ibid., (CSEL 54:295; NPNF 6:49).

117. Palladius, *The Lausiac History* 61.7 and 62 (ACW 34:143 and 144).

118. Jones, Martindale and Morris, *The Prosopography of the Later Roman Empire*, 1:1138 and 1152. Arnheim (*The Senatorial Aristocracy in the Later Roman Empire*, pp. 129 and 130) accepts as genuine the following which Jones et al. consider conjectural—that Pammachius' father was a descendant of the Furian line and that his mother was a sister of Marcella's mother, both of whom were offspring of the prestigious Ceionius Rufius Albinus.

119. Jerome, Letter LXVI,6 (CSEL 54:654; NPNF 6:136).

120. Jones, *The Later Roman Empire*, 1:528.

121. Palladius refers in the same paragraph to Macarius, an ex-vicar, and Constantius, a prospective prefect of Italy, but mentions Pammachius without similar qualifying information about his office (Palladius, *The Lausiac History* 62 [ACW 34:144]).

122. Jerome, Letter LXVI,7 (CSEL 54:655; NPNF 6:137). "praecedebat alios dignitate, sed et alios sequebatur."

123. Jones, *The Later Roman Empire*, 1:550.

124. Ibid.

125. Ibid. Cf. Yarbrough's use of Jones: delineation of an "inner aristocracy" among the senatorial order in "Christianization in the Fourth Century."

126. Jerome, Letter LXVI,9 (CSEL 54:658 and 659; NPNF 6:138).

127. Ibid.

128. Paulinus of Nola, Letter 13, *Letters of St. Paulinus of Nola* vol. 1 (ACW 35), trans. P. G. Walsh, Westminster, Md.: The Newman Press; London: Longmans, Green and Co., 1966).

129. Augustine, Letter 58, *Saint Augustine: Letters,* trans. Sister Wilfrid Parsons, vol. I, *Fathers of the Church* (New York: Fathers of the Church, Inc., 1951), p. 296.

130. Jones, *The Later Roman Empire*, 1:554.

131. Jerome, Letter LXVI,3 (CSEL 54:650; NPNF 6:135).

132. Ibid., 1 (CSEL 54:648; NPNF 6:135).

133. Jerome, Letter CVIII,6 (CSEL 55:312; NPNF 6:197).

134. Ibid., 14 (CSEL 55:325; NPNF 6:202) for reference to Eustochium's presence.

135. Ibid., 26 (CSEL 55:345; 27 NPNF 6:210).

136. Ibid., 29 (CSEL 55:348; 30 NPNF 6:211). At Paula's funeral "Paula's daughter . . . could not be torn away from her parent. She kissed her eyes, pressed her lips upon her brow, embraced her frame, and wished for nothing better than to be buried with her."

137. Jerome, Letter XXII,17 (CSEL 54:165; NPNF 6:28).

138. Jerome, Letter CVIII,26 (CSEL 55:345; 27 NPNF 6:210).

139. Jones, Martindale and Morris, *The Prosopography of the Later Roman Empire*, 1:312.

140. Cf. Jerome's Letter CVII (CSEL 55:290f).

141. Jerome, Letter CVIII,6 (CSEL 55:311; NPNF 6:197).

142. Jones, Martindale and Morris, *The Prosopography of the Later Roman Empire*, 1:34 and Jones, *The Later Roman Empire*, 1:529.

143. Macrobius, *The Saturnalia*, trans. Percival Vaughan Davies (New York: Columbia University Press, 1969), 1. 2. 15, p. 33.

144. Jones, Martindale and Morris, *The Prosopography of the Later Roman Empire*, 1:36.

145. Jerome, Letter CVII,1 (CSEL 55:290; NPNF 6:189).

146. Cf. Arnheim, *The Senatorial Aristocracy in the Later Roman Empire*, p. 107, 121, and 125.

147. Jerome, Letter CXXVII,2 (CSEL 56:146; NPNF 6:253).

148. Ibid., 1 (CSEL 56:245; NPNF 6:253).

149. Jones, Martindale and Morris, *The Prosopography of the Later Roman Empire*, 1:32.

150. Ibid.

151. Jerome, Letter CXXVII,2 (CSEL 56:146).

152. Jones, Martindale and Morris, *The Prosopography of the Later Roman Empire*, 1:197.

153. Cf. Pomeroy, *Goddesses, Whores, Wives, and Slaves*, pp. 164–66 for claim about the dearth of women in Roman society.

154. Jerome, Letter XLVII,3 (CSEL 54:346; NPNF 6:66).

155. *The Dictionary of Greek and Roman Geography*, 2:812.

156. Jerome, Letter CXXVII,8 (CSEL 56:151; NPNF 6:256).

157. Cf. Jerome Letters XXII and XXIV,12 (CSEL 54).

158. Jerome, Letter XLV,7 (CSEL 54:328; NPNF 6:60).

159. Jerome, Letter CXXVII,14 (CSEL 56:156; NPNF 6:258).

160. Ibid., 5 (CSEL 56:149; NPNF 6:254).

161. Jerome, Letter CXXVII,7 (CSEL 56:151; NPNF 6:255).

162. Ibid.

163. Ibid., 9 (CSEL 56:152; NPNF 6:256).

164. *Codex Theodosianus, The Theodosian Code and Novels and the Surmondian Constitutions,* trans. Clyde Pharr with Theresa Sherrer Davidson and Mary Brown Pharr (Princeton: Princeton University Press, 1952), p. 443.

165. Jerome, Letter LXXVII,2 (CSEL 55:38; NPNF 6:158). "Another writer, mindful of the school, would perhaps bring forward Quintus Maximus, . . . and the whole Fabian family; he would describe their struggles and battles and would exult that Fabiola had come to us through a line so noble."

166. Ibid., 3 (CSEL 55:39; NPNF 6:159).

167. Ibid., 6 (CSEL 55:42; NPNF 6:160).

168. Ibid. (CSEL 55:44; NPNF 6:160, 161 and 162). Cf. map 23 *The Atlas of the Early Christian World* for location of Volscian district.

169. Ibid., 7 (CSEL 55:44; NPNF 6:161).

170. Ibid., 11 (CSEL 55:48; NPNF 6:162).

171. Ibid.

172. Jerome, Letter CXXIII,1 (CSEL 56:72; NPNF 6:230).

173. *A Dictionary of Christian Biography*, vol. 2, ed. William Smith and Henry Wace (New York: AMS Press, Inc. and Kraus Reprint Corp., 1967), p. 875. Source of the claim is Ausonius.

174. Jerome, Letter LXXV (CSEL 55:29f; NPNF 6:154f).

175. Jerome, Letter LXXIX,1 (CSEL 55:87; NPNF 6:163).

176. *Codex Theodosianus*, 7. 8. 7 dubs Gildo a "public enemy" and calls for the confiscation of his vast estates.

177. Jones, Martindale and Morris, *The Prosopography of the Later Roman Empire*, 1:736.

178. Ibid., p. 639.

179. Jerome, Letter CXXX,6 (CSEL 56:181; NPNF 6:263).

180. Ibid.

181. Ibid., 2 (CSEL 56:176; NPNF 6:261).

182. Ibid., 5 (CSEL 56:180; NPNF 6:262).

183. Palladius, *The Lausiac History*, 46 (ACW 34:123). Jerome in his *Chronicles* s.a. 377 claims Marcellinus as Melania's father (*The Prosopography of the Later Roman Empire*, 1:592).

184. Paulinus of Nola, Letter 29 (ACW 36:108), trans. P. G. Walsh (Westminster, Maryland: The Newman Press; London: Longmans, Green and Co., 1968).

185. F. X. Murphy, "Melania the Elder," p. 62 and Jones, Martindale and Morris in *The Prosopography of the Later Roman Empire*, 1:592.

186. Palladius, *The Lausiac History*, 46 (ACW 34:123).

187. Paulinus of Nola, Letter 29 (ACW 36:106).

188. Ibid., p. 107.

189. Palladius, *The Lausiac History*, 46 (ACW 34:123).

190. Murphy, "Melania the Elder," p. 64.

191. Murphy refers to Rampolla as the source of this claim. Cf. M. Cardinale Rampolla del Tindaro, *Santa Melania giuniore, senatrice Romana: documenti contemporanei e note* (Rome, 1905), pp. 115 and 116.

192. Palladius, *The Lausiac History*, 54 (ACW 34:134).

193. Jones, Martindale and Morris, *The Prosopography of the Later Roman Empire*, 1:754.

194. Paulinus of Nola, Letter 45 (ACW 36:246). Paulinus refers to the death of Publicola while "still preoccupied by worldly foolishness."

195. Jones, Martindale and Morris, *The Prosopography of the Later Roman Empire,* 1:558.

196. Ibid., 1:33.

197. Cf. Stemma 13 in *The Prosopography of the Later Roman Empire,* 1:1138 for Jones' assessment of the links of Laeta and Albina to the Ceionii Rufii.

198. Paulinus of Nola, Letter 29 (ACW 36:106).

199. Murphy, "Melania the Elder," p. 62. For assessment of scholarly divergence on the date of Melania's birth, see Moine, "Melaniana," *Recherches Augustiniennes* 15 (Paris: Etudes Augustinennes, 1980):4.

200. Jerome, Letter XXXIX,5 (CSEL 54:305; NPNF 6:53).

201. Murphy, "Melania the Elder," p. 65.

202. Moine wonders whether Jerome could have praised a widow whose ascetic conversion required so much time to be realized and questions the necessity of setting sail just before the onset of winter, if Melania had had years to plan her journey (Nicole Moine, "Melaniana," *Recherches Augustiniennes* 15 [Paris: Etudes Augustiniennes, 1980]:36 and 37).

203. Palladius, *The Lausiac History,* 46 (ACW 34:123).

204. Paulinus of Nola, Letter 29 (ACW 36:110 and 111).

205. Cf. Moine, "Melaniana," p. 6 for an account of the disagreement.

206. Palladius, *The Lausiac History,* 46 (ACW 34:123).

207. Paulinus of Nola, Letter 29 (ACW 36:113).

208. Cf. Jones, *The Later Roman Empire,* 1:152.

209. Palladius, *The Lausiac History,* 46 (ACW 34:124).

210. Paulinus of Nola, Letter 29 (ACW 36:113).

211. Palladius, *The Lausiac History,* 46 (ACW 34:123).

212. Paulinus of Nola, Letter 29 (ACW 36:113).

213. Ibid., p. 105.

214. Palladius, *The Lausiac History,* 46 (ACW 34:124).

215. Ibid.

216. Murphy, "Melania the Elder," p. 70.

217. Palladius, *The Lausiac History,* 54 (ACW 34:134).

218. Moine, "Melaniana," p. 9.

219. Palladius, *The Lausiac History,* 55 (ACW 34:136 and 137).

220. Paulinus of Nola, Letter 29 (ACW 36:116).

221. Palladius, *The Lausiac History,* 38 (ACW 34:112).

222. Ibid.

223. Cf. Moine, "Melaniana," p. 25f. for a discussion of theories regarding the date of Melania's return to Italy. The major stumbling block to Murphy's dating of the return in late A.D. 399 has to do with such a late dating of the conversion of Apronianus, apparently effected by Melania upon her return to Italy.

224. Paulinus of Nola, Letter 29 (ACW 36:114).

225. Ibid., p. 115.

226. Ibid.

227. Ibid., p. 116.

228. Ibid.

229. Murphy, "Melania the Elder," p. 77.

Chapter 4

1. Pomeroy, *Goddesses, Whores, Wives, and Slaves: Women in Classical Antiquity* (New York: Schocken Books, 1975), p. 153.

2. J. P. V. D. Balsdon, *Roman Women: Their History and Habits* (London: The Bodley Head, 1962), p. 180.

3. R. W. Leage, *Roman Private Law,* 2d edition by C. H. Ziegler (London: Macmillan and Co., 1951), pp. 100 and 101.

4. Ibid., p. 100.

5. Ibid., p. 90f.

6. Ibid., p. 103.

7. Pomeroy, *Goddesses, Whores, Wives, and Slaves,* p. 155. W. Warde Fowler in *Social Life at Rome in the Age of Cicero* (New York: Macmillan Company, 1924), p. 146f., agrees with Pomeroy's view that the decrease in the male population resulting from the Punic Wars enhanced the position of women.

8. Pomeroy, *Goddesses, Whores, Wives, and Slaves,* p. 155.

9. Leage, *Roman Private Law,* p. 91f.

10. *Codex Theodosianus* (8. 18), p. 218.

11. *Codex Theodosianus* (3. 7. 1), p. 70.

12. Leage, *Roman Private Law,* p. 120.

13. Hugh Last, "The Social Policy of Augustus," chap. 14, *The Cambridge Ancient History,* vol. 10, S. A. Cook, F. E. Adcock and M. P. Charlesworth, eds. (Cambridge: Cambridge University Press, 1934), p. 455.

14. Pomeroy, *Goddesses, Whores, Wives, and Slaves,* p. 151.

15. Ibid., p. 152.

16. *Codex Theodosianus* (17. 4) p. 78. The intent of the edict is not to grant women a privilege but to provide for the protection of the paternal property of her minor children if she assumes guardianship of them. However, the explicit recognition of the right of a widowed woman to fill the tutor's role is significant.

17.   Jerome, Letter CVIII,15 (CSEL 55:326 and 327; NPNF 6:203).

18.   Jerome, Letter CXXVII,4 (CSEL 56:148 and 149; NPNF 6:254).

19.   The following advice of Jerome to Eustochium, referring to envy of an apparently independent female economic status, points toward the possibility of independent status in the Late Empire: "Say not: 'So-and-so enjoys her own property, she is honored of men, her brothers and sisters come to see her'" (Jerome, Letter XXII,38 [CSEL 54:203; NPNF 6:39]).

20.   Corbett, *The Roman Law of Marriage,* p. 117.

21.   Ibid., p. 118.

22.   Ibid., p. 120.

23.   Pomeroy, *Goddesses, Whores, Wives, and Slaves,* p. 162.

24.   Last, "The Social Policy of Augustus," p. 443.

25.   While the *Lex Julia* defined all extramarital relations of a married woman as adultery, a man was subject to penalties for adultery only if his liaison were with a married woman (Corbett, *The Roman Law of Marriage,* p. 141).

26.   Last, "The Social Policy of Augustus," p. 444.

27.   Ibid.

28.   Ibid., p. 445. These two moments continue to be recognized in the *Codex Theodosianus* (9. 7. 7), although the order is reversed.

29.   Ibid., p. 446.

30.   Ibid., p. 447.

31.   Balsdon, *Roman Women,* p. 218. The *Codex Theodosianus* (9. 40. 1) indicates that adultery is considered a capital offense. In Roman law not only death but deprivation of freedom and banishment were included under the rubric of capital punishment. However, sources indicate Constantine's use of capital punishment in the case of adultery meant death. Cf. Hunter's *A Systematic and Historical Exposition of Roman Law* (p. 1072) which points to the *Code of Justinian* (9. 9. 30. 1) as evidence that Constantine imposed the death penalty for adultery.

32.   *Codex Theodosianus* (9. 7. 2), p. 231.

33.   *Ammianus Marcellinus* 28. 1 (LCL 3), is devoted to the havoc wreaked by Maximinus in Rome.

34.   Ibid., 28. 1. 11 (LCL 3:95).

35.   Ibid., 28. 1. 16–50 (LCL 3:97–119).

36.   Ibid., 28. 1. 15 (LCL 3:97).

37.   Jerome, Letter CXXVII,3 (CSEL 56:147; NPNF 6:254).

38.   Ibid. (CSEL 56:148; NPNF 6:254).

39.   Jerome, Letter I (CSEL 54:1–9; NPNF 6:1–4).

40.   Corbett, *The Roman Law of Marriage,* p. 239. Also Last, "The Social Policy of Augustus," p. 444.

41. Last, "The Social Policy of Augustus," p. 445.

42. This case is described by Pomeroy in *Goddesses, Whores, Wives, and Slaves,* p. 156.

43. *Codex Theodosianus* 3. 16. 1, p. 76. However, divorce by mutual consent was not restricted by the State until the time of Justinian. Cf. W. A. Hunter, *A Systematic and Historical Exposition of Roman Law,* trans. J. Ashton Cross (London: William Maxwell's Sons, 1885), p. 689.

44. *Codex Theodosianus* 3. 16. 1, p. 76.

45. Ibid., p. 77.

46. Ibid.

47. Ibid.

48. Ibid., 3. 16. 2, p. 77.

49. Ibid.

50. Ibid.

51. Ibid.

52. Corbett, *The Roman Law of Marriage,* p. 244.

53. Ibid., p. 245.

54. Pomeroy (*Goddesses, Whores, Wives, and Slaves,* p. 161) notes the tension between Augustan legislation and the ideal Roman *matrona.*

55. Last, "The Social Policy of Augustus," p. 450.

56. Ibid.

57. Cf. Gordon Williams, "Some Aspects of Roman Marriage Ceremonies and Ideals," *The Journal of Roman Studies* 48 (1958). Williams points to the Roman ideal of marriage to only one husband as a uniquely Roman (as opposed to Greek) attitude. Pomeroy notes the contradiction between Augustan aims and Roman esteem for the *univira.*

58. Whereas the *Lex Julia* required a woman to remarry six months after a divorce or a year after widowhood, the *Lex Papia* allowed eighteen months and two years, respectively, for contracting another marriage before penalties began (Last, "The Social Policy of Augustus," p. 454).

59. Yarbrough in "Christianization in the Fourth Century," (p. 160) claims that depopulation and asceticism probably occurred "in response to the same social conditions."

60. Marjorie Lightman and William Zeisel, *"Univira:* An Example of Continuity and Change in Roman Society," *Church History* 46 (March 1977):20.

61. Ibid.

62. Ibid., p. 25.

63. Lightman and Zeisel in *"Univira,"* refer to Fabia who died at twenty-four as an *univira* (*Corpus Inscriptionum Latinarum* 6:31711 [Berline: Wide Gruyter, 1863–1975]). Aurelia Domitia died as an *univira* at the age of thirty-six (*CIL* 6:13303). In contrast, later inscriptions describing Christian widows as *univirae* refer to deaths of much older women.

64. Lightman and Zeisel, *"Univira,"* p. 26.

65. Pomeroy, *Goddesses, Whores, Wives, and Slaves,* p. 150.

66. Ibid., p. 161.

67. Lightman and Zeisel, *"Univira,"* p. 31.

68. Jerome, Letter LIV,1 (CSEL 54:466; NPNF 6:102). Jerome finds it shameful that Christian women might remarry, while their pagan counterparts according to the custom of the *univira* marry only once: "Therefore it will not redound so much to your praise if you continue a widow as to your shame if being a Christian you fail to keep what heathen women have jealously guarded for so many centuries."

69. *Dictionary of Greek and Roman Biography and Mythology,* vol. I, p. 592.

70. Jones, *The Later Roman Empire,* 1:1040. Jones points to the major exponent of the depopulation theory (p. 1409)—A. E. R. Boak in *Man-Power Shortage and the Fall of the Roman Empire in the West* (London, 1955). Also cf. Martin P. Nilsson, *Imperial Rome,* bk. II, chap. IV. (Chicago: Ares Publishers, 1974) for a racial perspective on the demographic question.

71. Last, "The Social Policy of Augustus," p. 451.

72. Ibid., p. 452.

73. Ibid.

74. Ibid., p. 453.

75. Ibid., p. 455. Last refers to records of the first century jurist Gaius (III, 46. 47. 50, and 52).

76. Ibid. Cf. Gaius III, 42 and 44.

77. John T. Noonan, Jr., *Contraception: A History of Its Treatment by the Catholic Theologians and Canonists* (Cambridge, Mass.: Harvard University Press, 1965), p. 22.

78. Ibid.

79. Balsdon, *Roman Women,* p. 194.

80. M. K. Hopkins, "Contraception in the Roman Empire," *Comparative Studies in Society and History* 8 (1965):126.

81. M. K. Hopkins, "The Age of Roman Girls at Marriage," *Population Studies* 18 (1965):313.

82. Ibid., p. 317.

83. Hopkins, "Contraception in the Roman Empire," p. 126.

84. I am indebted to Noonan for this reference.

85. *Pliny: Letters and Panegyricus* (LCL), ed. E. H. Warmington, trans. Betty Radice (Cambridge, Mass.: Harvard University Press; London: William Heinemann, 1969), p. 287.

86. Tacitus, *The Annals* (LCL), trans. John Jackson (Cambridge, Mass.: Harvard University Press; London: William Heinemann, 1962), p. 563. As cited by Noonan in *Contraception.*

87. Balsdon, *Roman Women* chap. 8, p. 192.

88. Ibid.

89. In his *Confessions*, 6. 12. 22, Augustine expresses his preconversion view of marriage: "Whatever conjugal grace there be in the duty of regulating the married state and in the bringing up of children, this moved the two of us [Alypius and Augustine] but vaguely" (*Confessions*, 6. 12. 22. Fathers of the Church, trans. Vernon Bourke [New York: Fathers of the Church, Inc., 1953], p. 155).

90. Balsdon, *Roman Women*, p. 196. Hopkins in "Contraception in the Roman Empire," p. 127, questions whether aristocrats practiced exposure.

91. Hopkins, "Contraception in the Roman Empire," p. 129.

92. Ibid., p. 131.

93. Ibid., p. 134.

94. Noonan, *Contraception*, p. 20.

95. Hopkins, "Contraception in the Roman Empire," p. 149.

96. Ovid, *Artis Amatoriae* 3, *Ovid* 2 (LCL), ed. E. H. Warmington and trans. J. H. Mozley (Cambridge, Mass.: Harvard University Press; London: Willian Heinemann, LTD, 1969), p. 143. Marrou in *A History of Education in Antiquity* (p. 249) notes that in Rome's adoption of Greek standards of pedagogy music was not incorporated into the serious educational curriculum; therefore, the musical accomplishments of the women of elegiac poetry may have been devalued by more serious literati.

97. Ovid, *Artis Amatoriae* 3, pp. 293–96. *Ovid* 2 (LCL), p. 139. Jerome in Letter XXII, 29 refers to this curious, but obviously tenacious, practice of assuming a feigned lisp.

98. Pomeroy, *Goddesses, Whores, Wives, and Slaves*, p. 173.

99. Cf. Pomeroy's description of her poetic style and literary production, *Goddesses, Whores, Wives, and Slaves*, p. 175.

100. Pomeroy, *Goddesses, Whores, Wives, and Slaves*, p. 174.

101. *Dictionary of Greek and Roman Biography and Mythology*, ed. William Smith (Boston: Little, Brown, and Co., 1870), 1:1063.

102. Jones in *The Later Roman Empire*, vol. 2:1004, describes the typical Roman education of our period: "The learning that he [the average man] of late Roman society acquired was a jumble of miscellaneous lore, mainly mythological and antiquarian, but containing odd pieces of history, geography and natural or more often unnatural history."

103. H. I. Marrou, *A History of Education in Antiquity*, trans. George Lamb (New York: Sheed and Ward, 1956), p. 250f.

104. Ibid., p. 265.

105. Ibid., p. 275.

106. Ibid., pp. 277 and 278.

107. Ibid., p. 284f.

108. In Jerome's dream recounted in Letter XXII, a judge calls him a liar for claiming to be a follower of Christ: "Thou liest, thou art a follower of Cicero, not of Christ" (Letter XXII, 30 [CSEL 54:190; NPNF 6;35]).

109. Cf. Ovid, *Tristia* 2, pp. 369–70, and Martial, 8. 3. 16.

110. Marrou, *A History of Education in Antiquity*, p. 274.

111. Quintilian, 1. 2. From *The Institutio Oratoria of Quintilian*, vol. 1, trans. H. E. Butler (LCL) (William Heinemann and Harvard University Press, 1969), p. 39f.

112. Marrou, *A History of Education in Antiquity*, p. 266.

113. "Maria...was listening with rapt attention to the discourse of her saintly mother...nor does she cease under that mother's guidance to unroll the writers of Rome and Greece" (*Epithalamium De Nuptiis Honorii Augusti, Claudian*, vol. 1, trans. Maurice Platmauer [LCL], [1963], p. 259. As cited by Clark in *Jerome, Chrysostom, and Friends*).

114. Marrou, *A History of Education in Antiquity*, p. 265.

115. Jones, *The Later Roman Empire*, 2:998.

116. Claudian, *Epithalamium de Nuptiis Honorii Augusti, Claudian*, vol. I (LCL), p. 259. As cited by Clark in *Jerome, Chrysostom, and Friends*.

117. Jerome, Letter XXII,29 (CSEL 54:189; NPNF 6:35). Elizabeth Clark aptly suggests that Jerome should be posing these questions to himself rather than to Eustochium (Clark, *Jerome, Chrysostom, and Friends*, p. 72).

118. Jerome, Letter CXXVII,6 (CSEL 56:150; NPNF 6:255).

119. Pomeroy, *Goddesses, Whores, Wives, and Slaves*, p. 171.

120. Clark, *Jerome, Chrysostom, and Friends*, p. 74.

Chapter 5

1. Parsons' theory of action needs to be defined in terms of its relationship to other theoretical perspectives in sociology in order to elucidate some of its presuppositions. As Jonathan Turner has noted, distinguishing between perspectives in sociological theory is somewhat arbitrary in view of the often common sources and convergence between the different perspectives (Turner, *The Structure of Sociological Theory*, p. 9). However, for expository purposes, Turner has distinguished four major thrusts in sociological theory: (1) functionalist theory, (2) conflict theory, (3) symbolic interactionism and role theory, and (4) exchange theory (Turner, p. 9). Functionalist theory has its intellectual roots in Emile Durkheim and tends to carry on the legacy of his view of the social system as seeking equilibrium, in a fashion analogous to a biological organism. Emerging as a critique of functionalist concern with homeostasis and the consequent casting of change and conflict as pathological, conflict theory has emphasized the reality and normalacy of conflict within the social order. (Turner, p. 78) Its, perhaps, most noted proponent, Lewis Coser, represents the convergence of perspectives insofar as he (in the legacy of George Simmel) stresses the equilibrating function of conflict, thereby earning the label of a functional conflict theorist. Symbolic interactionism and role theory have also criticized the conservative presuppositions of functionalist theory and (in the legacy of George Herbert Mead) stressed the potential of the human actor to create and affect the social world (Turner, p. 158). The concepts of symbolic interactionism and role theory have centered around the ideas of status, norms, and social expectations. While Turner designates Talcott Parsons' theory of action as "functional imperativism," he notes its theoretical convergence with symbolic interactionism at the level of concepts but departure at the level of methodology for building sociological theory (Turner, pp. 193–207). It is at their point of convergence that my use of Parsons is located. However, the functionalist roots in

Parsons' theory of action should be noted in order to bring to light the tendency of his view of the social process to emphasize orientation toward equilibrium. The theoretical attractiveness of the Parsonian model for my purposes is its attention to the individual in his or her relationship to the larger social order, for, obviously, I am not trying to provide a social construct to characterize the social order of late antiquity. Rather, I am attempting to use social theory to discern possible sources of motivation to a particular action—ascetic renunciation.

2. Peter Brown, "Aspects of the Christianization of the Roman Aristocracy," *Journal of Roman Studies* 51 (1961):4. Cf. Sir Samuel Dill, *Roman Society in the Last Century of the Western Empire* bk. 1, chaps. 1 and II (1899; reprint, New York: Meridian Books, Inc.) for another account of the close mingling of pagan and Christian of the senatorial class of late Rome.

3. Cf. W. H. C. Frend, "The Two Worlds of Paulinus of Nola," *Latin Literature of the Fourth Century*, ed. J. W. Binns (Boston: Routledge and Kegan Paul, 1974). However, A. H. M. Jones focuses analysis of the pagan/Christian conflict on social origins in "The Social Background of the Struggles Between Paganism and Christianity," *The Conflict Between Paganism and Christianity in the Fourth Century*, ed. Arnaldo Momigliano (Oxford: Clarendon Press, 1963).

4. Cf. Jonathan Turner, "Interaction Theory," *The Structure of Sociological Theory* (The Dorsey Press, 1974). For a more differentiated model cf. Talcott Parsons, "The Position of Identity in the General Theory of Action," *The Self in Social Interaction*, ed. Chad Gordon and Kenneth J. Gergen (New York: John Wiley and Sons, Inc., 1968).

5. Talcott Parsons, *The Social System* (Free Press of Glencoe, 1951), pp. 204 and 205.

6. Ibid., p. 27.

7. Ibid., p. 38. "In so far as . . . conformity with a value-orientation standard . . . is both a mode of the fulfillment of his own need-dispositions and a condition of 'optimizing' the reactions of other significant actors, that standard will be said to be 'institutionalized.'"

8. Ibid., p. 42.

9. Ibid.

10. Talcott Parsons and Edward A. Shils eds., *Toward a General Theory of Action* (Cambridge, Mass.: Harvard University Press, 1967), pp. 105 and 106.

11. Peter Brown, "Aspects of the Christianization of the Roman Aristocracy," *Journal of Roman Studies* 51 (1961):4.

12. Ibid., p. 10. Christian art reflects this syncretism, e.g., a gold coin of about 417 A.D. portrays Galla Placida, daughter of Theodosius I., as a winged victory holding a Christian cross. (*Prefect and Emperor: The "Relationes" of Symmachus*. Oxford: Clarendon Press, 1973, frontispiece.)

13. Jerome's barb at made-up Christian women centers on his critique that the Creator won't recognize the face He has created (Jerome, Letter LIV,7 [CSEL 54:473; NPNF 6:104]).

14. Jones, *The Later Roman Empire*, 1:163.

15. Ibid., 2:940. Cf. "Relatio III," *Prefect and Emperor: the "Relationes" of Symmachus*, trans. R. H. Barrow (Oxford: Clarendon Press, 1973), p. 32 and Samuel Dill, *Roman Society in the Last Century of the Western Empire* bk. 1.

16. Ibid., 2:941.

17. Cf. Theodosius' reference to the pagan claim on entry into illustrious office: "Our good leader [Theodosius] gives a fair return for services in the earthy sphere to the worshippers of idols, grants them the highest honours and allows them to compete with the distinctions of their own families." (Theodosius' address to Rome as recorded in Prudentius' *Contra Orationem Symmachi*, 618–19 *Prudentius* 1 [LCL], p. 397.)

18. Jones, Martindale and Morris, *The Prosopography of the Later Roman Empire*, 1:1055.

19. Ibid., p. 348.

20. Cf. Brown, "Aspects of Christianization of the Roman Aristocracy," (p. 7) for claims about the solidarity of male pagans.

21. Alan Cameron in "Paganism and Literature in Late Fourth Century Rome" (*Christianisme et formes littéraires de l'antiquité tardive en occident*, Fondation Hardt, Geneve 1977) notes the closeness of Christians to pagan literature. Christians may have provided more patronage for the preservation of the classical tradition than the pagans, resulting in the prevalence of a Christian slant on the preserved classics.

22. *Dictionary of Greek and Roman Biography and Mythology*, 2:926.

23. Jones notes that under Constans senators, often from the most elite families, virtually monopolized the praetorian prefecture of Italy (Jones, *The Later Roman Empire*, 1:134). Also cf. "Antonius Marcellinus 16," *The Prosopography of the Later Roman Empire*, 1:548.

24. Jones, Martindale and Morris, *The Prosopography of the Later Roman Empire*, 1:582.

25. Ibid., p. 590.

26. "On their return he [Julian] received them with honour, and passing over the better man...made Maximus prefect...to please Rufinus Vulcatius [*sic*], whose nephew he knew him to be." (*Ammianus Marcellinus* 21. 12. 24 [LCL 2:155]).

27. Macrobius, *The Saturnalia*, pp. 7 and 8.

28. Jones, Martindale and Morris, *The Prosopography of the Later Roman Empire*, 1:593. Jones cites the *Vita S. Melaniae* Gr. 34–35 and Latin II 2–4.

29. Ibid., p. 88.

30. Paulinus of Nola, Poem 21 (ACW 40:180).

31. *Ammianus Marcellinus* 28. 1. 17–23 (LCL 3:99–101).

32. Jones, Martindale and Morris, *The Prosopography of the Later Roman Empire*, 1:721.

33. *Corpus Inscriptionum Latinanum* (CIL) VI.1779 (also ILS 1259) in *Religious Conflict in Fourth-Century Rome* by Brian Croke and Jill Harris (Sydney University Press, 1981), p. 106. Brackets in secondary text.

34. Cf. Macrobius, *The Saturnalia* 1. 7. 17 (p. 57) and 1. 17–23.

35. Cf. Jerome, Letter CVII,5 (CSEL 55:296; NPNF 6:191).

36. Ibid., 1 (CSEL 55:291; NPNF 6:190).

37. Ibid. (NPNF 6:189). Yarbrough cites this passage to claim that Toxotius converted from paganism to Christianity ("Christianization in the Fourth Century," p. 156).

38. Ibid.

39. Jones, Martindale and Morris, *The Prosopography of the Later Roman Empire,* 1:36.

40. Jerome, Letter LIV,6 (CSEL 54:471 and 472; NPNF 6:104).

41. Jones, Martindale and Morris, *The Prosopography of the Later Roman Empire,* 1:198.

42. Ibid., p. 782. Cf. *Corpus Inscriptionum Latinarium* VI 32051 and *Inscriptiones Latinae Selectae* (Dessau) 1237.

43. Jerome, Letter XXII,32 (CSEL 54:193; NPNF 6:36).

44. Jerome, Letter XXXVIII,3 (CSEL 54:291; NPNF 6:48). "nimio candore deformes idola."

45. Paulinus of Nola, Letter 13 (ACW 35:134).

46. Ibid.

47. Also printed in C. P. Caspari, *Briefe, Abhandlungen und Predigten* (Christiana, 1870) and translated into English by R. S. T. Haslehurst in a book called *The Works of Fastidius* (Westminster: Society of SS. Peter and Paul, 1927).

48. Morris, "Pelagian Literature," p. 43f.

49. Cf. Augustine, Letter 156, The Fathers of the Church Vol. III, trans. Sister Wilfrid Parsons, S.N.D. (New York: Fathers of the Church, Inc., 1953). Cf. Morris, "Pelagian Literature," p. 37f.

50. Morris comments on this sociologically sophistocated line of argumentation ("Pelagian Literature," pp. 48–51).

51. *De Divitiis* (*PL* supplement 1); *The Works of Fastidius,* ed. and trans. R. S. T. Haslehurst (London: The Society of SS. Peter and Paul, 1927), p. 73.

52. Cf. Peter Brown, "The Patrons of Pelagius: The Roman Aristocracy between East and West," *Journal of Theological Studies,* vol. XXI, April 1970.

53. Cf. John Morris, "Pelagian Literature," pp. 40 and 45.

54. Peter Brown, "The Patrons of Pelagius," p. 60.

55. Jerome, Letter XXXIX,6 (CSEL 54:306; NPNF 6:53).

56. Parsons, *The Social System,* p. 250.

57. Ibid., pp. 252–53.

58. Ibid.

59. Ibid., p. 254.

60. Ibid.

61. Ibid., p. 257n.3.

62. Ibid., p. 259.

63. Ibid.

64. Jerome, Letter CVIII,6 (CSEL 55:310; NPNF 6:197). "Nor was she long able to endure the visits and crowded receptions, which her high position in the world and her exalted family entailed upon her."

65. Jerome, Letter XXII,16,17 (CSEL 54:327–29; NPNF 6:27 and 28).

66. Jerome, Letter CVIII,6 (CSEL 55:311; NPNF 6:197).

67. Ibid., 21 (CSEL 55:337; NPNF 6:207).

68. Ibid., 15 (CSEL 55:325; NPNF 6:202).

69. Parsons, *The Social System,* p. 259.

70. Jerome, Letter CVIII,18 (CSEL 55:329; NPNF 6:204).

71. Ibid.

72. Ibid., 15 (CSEL 55:326; NPNF 6:203).

73. Ibid., 17 (CSEL 55:328; NPNF 6:204).

74. Ibid., 20 (CSEL 55:336; NPNF 6:206).

75. Ibid., 21 (CSEL 55:336 and 337; NPNF 6:207).

76. Parsons, *The Social System,* p. 261.

Chapter 6

1. I must express my appreciation to Loretta Ross-Gotta for directing me to the attitudes toward women in classical literature which she used in an original religious drama about our Roman monastic women.

2. One of several ventures into sociological literature in search of suitable categories for interpreting the ascetic choice of the subjects of this inquiry was an examination of the ideal type method of Max Weber. In view of the fact that this investigation inspired my use of a typology for thesis building, a word about my typology as it relates to Weber's typological method is in order. My typology follows the Weberian mode in a limited way, being more classificatory than what Weber means by an ideal type in the essay " 'Objectivity' in Social Science and Social Policy." While Weber's writing on the ideal type is a highly complex and controverted area of scholarship (cf. Thomas Burger, *Max Weber's Theory of Concept Formation: History, Laws, and Ideal Types* [Durham, N.C.: Duke University Press, 1976], especially pp. 58 and 119, and Rolf E. Rogers, *Max Weber's Ideal Type Theory* [New York: Philosophical Library, Inc., 1969]), some general comments will highlight the links between my typological constructions and Weber's ideal type method. The following summary primarily reflects Weber's application of the methodological status of the ideal type in " 'Objectivity' in Social Science and Social Policy" (trans. Shils and Finch in *The Methodology of the Social Sciences* [Glencoe, Ill.: The Free Press, 1949]). Weber's methodological concern was with how the historian (or sociologist) can acquire meaningful knowledge given the infinite complexity and actual irreducibility of any phenomenon whether historical, contemporary, or even subjective. His solution was found by exploring the logical relationship between interpretive generalizations, interpretive concepts, and other such constructs of the investigator and their referent. He called this relationship ideal typical in order to indicate that the language and conceptuality we use to grasp a phenomenon does not fully account for its complexity but rather plucks out one aspect on the basis of our interest. Thus, meaningful knowledge is obtained because the object of investigation has relevance to our values. At the same time, objectivity is possible for the investigator despite the role of value in interpretation by recognizing the ideal typical (not absolute) relationship of his/her interpretive generalizations to their empirical

referent. My typology is not fully in this mode. My types are not synthetic concepts like the common Weberian example, bureaucracy, which is ideal typical in the sense that no historical referent fully embodies the definitional elements of a bureaucracy but, rather, approaches the definition in gradations. My typology rather serves as an organizing device which classifies the images current in the classical and ecclesiastical literature so that they can be compared. My types, however, have a Weberian element insofar as they are to a certain extent synthetic, formed as a composite of elements from various sources.

3. Kelly, *Jerome*, p. 11. Cf. *Quintilian's Institutes of Oratory.*

4. Cf. Jones, *The Later Roman Empire*, 2:1003 for reiteration of the curriculum of the standard rhetorical education in the Late Roman Empire.

5. Kelly lists the following authors as the basis of Jerome's classical education at Rome under Donatus: Vergil, Terence, Sallust, Cicero, Plautus, Lucretius, Horace, Persius, Lucan, Ovid, Martial, Quintilian, and Seneca (Kelly, *Jerome*, pp. 11 and 12).

6. Kelly, *Jerome*, p. 11. Cf. footnote 10.

7. *Ammianus Marcellinus* 28. 4. 14 (LCL 3:145).

8. Gilbert Highet, *Juvenal the Satirist: A Study* (Oxford: Clarendon Press, 1955), p. 186.

9. Ibid., pp. 185 and 186.

10. Susan Treggiara, "Libertine Ladies," *The Classical World* 64 (1971):196.

11. Saara Lilja, "The Roman Elegists' Attitude to Women," *Annales Academiae Scientiarum Fennicae* B 134 (Helsinki: Suomalainen Tiedeakatemia, 1965), p. 41.

12. Lilja, "The Roman Elegists' Attitude to Women," p. 42.

13. Cf. the general index of Macrobius' *Saturnalia*, p. 554.

14. Cf. Harold Hagendahl's *Latin Fathers and the Classics* (Göteborg, 1958), pp. 253 and 258.

15. Jerome, Letter CXXIII,4 (CSEL 56:75; NPNF 6:231). My italic.

16. Macrobius, *The Saturnalia*, index of citations, p. 535f.

17. Hagendahl, *Latin Fathers and the Classics*, p. 276.

18. Ibid. Cf. Aemilius Luebeck, *Hieronymus quos noverit scriptores et ex quibus hauserit* (Lipsiae, 1872).

19. Jones, *The Later Roman Empire*, 2:1003.

20. Hagendahl, *Latin Fathers and the Classics*, p. 270.

21. Ibid., pp. 271–72. Luebeck in the study cited above found six passages from *Andria* (*The Woman of Andros*), eight from *Eunuchus* (*The Eunuch*), five from *Heauton Timorumenos* (*The Self-Tormentor*), four from *Phormio* (*Phormio*), one from *Hecyra* (*The Mother-in-law*), and two from *Adelphoe* (*The Brothers*).

22. Hagendahl, *Latin Fathers and the Classics*, p. 273.

23. Ibid.

24. Lightman and Zeisel, "Univira," p. 19.

25. Williams, "Some Aspects of Roman Marriage Ceremonies and Ideals," p. 23f. Sarah Pomeroy (*Goddesses, Whores, Wives, and Slaves*, p. 161) also characterizes the *univira* ideal as distinctly Roman with no equivalent parallel in Greece.

26. Cf. Pomeroy, *Goddesses, Whores, Wives, and Slaves,* p. 161, and Williams, "Some Aspects of Roman Marriage Ceremonies and Ideals," p. 23.

27. Vergil, *The Aeneid* 4. 15–20, trans. Frank O. Copley (Indianapolis: The Bobbs-Merrill Co., Inc., 1965), p. 70. "Had I not fixed it firm within my heart never to yield myself to marriage bond since that first love left me cheated by death, did I not sicken at thought of bed and touch, to this one sin, this once, I might succumb." Further references to *The Aeneid* will be to this edition.

28. Vergil, *The Aeneid* 4. 170–72.

29. Williams, "Some Aspects of Roman Marriage Ceremonies and Ideals," p. 33, writes that "the ideal and eternal nature of her one marriage to Sychaeus is the big factor in her tragedy."

30. Another way of interpreting the Vergilian treatment of Dido (to which Williams alludes) is to see it as an indictment of her pseudo-marriage. This would be consistent with Augustan concerns to reform the disintegrated state of matrimony.

31. Williams, "Some Aspects of Roman Marriage Ceremonies and Ideals," p. 19f.

32. Translation by Sir Robert Allison appears in *The Complete Roman Drama* (New York: Random House, 1942), 1:43.

33. Williams cites in particular the *laudatio Turiae* in *Corpus Inscriptionum Latinarum* VI, 1527.

34. From *Religious Conflict in Fourth-Century Rome,* (p. 106) by B. F. Croke and J. D. Harries (Forest Grove, Oreg.: International Scholarly Book Service, Inc., 1981). Quoted from *Corpus Inscriptionem Latinarum* VI, 1779. The traditional image of woman also informs Claudian's portrayal of Maria, fiancée of Honorius, who, if modern in the sense of being educated, nonetheless was "learning to follow her mother's example of old-world chastity (*prisca pudicitiae*) (Claudian, "Epithalamium De Nuptiis Honorii Augusti," *Claudian* 1, trans. Maurice Platmauer (LCL) 1922, p. 259). *Prisca pudicitiae* might better be translated as "old-fashioned virtue."

35. Terence *The Mother-in-law (Hecyra)* 2. 2. 166f. Translator Anonymous. *The Complete Roman Drama,* 2:370.

36. Cf. Pomeroy, *Goddesses, Whores, Wives, and Slaves,* p. 199, and Williams, "Some Aspects of Roman Marriage Ceremonies and Ideals," footnote 20, p. 21.

37. Pomeroy, *Goddesses, Whores, Wives, and Slaves,* p. 199.

38. Pomeroy (*Goddesses, Whores, Wives, and Slaves,* p. 149) notes the tension between the ideal *matrona* of social myth and the real Roman matron.

39. Juvenal, Satire Six, lines 76 and 77, *Juvenal and Persius* (LCL), p. 89.

40. Ibid., lines 594–600 (LCL), p. 133.

41. Ibid., lines 166–69 (LCL), p. 97.

42. Cf. Treggiari, "Libertine Ladies," and Lilja, "The Roman Elegists' Attitude to Women," p. 36f.

43. Ovid "De Medicamine Faciei Liber," lines 11 and 12. *Ovid* 2, trans. J. H. Mozley (LCL) 1969, p. 3.

44. How large a factor the *Artis Amatoriae* was in Ovid's banishment from Rome by Augustus is a point of scholarly dispute. Cf. John C. Thibault, *The Mystery of Ovid's Exile* (Berkeley and Los Angeles: University of California Press, 1964).

45. Ovid *Artis Amatoriae* 2. 153–55. *Ovid* 2 (LCL), p. 77.

46. Ovid *Artis Amatoriae* 3. 585–87. *Ovid* 2 (LCL), pp. 159 and 161.

47. Ibid., lines 137–40. *Ovid* 2 (LCL), p. 127.

48. Ibid., lines 199–200. *Ovid* 2 (LCL), p. 133.

49. Ibid., lines 267–68. *Ovid* 2 (LCL), p. 137.

50. Lilja, "The Roman Elegists' Attitude to Women," p. 65f.

51. Ibid., pp. 185 and 186.

52. Lightman and Zeisel, *"Univira,"* p. 25, and Williams, "Some Aspects of Roman Marriage Ceremonies and Ideals," p. 24.

53. Lilja, "The Roman Elegists' Attitude to Women," p. 73.

54. Ovid *Artis Amatoriae* 2. 198–202. *Ovid* 2 (LCL), p. 79.

55. Terence *The Mother-in-law* (*Hecyra*) 2. 1. 197, *The Complete Roman Drama*, 2:371.

56. Ibid., 5. 1, p. 392f.

57. Ibid., 4. 2, p. 387f.

58. Ibid., 4. 1, p. 385f.

59. Jerome, "The Perpetual Virginity of Blessed Mary," (NPNF) 2d ser., vol. 6 (1893), p. 345.

60. Cf. Lightman and Zeisel, *"Univira,"* p. 31f.

61. *Monogamia* or its derivative is found in the following letters of Jerome: Letter XLVIII,18 (*PL* vol. 22, p. 508); Letter LII,16 (*PL* vol. 22, p. 539); Letter LIV,6 (*PL* vol. 22, p. 552); Letter LXXXV in referring to Tertullian's tract *De Monogamia*; and most prominently in Letter CXXIII in Jerome's letter to Ageruchia entitled *De Monogamia* (*PL* vol. 22, p. 1046f).

62. Jerome, Letter CXXIII,5 (CSEL 56:79; NPNF 6:232).

63. Lightman and Zeisel, *"Univira,"* p. 32.

64. Jerome, "Against Jovinianus," 1, 43 (NPNF) 2d ser., vol. VI (1893), p. 381. Jerome repeats this assessment of Dido in Letter CXXIII,8.

65. Cf. Vergil *The Aeneid* 4. 305–705.

66. Cf. Mary Louise Lord, "Dido as an Example of Chastity: The Influence of Example Literature," *Harvard Library Bulletin* vol. 17 (1969):22–44.

67. Plautus *The Amphitryon* 2. 2. 840, trans. Paul Nixon. *Plautus* 1 (LCL) 1950, pp. 88 and 89.

68. Livy 10. 23. *Livy* 4, trans. B. O. Foster (LCL) 1958, p. 442f.

69. Ibid., p. 444.

70. Ibid.

71. Juvenal, Satire Six, lines 1–7, (LCL), p. 82–85.

72. Jerome, Letter CXXX,12 (CSEL 56; NPNF 6:267).

73. Ibid., 6 (CSEL 56; NPNF 6:181).

74. Ibid., 2 (CSEL 56:176; NPNF 6:261).

75. Jerome, Letter CVII,10 (CSEL 55; NPNF 6:193). Cf. also Jerome's advice to Pacatula to learn to spin wool in Letter CXXVIII,1 (CSEL 56; NPNF 6:258) and his similar advice to Demetrias in Letter CXXX (CSEL 56:157; NPNF 6:269).

76. Ovid The *Amores* 2. 4. 17. *Ovid* 1 (LCL), p. 391.

77. Ovid *Artis Amatoriae* 3. 479–82. *Ovid* 2 (LCL), p. 153.

78. Ibid., lines 333–77, pp. 141 and 143.

79. Ibid., lines 341–45, p. 143.

80. Ibid., lines 293–96, p. 139.

81. Lilja, "The Roman Elegists' Attitude to Women," p. 141.

82. Ibid.

83. Clark alludes to the unsuitable nature of the Roman rhetorical education for women (Clark, *Jerome, Chrysostom, and Friends,* p. 72).

84. Ovid *Artis Amatoriae* 1. 459–62. *Ovid* 2 (LCL), p. 45.

85. Lilja, "The Roman Elegists' Attitude to Women," p. 138.

86. Juvenal, Satire Six, lines 444–51, (LCL), pp. 119 and 121.

87. Ibid., lines 187–88, p. 99.

88. Jerome, Letter CVII,4 (CSEL 55:295; NPNF 6:191).

89. Quintilian, *Institutes of Oration in Twelve Books* vol. I, trans, John Selby Watson (London and New York: George Bell & Sons, 1892), p. 10.

90. E. E. Best, "Cicero, Livy and Educated Roman Women," *Classical Journal* 65 (1970):pp. 200 and 201.

91. Jerome, Letter CVII,4 (CSEL 55:293; NPNF 6:190).

92. Jerome, Letter XXII,17 (CSEL 54:165; NPNF 6:28).

93. Clark, *Jerome, Chrysostom, and Friends,* p. 72. Clark has commented repeatedly on the positive view of women monastics as intellectuals. In *Jerome, Chrysostom, and Friends* (p. 70f.), she views monastic education as exempting them from inferiority as females and in "Ascetic Renunciation and Feminine Advancement: a Paradox of Late Ancient Christianity," she argues that education elevates ascetic women above the level of other Christian women.

94. Jerome, Letter CVII,4 (CSEL 55:295; NPNF 6:191). "unde et tibi est prouidendum, ne ineptis blanditiis feminarum dimidiata dicere filiam verba consuescas."

95. The *Octavia,* according to prevailing scholarly opinion, was most likely written shortly after Nero's death in A.D. 62 by an observer of imperial intrigue (*The Complete Roman Drama,* 2:854).

96. The *Octavia* 2. 2. 54f. *The Complete Roman Drama,* 2:873.

97. Lilja, "The Roman Elegists' Attitude to Women," p. 42.

98. Ovid "De Medicamine Faciei Liber," lines 43–45. *Ovid* 2 (LCL), p. 5.

99. Referring to Alceste and other self-sacrificing wives, Ovid says not these but "wanton loves are learnt through me." (Ovid, *Artis Amatoriae* 3. 165. *Ovid* 2 (LCL), p. 121.)

100. Lilja, "The Roman Elegists' Attitude to Women," p. 130.

101. Ovid *Artis Amatoriae* 3. 165. *Ovid* 2 (LCL), p. 129.

102. Ibid., lines 163 and 164, p. 129. "A woman stains her whitening locks with German juices, and by skill seeks a hue better than the real."

103. Ibid., lines 199–201, p. 133.

104. Ovid "De Medicamine Faciei Liber," line 59. *Ovid* 2 (LCL), p. 7.

105. Ovid *Artis Amatoriae* 3. 216f. *Ovid* 2 (LCL), p. 133.

106. Ovid The *Amores* 1. 14. 25. *Ovid* 1 (LCL), p. 375.

107. Ibid., 31f.

108. Lilja, "The Roman Elegists' Attitude to Women," p. 130.

109. Juvenal, Satire Six, lines 161–65, (LCL), p. 121.

110. Juvenal, Satire Six, lines 501–4, (LCL), p. 125. Cf. Balsdon's "Women in Imperial Rome," *History Today* 10 (1960):24 for a picture of a sculpted head in the Capitoline Museum which must represent the coiffure of Juvenal's image.

111. Jerome, Letter XXXVIII,4 (CSEL 54:291; NPNF 6:48).

112. Jerome, Letter CVIII,15 (CSEL 55:326; NPNF 6:203).

113. Jerome, Letter XXXVIII,3 (CSEL 54:291; NPNF 6:48).

114. Jerome, Letter XXII,29 (CSEL 54:187; NPNF 6:34).

115. Ibid., 27 (CSEL 54:183; NPNF 6:33).

116. Tertullian, "On the Apparel of Women," 2. 5 (ANF) vol. 4, trans. the Rev. S. Thelwall and ed. by the Rev. Alexander Roberts and James Donaldson (Grand Rapids, Mich.: Wm. B. Eerdmans Publishing Co., 1956), p. 21.

117. Ibid., 2. 7 (ANF 4:21).

118. Ibid., 2. 6 (ANF 4:21).

119. Lilja, "The Roman Elegists' Attitude to Women," pp. 120, 123, and 129.

120. Tertullian, "On the Apparel of Women," 2. 5 (ANF 4:20).

121. Ibid., 2. 3 (ANF 4:20).

122. Ibid., 2. 11 (ANF 4:24).

123. Ovid *Artis Amatoriae* 3. 421. *Ovid* 2 (LCL), p. 149.

124. Jerome, Letter XXII,25 (CSEL 54:179; NPNF 6:32).

125. Ibid., 29 (CSEL 54:188) and (NPNF 6:35).

Chapter 7

1. Cf. Brown, "Aspects of the Christianization of the Roman aristocracy," and Dill, *Roman Society in the Last Century of the Western Empire,* bk. 1, chap. 1.

2. Sir Samuel Dill thought Paula's husband, Toxotius, was pagan (*Roman Society in the Last Century of the Western Empire,* p. 13).

3. Cf. "On the Reason for Withdrawing from the World," Seneca's Epistle XIV.

4. Parsons, *The Social System,* p. 280.

5. Ibid., p. 293.

Bibliography

Ammianus Marcellinus. Trans. John C. Rolfe. In three vols. (especially vol. III, bk. XXVIII). The Loeb Classical Library. Ed. E. H. Warmington. Cambridge, Mass.: Harvard University Press, and London: William Heinemann, 1971.

Arnheim, M. T. W. *The Senatorial Aristocracy in the Later Roman Empire.* Oxford: The Clarendon Press, 1972.

Balsdon, J. P. V. D. "Women in Imperial Rome." *History Today* 10 (1960):24–31.

Berger, Peter, and Luckmann, Thomas. *The Social Construction of Reality: A Treatise in the Sociology of Knowledge.* Garden City, N.Y.: Doubleday and Co., 1966.

Best, E. E. "Cicero, Livy and Educated Roman Women." *Classical Journal* 65 (1970):199–204.

Binns, J. W., ed. *Latin Literature of the Fourth Century: Classical Literature and Its Influence.* Boston: Routledge and Kegan Paul, 1974.

Brown, Peter. "Aspects of the Christianization of the Roman Aristocracy." *The Journal of Roman Studies* 51 (1961):1–11.

_____. "The Patrons of Pelagius: The Roman Aristocracy between East and West." *Journal of Theological Studies,* n.s., vol. 21, pt. 1 (April 1970):56–72.

_____. "Pelagius and His Supporters: Aims and Environment." *Journal of Theological Studies,* n.s., vol. 19, pt. 1 (April 1968):93–114.

Burger, Thomas. *Max Weber's Theory of Concept Formation: History, Laws, and Ideal Types.* Durham: Duke University Press, 1976.

Cameron, Allan. "Paganism and Literature in Late Fourth Century Rome." *Christianisme of Formes Littéraires de L'Antiquité Tardive en Occident.* Geneve: Fondation Hardt, 1977.

Campbell, Gerald J. "St. Jerome's Attitude toward Marriage and Woman: II." *The American Ecclesiastical Review* 143 (July-December 1960):384–94.

Clark, Elizabeth. "Ascetic Renunciation and Feminine Advancement: a Paradox of Late Ancient Christianity." *Anglican Theological Review* 63 (July 1981):240–57.

_____. *Jerome, Chrysostom, and Friends.* Essays and Translations. New York: The Edwin Mellen Press, 1979.

Claudian. "Epithalamium De Nuptiis Honorii Augusti," *Claudian* 1. Trans. Maurice Platnauer. The Loeb Classical Library. Ed. Capps, Page, and Rouse. London: William Heinemann, and New York: G. P. Putnam's Sons, 1922.

Coyle, John Kevin. "Augustine's 'De Moribus Ecclesiae Catholicae.'" *Paradosis* 25. Fribourg, Switzerland: The University Press (1978):226–37.

Croke, B. F., and Harries, J. D. *Religious Conflict in Fourth Century Rome.* Forest Grove, Oreg.: International Scholarly Book Service, 1981.

Crook, J. A. "Family and Succession." Chap. 6. in *Law and Life of Rome: Aspects of Greek and Roman Life.* London: Thames and Hudson, 1967.

Dahrendorf, Ralf. "Out of Utopia: Toward a Reorientation of Sociological Analysis." *American Journal of Sociology* 64 (September 1958):127f.

Daube, David. *Roman Law: Linguistics, Social and Philosophical Aspects.* Chap. 2. The Gray Lectures, 1966. Edinburgh: The University Press, 1969.

Dill, Sir Samuel. *Roman Society in the Last Century of the Western Empire.* Book 1, Chaps. 1 and 2. New York: Meridian Books, Inc. A reprint of 1899 edition.

Field, James, Jr. "The Purpose of the Lex Julia et Papia Poppaea." *Classical Journal* 40 (1944–45):398–416.

Finley, M. I. "The Silent Women of Rome." *Horizon* 7 (1965):57–64.

Fiorenza, Elisabeth Schüssler. "Word, Spirit, and Power: Women in Early Christian Communities." *Women of Spirit.* Ed. Rosemary Ruether and Eleanor McLaughlin. New York: Simon and Schuster, 1979.

Hagendahl, H. *Latin Fathers and the Classics.* Göteborg: Almquist and Wiksell, Stockholm, 1958.

Hieronymus, Saint. *Sancti Eusebii Hieronymi Epistulae.* Recensuit Isidorus Hilberg. New York: Johnson, 1961. A reprint of the 1910–18 edition, published by F. Tempsky, Vindobonae.

Highet, Gilbert. *Juvenal the Satirist: A Study.* Oxford: At the Clarendon Press, 1955.

Hopkins, M. K. "The Age of Roman Girls at Marriage." *Population Studies* 18 (1965):309–27.

———. "Contraception in the Roman Empire." *Comparative Studies in Society and History* 8 (1965):124–51.

Hunter, W. A. *A Systematic and Historical Exposition of Roman Law.* Book 2, pt. 3, B, "Status." Trans. J. Ashton Cross. London: William Maxwell's Sons, 1885.

Jerome. *Letters.* Trans. W. H. Fremantle. *A Select Library of Nicene and Post-Nicene Fathers of the Christian Church.* 2d ser., vol. 6. St. Jerome: Letters and Select Works. Ed. Philip Scharff and Henry Ware. New York: The Christian Literature Co.; London: Parker and Co., 1983.

Jones, A. H. M. *The Later Roman Empire, 284–602: A Social, Economic and Administrative Survey.* Vols. 1 and 2 (especially vol. 1, pts. 2, 15, and 16, and vol. 2, pts. 22, 23, 24, and 25). Norman: University of Oklahoma Press, 1964.

Jones, A. H. M.; Martindale, J. R.; and Morris, J. *The Prosopography of the Later Roman Empire,* vol. 1, A.D. 260–395. Cambridge: Cambridge University Press, 1971.

Juvenal. *Juvenal and Persius.* Satire Six. Trans. G. G. Ramsay. The Loeb Classical Library. Ed. E. H. Warmington. Cambridge, Mass.: Harvard University Press; London: Willian Heinemann, 1969.

Kelly, J. N. D. *Jerome: His Life, Writings, and Controversies.* New York: Harper & Row Publishers, 1975.

Klawiter, Frederick C. "The Role of Martyrdom and Persecution in Developing the Priestly Authority of Women in Early Christianity: A Case of Montanism." *Church History* 49, no. 3 (September 1980):251–61.

Kraemer, Ross Shepard. "Esctatics and Ascetics: Studies in the Functions of Religious Activities for Women in the Greco-Roman World." Ph.D. dissertation, Princeton University, 1976.

Last, Hugh. "The Social Policy of Augustus," *The Cambridge Ancient History,* vol. 10: *The Augustan Empire 44 B.C.-A.D. 70.* Ed. Cook, Adcock, and Charlesworth. Cambridge: Cambridge University Press, 1934.

Life of St. Melania. Trans. E. Leahy, and ed. H. Thurston. London, 1908.

Lightman, Marjorie, and Zeisel, William. "*Univira:* An Example of Continuity and Change in Roman Society." *Church History* 46 (March 1977):19–32.

Lilja, Saara. "The Roman Elegists' Attitude to Women." *Suomalaisen Tiedeakatemian Toimituksia, Annales Academiae Scientiarum Fennicae.* Helsinki: Suomalainen Tiedakaremia, 1965.

Lord, Mary Louise. "Dido as an Example of Chastity." *Harvard Library Bulletin* 17 (1962):22–44.

McDermott, W. C. "Saint Jerome and Pagan Greek Literature." *Vigiliae Christianae* 36, no. 4 (December 1982):372–82.

McNamara, Jo Ann (of Hunter College). "Chaste Marriage and Clerical Celibacy." An unpublished manuscript.

Macrobius. *The Saturnalia.* Trans. Percival Vaughan Davies. New York: Columbia University Press, 1969.

Meer, Frederik van der. *Augustine the Bishop: The Life and Work of a Father of the Church.* Part 1, 8. Trans. Brian Battershaw and G. R. Lamb. New York: Sheed and Ward, 1961.

Moine, Nicole. "Melaniana." *Recherches Augustinienne,* vol. 15. Paris: Etudes Augustiniennes (1980):1–65.

Morris, John. "Pelagian Literature." *Journal of Theological Studies,* n.s., vol. 16, pt. 1 (April 1965):26–60.

Murphy, Francis X. "Melania the Elder: A Biographical Note." *Traditio* 5 (1947):59–77.

_____. *Rufinus of Aquileia (A.D. 345–411): His Life and Works.* Studies in Mediaeval History. n.s., vol. 6. Washington, D.C.: The Catholic University of America, 1945.

Noonan, John T. *Contraception.* New York: Mentor, 1967.

Ortner, Sherry. "Is Female to Male as Nature Is to Culture?" *Woman, Culture and Society.* Ed. Rosaldo and Lamphere. Stanford: Stanford University Press, 1974.

Ovid. *The Amores.* Trans. Grant Shouerman. *Ovid* 1: *Heroides and Amores.* The Loeb Classical Library. Ed. E. H. Warmington. Cambridge, Mass.: Harvard University Press; London: William Heinemann, 1971.

_____. *Artis Amatoriae.* Trans. J. H. Mozley. *Ovid* 2: *The Art of Love and Other Poems.* The Loeb Classical Library. Ed. E. H. Warmington. Cambridge, Mass.: Harvard University Press; London: William Heinemann, 1969.

_____. "De Medicamine Faciei Liber." *Ovid* 2: *The Art of Love and Other Poems.* Trans. J. H. Mozley. The Loeb Classical Library. Ed. E. H. Warmington. Cambridge, Mass.: Harvard University Press; London: William Heinemann, 1969.

Palladius. *The Lausiac History.* Trans. Robert T. Meyer. Ancient Christian Writers Series, no. 34. Ed. Quasten, Burghardt, and Lawler. Westminster, Md.: The Newman Press; London: Longmans, Green and Co., 1965.

Parsons, Talcott. *The Social System.* Glencoe, Ill.: Free Press of Glencoe, 1951.

Paulinus of Nola. Letters 13, 29, and 45 in the *Letters of Paulinus of Nola,* vols. 1 and 2. Trans. P. G. Walsh. Ancient Christian Writers Series, nos. 35 and 36. Ed. Quasten, Burghardt, and Lawler. Westminster, Md.: The Newman Press; London: Longmans, Green and Co., 1966.

Plautus. *Amphitryon.* Trans. Sir Robert Allison.

_____. *The Rope.* Trans. Cleveland K. Chase.

_____. *The Two Bacchides.* Trans. Edward H. Sugden. All appearing in *The Complete Roman Drama,* vol. 1: *All the Extant Comedies of Plautus and Terence, and the Tragedies of Seneca, in a Variety of Translations.* Ed. George E. Duckworth. New York: Random House, 1942.

Pomeroy, Sarah. *Goddesses, Whores, Wives, and Slaves: Women in Classical Antiquity.* New York: Schocken Books, 1975.

Rogers, Rolfe. *Max Weber's Ideal Type Theory.* New York: Philosophical Library, 1969.

Rosaldo, Michelle Zimbalist. "Woman, Culture, and Society: A Theoretical Overview." *Woman, Culture, and Society.* Ed. Rosaldo and Lamphere. Stanford: Stanford University Press, 1974.

Rousseau, Philip. "Blood-Relationships among Early Eastern Ascetics." *Journal of Theological Studies,* n.s., 23 (1972):235f.

Ruether, Rosemary Radford. "Misogynism and Virginal Feminism in the Fathers of the Church." *Religion and Sexism: Images of Woman in the Jewish and Christian traditions.* Ed. Rosemary Radford Ruether. New York: Simon and Schuster, 1974.

_____. "Mothers of the Church: Ascetic Women in the Late Patristic Age." *Women of Spirit.* Ed. Rosemary Ruether and Eleanor McLaughlin. New York: Simon and Schuster, 1979.

Sanday, Peggy R. "Toward a Theory of the Status of Women." *American Anthropologist* 75 (1973):1682–1700.

Seneca (?). *Octavia.* Trans. Frank Justus Miller. *The Complete Roman Drama,* vol. 2: *All the Extant Comedies of Plautus and Terence, and the Tragedies of Seneca, in a Variety of Translations.* Ed. George E. Duckworth. New York: Random House, 1942.

Shils and Finch, eds. *Max Weber—On the Methodology of the Social Sciences.* Glencoe, Ill.: The Free Press, 1949.

Smith, Jonathan. "The Social Description of Early Christianity." *Religious Studies Review* 1, no. 1 (September 1975):19–23.

Smith, Margaret. *The Way of the Mystics.* Chapter 3: "Asceticism and the Monastic Life among Women." New York: Oxford University Press, 1978.

Symmachus. "Relatio III." *Prefect and Emperor: the "Relationes" of Symmachus.* Trans. R. H. Barrow. Oxford: The Clarendon Press, 1973.

Terence. *The Woman of Andros* and *The Mother-in-Law.* Translators anonymous. *The Complete Roman Drama,* vol. 2: *All the Extant Comedies of Plautus and Terence, and the Tragedies of Seneca, in a Variety of Translations.* Ed. George E. Duckworth. New York: Random House, 1942.

Tertullian. "On the Apparel of Women," and "To His Wife." *The Ante-Nicene Fathers,* vol. 4: *Tertullian, Part Fourth; Minucius Felix; Commodian; Origen, Parts First and Second.* Trans. Rev. S. Thelwall, and ed. Rev. Alexander Roberts and James Donaldson. Grand Rapids, Mich.: Wm. B. Eerdmans Publishing Co., 1956.

Thibault, John C. *The Mystery of Ovid's Exile.* Berkeley and Los Angeles: University of California Press, 1964.

Treggiari, Susan. "Libertine Ladies." *Classical World* 64 (1971):196–98.

Turner, Jonathan. *The Structure of Sociological Theory.* Homewood, Ill.: The Dorsey Press, 1974.

Walsh, P. G. "Paulinus of Nola and the Conflict of Ideologies in the Fourth Century." *Kyriakon: Festschrift Johannes Quasten,* vol. 3. Ed. Patrick Granfield and Josef A. Jungmann. Munster Westf.: Verlag Aschendorff, 1970.

Weber, Max. "The Interpretive Understanding of Social Action" and "'Objectivity' in Social Science." *Readings in the Philosophy of the Social Sciences.* Ed. May Brodbeck. New York: The Macmillan Co.; London: Collier-Macmillan, 1968.

Williams, Gordon. "Some Aspects of Roman Marriage Ceremonies and Ideals." *The Journal of Roman Studies* 48 (1958):16–29.

Yarbrough, Anne. "Christianization in the Fourth Century: The Example of Roman Women." *Church History* 45 (1976):149–65.

Index

Adultery, in Ancient Rome, 51–56, 129n.31
Ageruchia, 41
Ambivalent motivational structure, 79–81
Ancient Rome. *See* Rome
Ascetic conversion: Blaesilla, 33–34; literature
  of, 5–6; Melania the Elder, 46–47
Ascetic monasticism, and Jerome, 45
"Ascetic Renunciation and Feminine
  Advancement: A Paradox of Late Ancient
  Christianity" (Clark), 2, 3, 4, 18–20
Ascetic self-discipline, 47
Asceticism: appeal of to women, 1–2; in Asia
  Minor, 8–9; function of for women, 5–6;
  and gnosticism, 5–7; history of, 5–6; and
  maternity, 19, 24–25; and misogyny, 1;
  motivation for, 6–9, 67–69, 83–84, 88,
  108; as social advancement for women,
  18–19; and wealth, 52
The Atlas of the Early Christian World, 21, 28
Augustus, social policy of, 51–53

Blaesilla, 32–34; genealogy of, 22, 32–34; and
  Jerome, 16, 22; marriage of, 107; physical
  beauty of, 103; physical weakness of,
  33–34
Brown, Peter, 3, 14, 68, 71

Castitas, 96–97
Childcare subsidies in Ancient Rome, 60
"Christianization in the Fourth Century:
  The Example of Roman Women"
  (Yarbrough), 2
Clark, Elizabeth, 2–4, 16–20, 109, 141n.93.
  Works: "Ascetic Renunciation and
  Feminine Advancement: A Paradox of
  Late Ancient Christianity," 2, 3, 4, 18–20;
  Jerome, Chrysostom and Friends, 2–4,
  16–20; "John Chrysostom and the
  Subintroductae," 16
Codex Theodosianus, 29–30, 51, 52, 53–56, 60,
  73, 129n.31, 130n.43

Complementarity of expectations, 70
Contraception, in Ancient Rome, 60–61

Demetrias, 42–43
Deviant behavior and monasticism, 80–81
Divorce, in Ancient Rome, 52, 55–58, 130n.43

Education: and ascetic women, 61–64, 98–106,
  132nn.96, 102, 141n.93; and Jerome,
  97–98, 100–102, 111; and Juvenal, 100;
  and Marcella, 62; and Melania the Elder,
  62; and Ovid, 61–62; and Paula, 62
Eustochium, 36–37
Evagrius of Pontus, 47

Fabiola, 40–41
Functionalist theory, 15

Gnosticism: and asceticism, 6–7; and
  misogyny, 8–9
Gnostikos (Evagrius of Pontus), 47
Guardianship of women in Ancient Rome,
  51–52, 59

Harnack, 6, 115n.7
Hedibia, 41–42

Intellectual ability and ascetic women, 29–30,
  34, 46–47

Jerome: on adultery, 55; on Ageruchia, 41–42;
  attitude of toward social deviance, 78–79;
  on Blaesilla, 16, 22, 32–34; on Christian
  aristocrats, 76; on Demetrias, 42; on
  education, 87–88, 97–98, 100–101, 111; on
  Eustochium, 36–37; on Fabiola, 40–42; on
  female ascetic monasticism, 45; on
  Hedibia, 41; ideology of women of, 109;
  on intelligence, 19; vs. Jovinianus, 71; vs.
  Juvenal, 88–89; on liminality, 17–18; on

Marcella, 38–40, 52; on maternity, 18, 25, 111; on *matrona/univira,* 95–96; on Melania the Elder, 5, 45; on monastic ideology of womanhood, 105–6; on Paula, 21–22, 23–28, 29–30, 52, 84; on Paulina, 34–36; portrait of Rome of, 72; and the *proemptikon* form, 25; protegées of, 2; on remarriage, 131n.68; on Rufina, 37; on Salvina, 42; on Theodora, 42; on Toxitius, 37–38; women in the work of, 5, 9–10
Jerome, Chrysostom and Friends (Clark), 2, 3, 4, 16–20
"John Chrysostom and the Subintroductae" (Clark), 16
Jones, A.H.M., 34, 59, 72–73. Works: *The Later Roman Empire,* 21, 59; *The Prosopography of the Later Roman Empire,* 21–22, 34, 73
Juvenal: on education, 100; images of women in work of, 4–5, 88–89; on intelligence, 19; vs. Jerome, 88–89; on *matrona,* 92; on physical beauty, 103

The Later Roman Empire (Jones), 21, 59
The Lausiac History, 8, 45
Lex Julia de Adulteriis, 53, 55
Lex Julia de maritandis ordinibus, 57
Lex Papia Poppaea, 57, 59, 130n.58
Liminal state, in primitive *rites de passage,* 17–18

Manus, marriage with, 50–51
Marcella: and education, 62, 88; genealogy of, 38–40; and Jerome, 52; an originator of monasticism for Roman women, 38–40; reputation of, 54; as scriptural authority, 40; wealth of, 52
Marriage, in Ancient Rome, 59–60, 91–95
Maternity: and Jerome, 111; and Paulina, 36; in Rome, 58–61
Matrona: images of in Ancient Rome, 91; in work of Jerome, 95–96; in work of Juvenal, 93; in work of Ovid, 93, 94; and women of monastic ideology, 105–6
Melania the Elder: birth of, 45; clashes with civil authorities, 46; education of, 62, 88; genealogy of, 43–44, 74; intelligence of, 46–47; and Jerome, 5, 43; marriage of, 108; monastery of, 46, 117n.1; monastic journey of, 45–46; self-discipline of, 47; social position of, 77; values of, vs. Roman society, 79–80
Melania the Younger: conversion of, 74; genealogy of, 74; and Jerome, 43; wealth, 23–24
Misogyny, 1, 19–20

The Mission and Expansion of Christianity in the First Three Centuries (Harnack), 5
Monastic behavior and social deviance, 68, 80, 108–9
Monastic ideology of womanhood, 104–6
Monastic mores, 79
Monastic movement, 9, 21–49
Monastic pilgrimages: Melania the Elder, 45; Paula, 25–30, 31
Monastic women and St. Thecla, 27
Monasticism: and intellectual accomplishment, 19; as liberation, 110, 122n.86; and misogyny, 20; and paganism, 108; and physical beauty, 110; and psychology, 31–32; privileges of, 19; and self-denial, 32; and social advancement, 18, 30, 109

Ovid: on education, 61–62; on *matrona,* 93–94; on physical beauty, 102–3; women in work of, 4, 105; work of, 89

Paganism, v. Christianity, 69, 71–74, 75, 87, 104–5, 108–11, 131n.68, 134nn.2,3; and Melania the Elder, 79–80; and Paula, 80–81
Pagels, Elaine, 6–7
Parsons, Talcott, 11; interactive model of, 69–70, 78–85, 108, 109, 133–32n.1. Works: *The Social System,* 4, 69, 85, 109
Patria potestas, 50
Paula, 21–32; ascetic conversion of, 82; asceticism of, 83–84; education of, 62, 88; and Eustochium, 36; family of, 32–37, 74–75; genealogy of, 22–23, 43, 67, 73–75, 81–83, 84, 107; generosity of, 21–25, 52; intelligence of, 30; and Jerome, 29–30, 52; marriage of, 107; maternity of, 24–26, 82–83; monastic pilgrimage of, 26–31; motivation for choosing asceticism, 67, 83–84; organization of a monastery by, 30–32; and Parsons' analysis of deviant orientation, 80–82; and physical beauty, 105; and self-denial, 31–32; values of, vs. Roman society, 81–83; wealth of, 22–24, 52
Paulina, 34–36; and wifely subordination, 92
Perpetual marriage in Ancient Rome, 57
Physical beauty: images of in Ancient Rome, 101–6; monastic attitudes towards, 111
Praktikos (Evagrius of Pontus), 47
Proemptikon, 25
The Prosopography of the Late Roman Empire (Jones), 21–22, 34, 73
Pudicitia, 96–97

Rome, Ancient: ascetic women in, definition

of, 13; childcare subsidies in, 60; consular
status in, 35; contraception in, 60; divorce
in, 52–53, 55–57; guardianship of women
in, 50–52, 59; marriage in, 49–52, 56–58,
60, 91–96, 131n.68; matron in, 4–5, 49–65;
patria potestas in, 50; senatorial mores in,
22; social context of, 4, 49, 77, 78–79
Ruether, Rosemary, 2–3, 15, 110. Works:
Women of Spirit, 2, 3
Rufina, 37

St. Thecla, 27
Salvina, 42
Saturnalia (Macrobius), 62, 89, 90
Senatorial mores in Ancient Rome, 22, 69–78
Social structure in Ancient Rome, 67–69, 77
The Social System (Parsons), 4, 69, 85, 109
Syria, Christian asceticism in, 8

Terence, 90, 94–95

Tertullian, 104
Theodora, 42
Toxotius, 37–38
Turner, Victor, 17

Univira: as ideal, 71; in Jerome, 95; and
matrona, 91–92; in Rome, 57

Values of Ancient Roman women, 72
Van Der Meer, F., 1, 116n.23

Wealth and Marcella, 39; and Paulina, 35–36
Weber, Max, ideal type method of, 137–38n.2
Women, images of in Roman Antiquity,
87–101
Women of Spirit (Reuther), 2, 3

Yarbrough, Anne, 2–3, 14, 19. Work:
"Christianization in the Fourth Century:
The Example of Roman Women," 2, 14